W9-BBF-653

FROM

THE LAND OF SHADOWS

by the same author

Autobiography

UNRELIABLE MEMOIRS

Verse

PEREGRINE PRYKKE'S PILGRIMAGE
THROUGH THE LONDON LITERARY WORLD

THE FATE OF FELICITY FARK
IN THE LAND OF THE MEDIA

BRITANNIA BRIGHT'S BEWILDERMENT
IN THE WILDERNESS OF WESTMINSTER

CHARLES CHARMING'S CHALLENGES
ON THE PATHWAY TO THE THRONE

FAN-MAIL

Criticism

VISIONS BEFORE MIDNIGHT

THE CRYSTAL BUCKET

THE METROPOLITAN CRITIC

AT THE PILLARS OF HERCULES

FIRST REACTIONS

Collections of lyrics set and sung by
Pete Atkin on the RCA label

BEWARE OF THE BEAUTIFUL STRANGER

DRIVING THROUGH MYTHICAL AMERICA

A KING AT NIGHTFALL

THE ROAD OF SILK

SECRET DRINKER

THE RIDER TO THE WORLD'S END

LIVE LIBEL

MASTER OF THE REVELS

Song-book (written with Pete Atkin)

A FIRST FOLIO

Clive James

FROM THE LAND OF SHADOWS

JONATHAN CAPE
THIRTY BEDFORD SQUARE LONDON

First published 1982

Jonathan Cape Ltd, 30 Bedford Square, London WC1

British Library Cataloguing in Publication Data
James, Clive
From the land of shadows.
I. Books – Reviews
I. Title
028.1 Z1035.A1

ISBN 0-224-02021-8

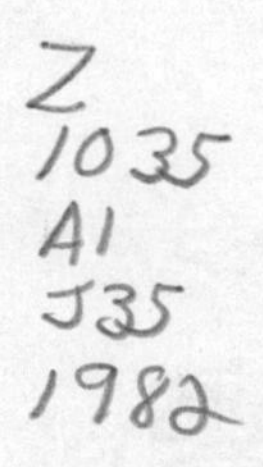

Photoset in Great Britain by
Rowland Phototypesetting Ltd
Bury St Edmunds, Suffolk
and printed by Butler & Tanner Ltd
Frome and London

for Diana Phipps

Alle Krystallisationen sind ein realisiertes Kaleidoskop

Author's Note

Thanks are due to the editors of the various periodicals in which these essays first appeared; and also to Anthony Thwaite, editor of *Larkin at Sixty* (Faber, 1982).

Contents

Introduction

The land of shadows is where we should be proud to live. In August 1946 Zhdanov launched an official attack on certain reactionary tendencies in the arts, with particular attention to the poetry of Anna Akhmatova. Called *The Report of Comrade Zhdanov on the Journals 'Zvezda' and 'Leningrad'*, his main speech on the subject is one of the dirtiest pieces of writing I have ever read. Long before finishing it you would be ready to sluice yourself down with used washing-up water just to get relatively clean. Pornography might feel dirty but most of it washes off the mind fairly easily. Political murder in written form has a dirtiness that you can't free yourself from merely by taking thought. From Zhdanov's smutty invective you get a feeling directly connected with what he would have liked to do to his victims once he got them alone. He was instinctively and rightly certain that the most degrading way to torment the poets was to bring them down to his level. Reading his smug prose is like being vouchsafed a glimpse into the mind of an obscene phone-caller, except that the range of ambition encompasses not merely the disturbance of your domestic innocence but includes starvation, torture, bitter cold and a broken back.

Yet for all the power that Zhdanov represented, he could not entirely destroy the deliberate poetry of talented people, and at least once he created accidental poetry himself. He found Akhmatova and the others guilty of sharing a Bohemian background. Vociferously echoing Gorky, he loathed that inventive, forward-looking, past-respecting, liberal-minded pre-revolutionary culture in which they had their roots and for which he correctly suspected they longed in their troubled sleep. An almost touchingly spiteful example of his censorious type, the type of the artist-*manqué* cultural commissar, he especially hated the very idea of Akhmatova in Paris. The cosmopolitan heritage of these backsliders he called their 'world of shadows'. (I have changed 'world' to 'land' in order to preserve the idea of its being a separate country.) The land of shadows was evidently a place where art was presumptuous enough to behave as if it had its own laws.

For other beginners in Russian, incidentally, the study of official Soviet speeches can be confidently recommended, since the restricted vocabulary and constant repetition make them even easier to cope with than *The Three Bears*, the Russian version of which is written by Tolstoy and thus features stylistic subtleties of a kind rigorously avoided by Central Committee spokesmen. The day I puzzled Zhdanov's unintentionally beautiful idea out of the original language and noted it down, I already knew that it was a special jewel. Zhdanov had set his precious stone in a knuckleduster. Time having chipped it loose, it was now free to be set in a ring, even if the ring had to be tinsel. By accomplishing such a transference, however maladroitly, I could symbolise what I regarded myself as good for in the role of literary critic. It might not be much but nor was it quite nothing. Even in the most conceited moments of youth, the average writer knows himself powerless to affect history as it happens. Whether through disappointment or a growing sense of realism, that conviction tends to become deeper with the years. But so does the conviction that the truth is objective after all and that in helping to tell it on even the most elementary levels resides an absolute merit. Max Weber defined the state as that organisation controlling a monopoly of legalised violence. When totalitarian mentalities are in charge there is a lot that a monopoly of legalised violence can do to rewrite the past, dictate the present and shape the immediate future. But in some areas violence is without the complete power it would like to have and language is one of them. Even the tyrant may inadvertently coin a phrase that can be used against him. He can't always calculate his future effect. (It should be said, however, that not every phrase intended as abuse can be redeemed as an unintentional felicity. In China at the time of writing, those concerned with intellectual matters are known officially as the Stinking Ninth. Try making a resonant title out of that.)

But what would depress the tyrant if he really knew himself should inspire the literary critic. The literary critic can't wholly calculate his future effect either, but in his case the uncertainty should be a source of courage. By saying what is so he might, for all he knows, help someone now to change the future, or someone in the future to rediscover the past. That he can never be quite certain he can't do these things should give him hope, if hope is what he needs. Ideally, of course, he should be capable of seeing that the truth is worth telling for its own sake, but most of us have luckily never lived in circumstances where that fact is made self-evident by the relentless virulence dedicated to calling it a lie.

So the title of this book means not quite what it at first might seem to mean. The land of shadows is the country we inhabit at those times when we admit the existence of a mental life independent of material determination. In the land of shadows there are only local patches, instead of a universal incidence, of that remorseless, enervating white light in which the Zhdanovs would prefer all mental life to take place, so that it could be checked up on in all its aspects. The West's best chance to endure is in staying true to its liberal heritage, and so far it still looks resigned, if not resolved, to doing that. If the West is ever in doubt as to what that liberal heritage actually consists of, all it has to do is take a long look at the Soviet Union, and ask itself how the alleged giant, which undoubtedly possesses a strapping pair of hairy thighs, ever came to have such a pin head. Teleological conclusions are bad ones to reach about history but there is some point to the contention that the totalitarian states came into being specifically to remind us that there is such a thing as liberty after all.

The contention that there is no such thing as objective truth is, or ought to be, self-refuting. (If there were no such thing as objective truth, the contention that there is no such thing as objective truth could not be objectively true.) But for some reason an obvious illogicality is not always enough to disprove a point. What's needed is a huge, unarguable, pitifully wasteful historical example. The Soviet Union should be enough to provide it. For more than sixty years the Soviet government has striven to extirpate the very notion of any reality independent of ideological precept. By now everyone who sincerely wants to has drawn the moral. You don't have to teach yourself the Russian language in order to appreciate the heroism of those who dared to say what was so even as the boot was coming down across their throats. The lesson of political tragedy is there for the learning, even if you can't read it in the Cyrillic alphabet. But what even the most elementary knowledge of the Russian language helps you towards realising, quite possibly against your will, is the magnitude of the *cultural* tragedy.

My own Russian studies, such as they are, I began when in 1975 I could no longer bear not to know something about how Pushkin actually sounded. I was ready for his grandeur when I got to him. Even Tolstoy's perspicuity did not come as a shock, since if you have read *War and Peace* and *Anna Karenina* in various English and French versions you are bound to have some idea of the transparency his translators, each hampered differently by an individual style, are trying to emulate. Chekhov's stories were a revelation, but they were a familiar revelation: already knowing him to be a genius helped prepare you for his being a genius on such a scale. The true shock came from the sheer richness of the immediate pre-revolutionary culture.

In those years between 1898 and 1917, Russia was not only industrialising itself at a rate which no five-year plan has since been able to equal, it was experiencing a cultural efflorescence for which the whole of the astonishingly vital nineteenth century would have looked like the mere preparation, and which would have needed the whole world in order to unfold its unprecedented wealth of blooms. We think we know something about this putative vigour from the history in exile of the *ballets russes*. We listen to Stravinsky and think we can guess at what Diaghilev stood for. But when you actually look into Diaghilev's magazine *Mir Iskustva* (*The World of Art*) you start getting some idea of what that aspect of Russian culture was like when it was still in Russia. You start getting some idea of why the very name of Petersburg should retain, even today, such emblematic importance for the Russian intelligentsia. Bely's symbolist novel *Petersburg*, like Joyce's *Ulysses*, presented a home city as a world capital, but what in Joyce had an element of defiant caprice was in Bely virtually a natural impulse, since Petersburg in those years must have felt like the actual, not just the metaphorical, centre of the world.

Diaghilev's energy can be interpreted along Marxist lines as a bourgeois impulse emerging belatedly from an ossified feudalist structure. The young poets who datelined their slim volumes 'Petropolis' can be regarded as revolutionary harbingers if you are prepared to stretch a point. But no amount of social analysis can reduce that total artistic upheaval to a formula. It took repression, physical extermination and a comprehensive rewriting of history to do that. So thoroughly has the job been done that even the most sceptical Westerner is still inclined to swallow the idea of a Soviet cultural exfoliation in the 1920s. Impressed by Malevitch, the Tatlin tower, Mayakovsky's poems, Eisenstein's films, Dzhiga-Vertov's newsreels and the heady prospect of agitprop trains steaming with the good news towards the cultural front, they blame the hardening bureaucracy for cracking down on a new Renaissance. But for all its energy and achievement, the Soviet post-revolutionary decade was already a stunted parody of what might have been. Not what might have been – what must have been.

Almost the entire mental life of a whole great nation was destroyed. Not even the famous names who lived on into the new era and were eventually snuffed out are typical of their kind. The typical poet was Gumilev, not Mandelstam. Mandelstam survived as far as the 1930s, where he at least had the dubious privilege of being done to death by known philistines and obscurantists. Gumilev was killed off straight away, in the era when the arts were supposedly being set free from their long bondage. We should be less impressed by the way Mayakovsky stood on the throat of his own song than by how Gumilev never really got a chance to open his mouth at all. Hope, without which we can't function, tells us that a civilisation is a hard thing to kill. But realism, without which hope is mere frivolity, should tell us that there is indeed such a thing as cultural extinction. The idea that the repressive conditions of the Soviet Union make poetry *mean more* to its citizens is essentially and insultingly frivolous. If poetry means more in the Soviet Union, it means more in the same way that air means more to a choking man. It is a peculiar kind of arrogance to suppose that Akhmatova, for instance, wrote her poem *Requiem* in order to reconcile us with history. The voice in *Requiem* (which has never been published in the Soviet Union, and of whose existence not even the most subversive of the young poets would dare make an open acknowledgment) is that of a traumatised child speaking the wreckage of a nursery rhyme. 'This woman is sick,/This woman is alone./Husband dead, son in gaol,/Pray for me.' When you have enough Russian to absorb that wounded, sobbing rhythm, you have already arrived at the heart of the great, irreparable disaster of modern history. It is a disaster not just of destruction but of loss. What has been wiped out would be frightening enough but is made more frightening by what has not happened at all. The reader walks out of a garden into a desert. Germany has never really recovered as a culture from the destruction of its Jews, but at least the generation now coming of age is able to contemplate the event in its fullness. The awful thing is all over bar the weeping. With the help of so imaginatively realistic a book as Golo Mann's *Deutsche Geschichte des 19. und 20. Jahrhunderts* a young German can establish the separation of the past and present and so connect them. But for the young citizen of the Soviet Union there is small chance of doing any such thing. For him or her, history is more easily ignored than come to terms with. The catastrophe goes on. That the regime should come to terms with its own past is beyond expectation, but for even the ordinary citizen to face the facts must entail coping with an intensity of deprivation that only the obsessive or the very brave could possibly support.

But with all that against it, the truth, as Nadezhda Mandelstam always said it would, goes on being reborn. Sometimes it is not easily recognised by those of us with incurably high expectations of life. In my essays on Zinoviev, for instance, I could see the originality of the social analysis underlying his comic invention but underestimated his intellectual consistency. The reader will see how relieved I was, when noticing *Sans illusions* (the French translation of *Byez illuzii*, not yet done into English at the time of writing), to find an apparent amelioration of the scepticism towards dissidence evident in *The Yawning Heights* and *The Radiant Future*. Actually Zinoviev's attitude towards dissidence is perfectly consistent and not to be taken as a source of comfort, although his views on the subject are expounded with the necessary thoroughness only in such later books as *Mi i zapad* (*We and the West*) and *Kommunizm kak realnost* (*Communism as Reality*), which will be some time reaching general circulation amongst the English-speaking reading public. Zinoviev can be accused of determinism but he has his answers ready ahead of time. If anybody is serious on the subject of the Soviet Union, Zinoviev is. He is perhaps even more serious than Solzhenitsyn, who wants the Soviet Union discredited, and Sakharov, who still so generously thinks, after having his life made misery by official persecution of the most disgusting brand, that technological necessity might bring liberal reforms. Zinoviev claims to be expounding an objective sociological view by which the Soviet Union is not an aberration but the natural and complete expression of the collectivist impulse in mankind. He thinks that even if the Soviet Union collapses it will collapse outwards. He argues as powerfully as Pareto. Reading him without a twinge of fear takes strong nerves. But at least you will know that you are reading someone fully engaged with his subject.

I was once told by a reviewer in whose radical politics I was not interested that I was not interested in politics. Similarly people are reluctant to call you serious if you do not take them seriously. I don't mind being called frivolous by the solemn: in fact it is a reputation I court. But I hope that the truly serious reader will be able to detect, in even the least grave of the following essays, a certain disinclination to make cheap jokes, or at any rate a determination to make only expensive ones if I can. I don't regard myself as a humorist and am slow to take it as a compliment when given the name. Not just by ambition, but by a sense of responsibility to those who have suffered innocently in the political catastrophes of the twentieth century, I consider myself debarred from the attitude of irreverence as it is commonly defined. T. S. Eliot defined humour as the weapon with which intelligence defends itself. What I believe is that those people capable of seeing the world as it is speak a common language of which the play of wit forms a part. The jokes of the obtuse are not worth hearing, but the laughter of the intelligent and sensitive is well worth trying to elicit. It comes when you put what they think into brief words without belittling what they see.

During my first years in London in the early 1960s I read through the transcripts of the Nuremberg trials and began at last, after a decade of horrified vagueness on the topic, to get some precise idea of the times we had all been living in. Until the advent in English translation of Solzhenitsyn, Nadezhda Mandelstam, Marchenko, Evgenia Ginzburg and all the others, the equivalent information on the Soviet Union was less readily available in the one spot, but there was no real excuse for not being aware of the truth, just as, at the present time, there is no real excuse for not being aware of the truth about Mao's China, even though the story is so short of detail that Shirley MacLaine's little cries of ecstasy at the alleged happiness of the Chinese under the Cultural Revolution can still, in retrospect, touch the heart more than they turn the stomach. So at the beginning of my career as a literary journalist I was already aware of the difference between politics in the totalitarian nations and politics as they are generally understood in conditions of freedom. Such an awareness *is* my politics. A specialist in political thought might find my attitude hopelessly simplistic. A young radical, should he or she happen to pick up this book, would no doubt be suitably disgusted at the thoroughness with which I have embraced reaction. But really it is not Pangloss speaking in these essays, although it might well be Candide. There is no sense in which I believe that the sweet calm of Paradise obtains in all the lands of the West. I am just suitably grateful for the fact that the democracies hold together, despite the strength of the forces operating to pull them to pieces. In this book the reader will find several Western prophets taken with what might appear to be undue levity, but there is such a thing as a sense of proportion and it is a kind of conceit to flout it. Solzhenitsyn has earned the right to fulminate unreasonably against what he conceives to be the West's lack of purpose. Westerners should start off by being thankful for waking up at liberty each morning.

Like most of my contemporaries I spent a good number of my young years being scared witless by the foreign policy of the United States, which seemed specifically designed to yield the moral advantage to the Eastern powers. By working on a global scale to help dictatorial regimes wipe out any democratic element brave enough to raise its head, the United States pursued a *Realpolitik* which didn't even have the merit of being real, since to give up the moral advantage almost invariably meant handing over the political advantage as well, as the communists recruited the non-aligned populace and expanded into the central vacuum. The Carter administration, which it is fashionable at the moment to laugh at, did something to reverse this policy and is thus likely to gain credit in the long view, especially now that President Reagan seems as determined to misunderstand the world he is living in as all his predecessors put together. There are, of course there are, changes one would like to see made in the Western democracies. But I am of the wrong generation, and have the wrong education, to believe in my heart that they should be radical changes. It is not just that I fear what havoc might be wrought by those I see around me if traditional restraints were to be removed. I fear what havoc might be wrought by myself. Once in conversation I was giving public thanks that I had never had my moral fibre tested as a prisoner in a concentration camp. Someone present reminded me, with a casual acerbity never to be forgotten, that I was being too confident: I might not have been a prisoner, I might have been a guard. Most of us don't have to examine our own characters for long before discovering such weaknesses as envy, bad faith or at least a certain thoughtlessness for the welfare of others. In conditions of freedom a shared sense of community keeps us up to the mark or near it, but in the forcing-house of a totalitarian state such weakness would *become* our character. Here in the West, in the tense but fortunate here and now, I can give a contemporary a bad notice without his imagining that he will be taken away in a plain van next morning, and he can do the same for me. To read a bad notice of your work and feel stung is one thing, but to read a bad notice of your work and know yourself doomed is quite another. As this world goes, the elementary conditions of civilised debate should be regarded as abnormal rather than otherwise, and not be voluntarily given up for any reason, however convincing it might happen to sound.

The ideological apparatus of a totalitarian state is run by people not entirely different from ourselves. We would be insulting ourselves unduly to think that we could ever have been Zhdanov, but most of us have had weak moments in which the conduct of someone like Ehrenburg becomes chasteningly understandable, and even the most independent of us should take warning from the behaviour of such a considerable mind as, say, Lukács, who sang hosannahs for the greatness of Stalinist literature at the very time when the real writers were having their knuckles crushed. Zhdanov, who was all spite, merely wrote the vile junk of which he was capable. Lukács, a man of immense culture, committed blasphemy. A wilderness was being created and he called it peace. Leszek Kolakowski, in the third volume of his great book *Main Currents of Marxism*, calls Lukács the most striking modern case of the betrayal of reason by those whose profession is to defend it. Lukács probably deserves the title but he had a lot of competition, and if our circumstances changed tomorrow he would undoubtedly have more competition still. How many among us could guarantee to answer for ourselves beyond the first year? Beyond the first month, week, day? Thank heaven for large mercies.

The first duty of the intellect is to extend, or if it cannot extend at least protect, the area of common reason. As a political force the intellect habitually fails to realise its limitations. Wanting intellect to limit itself does not necessarily make you an anti-intellectual. Indeed it is often the sign of an intellectual who knows his business. The same applies to academicism, which like intellect tends to get above itself because of its own impulse towards order. Wanting the academy to stay sane does not necessarily make you anti-academic. Even when I cockily styled myself a metropolitan critic it never occurred to me that metropolitan criticism would last long or mean much without a solid academic effort backing it up. But I meant a *solid* academic effort, not vaporous posturings adopted by baby dons desperate to mark out for themselves an area of legerdemain which might be mistaken for a literary personality. It is an unfortunate fact that the academic student of literature must be either properly humble or else very intelligent indeed. In the rare case of academic genius he will be both, and you will get such scholars as Ernst Robert Curtius, Menendez Pidal, Natolino Sapegno, Gianfranco Contini, George Saintsbury and W. P. Ker. But a student can usefully be one without being the other. A. E. Housman was by no means humble but such was his intelligence that his classical papers remain a vital repository of critical acumen even to a reader unqualified in that field. Conversely it is possible to have an intelligence of the second or third rank and still do essential work: all it takes is a suitably modest appraisal of one's own abilities. The danger – the very present and steadily growing danger – comes from those ambitious mediocrities who look for a marketable gadget and all too often find it, mainly because the demand continues to outpace the supply, so that if you have a quirk to peddle there will always be an audience to hear it. But there are worse aberrations for a society to suffer from than the average academic fad, and there is even something to be said for the dullards marking themselves out by all suddenly adopting the catch-phrases of, say, structuralism – at least you can hear them coming and take avoiding action. The voice of real life will usually cut through the hubbub, not for its being louder but for the way it sounds reasonable.

The present writer doesn't aspire to anything more than that, and doesn't think that anything more can legitimately be aspired to. In a glossy magazine one of my books of television criticism was accused of frivolity because it had nothing more to offer than common sense. I stood condemned because of my propensity for finding sententious expressions for what everybody knew already. Guilty, I hope. Common sense gets harder to have as the field of study becomes more complex, but it still remains common, even if common only to the qualified few. Most of us show enough common sense to run for a bus without falling under the wheels. Some of us show common sense about our trades and professions. A few of us show common sense about abstract speculation. Einstein showed common sense about the stars.

The necessary conceit of the essayist must be that in writing down what is obvious to him he is not wasting his reader's time. The value of what he does will depend on the quality of his perception, not on the length of his manuscript. Too many dull books about literature would have been tolerable long essays; too many dull long essays would have been reasonably interesting short ones; too many short essays should have been letters to the editor. If the essayist has a literary personality his essays will add up to something all of a piece. If he has not, he may write fancily titled books until doomsday and do no good. Most of the criticism that matters at all has been written in essay form. This fact is no great mystery: what there is to say about literature is very important, but there just isn't all that much of it. Literature says most things itself, when it is allowed to. In the land of shadows it is still allowed to, and we should bless our luck for being alive to listen.

Part One
IN A FREE SOCIETY

Misia and All Paris

Misia by Arthur Gold and Robert Fizdale (Macmillan, London, and Knopf, New York)

At the beginning of her life, Misia Sert met Liszt, whom she remembered for his warts, long hair and transvestite travelling companion. She lived almost long enough to meet two more piano-players, the co-authors of this book. In between, she knew just about everybody who counted in artistic Paris. The painters painted her and the composers aired their masterpieces at her piano, which she herself could play very well. But what gave her long life its fascination, and gives this book its strength, is that she was no mere dabbler. Her taste was original, penetrating and in most cases definitive. Without directly creating anything, she was some kind of artist herself – rather like Diaghilev, of whom she was the soul-mate and valued adviser. For most of her life she was too rich to be a true bohemian, and too passionate about art to be a true representative of high society. Instead, she was, for her time, the incarnation of that special energy released when talent and privilege meet. This book has several faults but at least one great merit: Arthur Gold and Robert Fizdale have seen that Misia's personality, even if it can never quite be captured, remains highly interesting for the light it casts on how talent can cohabit with gracious living and yet still keep its distance. *Misia* features a good deal of novelettish speculation about the way people long dead 'must have' thought and felt, but on the whole it is a refreshingly humane book about how creative work actually gets done. It would be praiseworthy at any time, but is particularly so now, when too many abstract treatises are being foisted on us by coldly able young academics who behave as if the arts, like their salaries, came out of a machine.

Misia's mother died giving birth to her – an inconvenience which her father, the fashionable Polish sculptor Cyprien Godebski, characteristically dealt with by pushing off. Growing up well-connected but abandoned, Misia gave of herself freely but remained hard to get at. In Paris she took piano lessons from Fauré (who regarded her as a prodigy) and lived by her wits. When she met Thadée Natanson she set a pattern by marrying him. From then on she took husbands rather than lovers, and expressed herself by running a menage in which the piano was something more than a prop but less than an instrument of devotion. Perhaps she was just too beautiful.

Thadée started the *Revue Blanche*. Verlaine, Mallarmé and the painters duly gathered. Those who couldn't paint the *ispiratrice* wrote poems for her. The painters had the privilege of immortalising her miraculous looks, which included a legendary pair of legs and a bosom that kept strong men awake at night thinking. The book reproduces the best of these portraits in good colour, thereby turning itself into something of a work of art. Vuillard, Bonnard, Lautrec and Renoir all painted her often, and later on there were plenty of drawings by such as Marie Laurencin and the omnipresent Cocteau. In addition, there are scores of photographs, the whole iconography adding up to a seductive visual record of her busily leisured life. I should mention at this point that the new picture book on Chanel* contains several interesting pictures of Misia which are not in Gold and Fizdale. There is a good photograph of *la belle Mme Edwards montant en voiture*, a superb one of *Misia Natanson en manteau à triple pèlerine*, and an extra Vuillard. But then there always seems to be an extra Vuillard: like Bonnard and Renoir, he never tired of painting her. Add all the pictures in both books together and you get a hint of what her beauty must have been like. She used to cut the paintings to size if they didn't fit the parts of the wall she wanted to put them on, but the painters loved her no less and probably all the more. At the time, we should remember, it must have been the painters' efforts which seemed capricious and Misia's volcanic personality which seemed the eternal

**Le Temps Chanel* by Edmonde Charles-Roux (Chéne/Grasset)

fact. And indeed she lives on, but through them.

Being published in the *Revue Blanche* was like getting into a party: you had to know Misia. But this condition was only mildly pernicious, because you had to be gifted before Misia wanted to know you. They all showed up. Gide didn't like Misia much but came anyway. Valéry liked her a lot. She adored Mallarmé, who reigned as the incorruptible grand old man. Fauré brought his bright young pupil Ravel. Debussy was there. So was Colette, sporting a waist nearly as enticing as Misia's, which was saying a great deal. At a party thrown by Misia's brother-in-law to celebrate the completion of nine large panels by Vuillard, Lautrec was the barman. Three hundred people were present, of whom a large proportion were already famous and all promptly became drunk, since Lautrec's cocktails consisted of several layers of different-coloured liqueurs. A room was set aside for casualties and ended up jammed with the bodies of Jarry, Vuillard, Bonnard, etc. It would be very easy to make a bad movie of all this. Misia was in the thick of it, stirring the magic, helping make life itself a work of art – something artists are usually too busy to do.

The century had not yet turned and high society still confined itself to the minutiae of dynastic self-perpetuation. In playing hostess to the artists, Misia was being more bohemian than grand. But she was a grand enough bohemian. She could give the artists a deep draught of luxury. She would probably have aroused the same sense of stylish comfort even if she had had nothing to offer except bread and cheese. But with Thadée's money she was able to offer country houses too. At the first of these, near Fontainebleau, Misia played Schubert to Mallarmé and every New Year's Day he gave her a fan with a poem on it. She instinctively respected his essential seriousness – an early instance of her knack for recognising creative intensity even at its most original.

Another, larger country house, at Villeneuve, inspired Vuillard, who was in love with her, to some of his finest panels. It also helped eat up Thadée's money. Misia didn't care about material things as long as she had plenty of them.

When she caught the eye of the vulgar press baron Alfred Edwards there seemed little chance that such a brute of a man could gain so sensitive a woman. But Thadée required bailing out and Misia was the price. There is also the possibility that she needed to be violated – the psychology of the book goes a bit hazy at this point.

Edwards was a coprophile, among his other charms, but he was also loaded. He knew how to appeal to the idleness that lay beneath Misia's energy. Bonnard's 'Misia aux Roses' portrayed her in her new luxury as Edwards's mistress. There were no more of the chintzes that had so appealed to Vuillard. Instead there were butlers, chandeliers and an endless supply of Louis XVI furniture. Misia played for Caruso while he sang Neapolitan songs, and told him to pipe down when she grew sick of them – her new equivalent of cutting up paintings. She had moved up a notch, or down, depending on how you view it. Some of her new acquaintances were less worthwhile than her old friends. On the other hand, she wielded her new power usefully. When Ravel failed for the third time to get the Prix de Rome, Misia used her husband's clout to make the director of the Conservatoire resign. Fauré took over. Ravel's *Le Cygne* is dedicated to Misia and she always called him *mon petit Ravel*. She was even more moved by Debussy. In 1902 Pierre Louÿs invited friends to hear Debussy play *Pelléas et Mélisande* at an upright piano. As so often happened, Misia was the only woman present. She was there by right, since the composers respected her not just as a Muse but as the ideally equipped listener. Later on she was kind to Debussy's ruthlessly abandoned wife, slipping her some money on the quiet but not afraid of Debussy's certain fury should he find out – an episode that speaks highly for her character. (In this respect, *Misia* is a valuable corrective to Frederick Brown's entertaining but unwarrantably malicious book on Cocteau, *An Impersonation of Angels*, where Misia is portrayed as a troublemaker who paid for admiration. It should now be clear that in her best years she sowed more harmony than discord and that she was loved for herself until the bitter end.)

Of her friends from the old days, many stuck around and at least one grew even closer. Renoir was without snobbery. Gold and Fizdale should have made more of his loyalty to Misia, since he was a deeply moral man whose approval of her must count as the single most convincing tribute to her character. In this regard, the book lacks proportion: it makes comprehensive lists of resonant names but lacks an economical sense of how to deploy facts in order to make points. A profoundly serious artist who had known real poverty and wasted no time on show, Renoir saw the importance of Misia's gift for bringing life alive. The authors know this well enough but lack the strategic sense to exploit it.

Renoir longed to paint Misia with the famous breasts naked, but she would never bare them to him, probably because Edwards was lurking heavily in the adjacent room, ready to exact jealous vengeance even though the artist by that time was an all but total cripple. At one point during her marriage to Edwards, Misia rewarded Renoir for a portrait by giving him a blank cheque. He filled it in with the going rate. Apparently he wrote love letters to her, but in her last days, on the advice of her literary agent, she destroyed them. Her agent had assessed them as 'too silly'.

Misia lost Edwards to the gorgeous young actress Geneviève Lantelme, who had started off as a whore at the age, say the authors, of fourteen. (In other books estimates go as low as twelve.) The break-up took a long time and Misia was able to go on enjoying a large income, but in the early stages she headed for the Normandy coast in order to get away from it all. She arrived to find that she was sharing the ozone with Edwards, Geneviève and her ex-husband Thadée. Proust was there too, and that night wrote to tell Reynaldo Hahn all about it. As Hahn had once said about the Normandy coast, it is so close to Paris and so far from the sea. When you read scenes like this it is no longer a question of whether the bad movie will be made, but of who will be in it.

Edwards was eventually replaced by José-Maria Sert, otherwise known as the Tiepolo of the Ritz. A colourful, muscular painter of colourful, muscular murals – Forain credited him with the invention of the collapsible fresco – Sert was a tirelessly fiery Spaniard with enough cash to keep Misia in the style to which she obviously had no real intention of becoming unaccustomed. Misia later said that Sert was the only man ever completely to arouse her sexually. Some men called her cold, but perhaps that was because they had missed out. Her sexuality remains something of a mystery, like anybody else's. Meanwhile Diaghilev had come to town. In the following years her drawing-room on the Rue de Rivoli became home from home for the Russians. Readers of Karsavina's book *Theatre Street* might not recall where it was that Proust drove her home from that night. It was Misia's.

Misia and Diaghilev were a royal couple. She opened doors for him while he broadened her horizons. They reigned as autocrats of taste, giving the word its full sense of adventurous critical discrimination. Diaghilev embodied the spirit that produces, whereas Misia embodied only the lesser spirit that consumes, yet she had virtues to complement his and her nose for quality was if anything even sharper. When Stravinsky first played the piano score of *Le Sacre du printemps* to Diaghilev – inevitably this took place in her apartment – she spotted it as a masterpiece before Diaghilev did. When the two Russians almost quarrelled over Diaghilev's proposed cuts she reconciled them. Debussy sat beside her on the first night. 'It's terrible,' he said. 'I don't understand it.' Misia's role was to understand both Debussy and Stravinsky even when they didn't understand each other. She would, it hardly needs saying, have played an important part in the Diaghilev enterprise even had she been obtuse, since Diaghilev's principal need was for money, not moral support. On the opening night of *Petrushka* it was Misia who handed over the 4,000 francs that saved the costumes from being impounded. The curtain went up late, but it went up. It is nice to know, however, that it went up to reveal a work of art which Misia understood in its full significance. She was the perfect audience.

But regrettably she had less time for old cronies, since as Diaghilev's friend she had begun to entertain *le gratin*, the top layer of Parisian society, which in the heady atmosphere generated by the Russian ballet had now for the first time risked contamination by the higher Bohemia. Misia was mobbed by the Comtesse Greffulhe, the Comtesse de Chevigné, and all the other ladies who served as models for Proust. She appears in Proust herself, as the lovely Princess Yourbeletieff in the Russian Ballet sequence of *La Prisonnière*, although some of her characteristics – the less pleasant ones – are given to Madame Verdurin. This last move was a snide one coming from Proust, since Misia was never a climber, whereas Proust, even when you make due allowances for the fact that he was using everything he found, was. In such moments one is reminded of Forster's objections to Proust. He said that Proust's analytical knife cut so deep it came out the other side. And certainly Proust could never do justice to the life-giving energy of a woman like Misia, who was fully capable of becoming interested in the world outside herself: all of Proust's grand women are egotists through and through.

The bad movie becomes a very bad movie. As Satie sits playing *Trois Morceaux en forme de poire* to Diaghilev in Misia's apartment, a friend bursts in to say that Austria has declared war on Serbia. Gold and Fizdale tell a sombre version of the famous ambulance expedition to the Front, with Misia in command and Cocteau featuring as a mascot. Frederick Brown's account is more savage. Probably our authors are closer to the truth about this absurd *beau geste*. Anybody could be excused for not guessing what the war was going to be like, even Cocteau in his specially tailored nurse's outfit. If the movie were good instead of bad, it would start, not with a scene of fifty famous artists all being introduced to one another, but with the visually sensitive Misia encountering a corpse whose face was a swarm of flies.

When the war blew away, Paris was still there but not even Diaghilev could stop time. In the era of Le Boeuf sur le Toit Misia remained a private arbiter of taste, cultivated by artists in the same way that critics were later on. She discovered Poulenc. But she couldn't persuade Diaghilev that Ravel's *La Valse* would make a ballet – a judgment on her part that Balanchine was later to vindicate, and a lapse on Diaghilev's that showed how the old impulse was growing diffuse. In addition, Misia had a rival for Diaghilev's intimacy: her friend Chanel. Misia and Sert helped open Chanel's eyes to art, but her eyes needed no opening to the main chance. She could write cheques for Diaghilev and Stravinsky just as fluently as Misia could. Misia remained influential to the end, but there was steadily less to influence – the great days did not return.

In Misia's circle between the wars, fashion steadily got the edge on art. Even though Sert carried on like a Renaissance man (and, according to Chanel, smelled like one), Misia knew that he was not Picasso, just as she knew that *Les Six* did not add up to Stravinsky. Cocteau, whose task in life was to be ahead of the game, became a more and more prominent part of the décor. Misia and Diaghilev presided over the gala in the Hall of Mirrors in Versailles in 1923. The parties grew ever more enormous but the old innocence drained away. When Balanchine auditioned for Diaghilev – in Misia's apartment, naturally – Diaghilev's days were already numbered. By this time Sert and Misia were both in love with the same girl, Roussy Mdivani, a junior member of the marrying Mdivanis. Roussy was chic as opposed to artistic. She was also young as opposed to old. The triangle lasted for as long as Misia's pride allowed, plus a bit longer. Then she consoled herself with Chanel, who now took her turn to assume the dominant role. At Diaghilev's funeral they were both in the first gondola.

Misia's legs were as lovely as ever but she grew less steady on them, not just from age but from a bad habit of injecting morphine straight through her clothes. During World War Two her record was good – certainly a lot better than Chanel's. Misia did her best to save Max Jacob's life, but not even her pull could rescue Jews from Nazis. At soirées after the war she invited *collaborateurs* and *résistants* on different days, but if they happened to bump into each other she left them to sort it out. She loved life too much to let go of it easily so the end was messy, but even in her most dire straits there was never anything mean about her. She was definitely never in it for the prestige: a lot of Proust's letters she didn't even bother to open.

The Banquet Years, *les beaux jours*: whatever you call those times, Misia Sert was at the heart of them, helping make life sweet for the artists who were busy enriching the future. She was unique in her period – her imitators, however grand their titles, had nothing like her certainty of taste – but not in cultural history, which shows many examples of fruitful interplay between creativity and a receptive social élite, with a stylish woman as the mediator. Catullus complains about being rejected by the high-stepping Clodia but not about the debilitating effects of being accepted: obviously he found in her comfortable surroundings a welcome relief from his lonely pushing of the stilus. Whether she was as thrilled by his poems as he was by her cushions is unknown. The friendship between Michelangelo and Vittoria Colonna brooks no romanticising but its balance of forces is familiar enough. Their mutual appreciation was a trade-off, in which the obsessed artist got a taste of grace and the lady fraternised with immortality. That she knew he was immortal was an indispensable part of the deal: a useful conjunction of high art and high living has always depended on the second respecting the first as much as the first the second.

Another case in point was Isabella d'Este, of whom the great Russian critic Muratov wrote in terms that might easily be applied to Misia. She existed, he says (and any pomposity is in my English, not his Russian),

> not so much for herself or for those near to her as for all epochs. Of her one thinks as of some living monument of the Renaissance. She didn't just live, she represented. In the literal sense she personified both the intellectuality of the Renaissance and the whole brilliance of its materialism.

Her taste, however, could be wobbly. She spurned Mantegna's portrait of her, preferring a more flattering one by the hack Giovanni Santi.

Isabella didn't get the point of Leonardo either, but if the artist got on the wrong side of her he could always move somewhere else. In the Renaissance, the artists could both enjoy aristocratic patronage and remain independent, since they constituted a high social stratum on their own account. On the ability of such a social stratum to form and grow has often depended the artist's freedom to thrive, and in some cases his survival. This social drama can be seen acting itself out in parallel with the accelerated history of musical Vienna. Haydn, though perfectly adjusted to court life, established what independence he could. Mozart might have lasted longer if he had had more earlier. Beethoven was free to fall hopelessly in love with fine young ladies because he had his own standards to fall back on and live by – those of an artistic calling grown self-sufficient. With Schubert, the independence acquired the support of the bourgeois nineteenth century, but it is still best regarded as characteristic of high Bohemia. What can happen to genius when there is no Bohemia to retreat to is exemplified by the fate of Pushkin, who was forced to live by aristocratic rules and rapidly died of them. In the literary civilisation that he called for in vain, he might have met the right kind of woman. In the Italian Renaissance, he could have skipped town and set up shop in a rival court. In Misia's Paris, the duel would have been fought with epigrams.

Goethe's Weimar saw the special relationship between the talented men and the well-born ladies so well established that the Misia Serts were jostling for compliments. On this subject I have attained temporary omniscience by means of *Frauen der Goethezeit*, an anthology of letters edited by Helga Haberland and Wolfgang Pehnt.* Caroline Schelling-Schlegel was praised by Novalis for her '*magisches Atmosphäre*' and complained of by Friedrich Schlegel for her '*hoher Corruptibilität*': i.e. they were all crazy about her. After a night at a bad inn, Goethe subsided with a purr into the well-judged ambience of Annalie Fürstin von Gallitzen. He commended the modesty of her surroundings, but obviously they were a vast improvement on the inn. She thanked him for helping kindle the Platonic spark that drives the shadows from the soul.

*Stuttgart, 1960

But for Goethe the most enchanting of them all was Anna Amalia Herzogin von Sachsen-Weimar-Eisenach, whose life, he recalled, was composed of '*mythologische Szenen.*' Goethe had a way with a thank-you letter that harked forward to the calculated humility of Rilke, who was likewise capable of telling his titled ladies that their lives were composed of mythological scenes. The titled ladies usually responded by inviting him back to their castles the following year. But Rilke's soul-mates should not be despised for allowing him to suck up to them. The *Duino Elegies* are dedicated to Marie von Thurn und Taxis-Hohenlohe as her 'possession'. The compliment might seem fulsome but she undoubtedly deserved something like it. The most you can say against her is that she might have done better to treat some of Rilke's letters the same way Misia treated Proust's.

As Arsène Houssaye has it in his memoirs, the aged Chateaubriand, walking in relaxed enjoyment of Madame Récamier's company, assured Sainte-Beuve that if he had his time again he wouldn't pick up a pen. This may have been rhetoric – if he had never picked up a pen he would not have met Madame Récamier – but it was understandable. It had not been all that long since Molière had died in harness. Great artists are always simple but rarely stupid. They usually realise that there is something distorted about the way they live for art, and are often attracted towards those who make an art of living. The same goes double when the artist is coming up from nowhere, devotes all his energy to his work, and finds at a late stage that he is without manners. There was nothing parodic about the Baroness Pannonica de Koenigswarter except her name. Emanating from the French branch of the Rothschild family, she was a jazz fan whose New York apartment served as *un fastueux logement de dépannage* for Charlie Parker. If he had met her earlier he might have lasted longer.

With the possible exception of Clodia, none of the women I have mentioned, least of all Misia, could possibly be described as a groupie. Sex hardly enters into it. Lou Andréas-Salomé, Alma Mahler, Peggy Guggenheim were out to establish a physical connection with the immortals.

The Misia Serts have always been concerned with a spiritual interchange in which aloofness underlines the intimacy and vice versa, with both hostess and guest being free to draw back. In any society where the middle class has expanded to the extent that the artist is no longer a hired member of the grand household, it has always been up to him how often he comes to dinner. It is true that high living is an enemy of promise, but whether it is succumbed to is a matter of will – and the will, as Chesterton pointed out, means nothing if not the willingness to give things up. Tom Moore sang for his supper until there was nothing left of him, but it was not the fault of Holland House, which could be walked away from, as Byron proved.

There is a crushing sort of determinism which tries to make social élites responsible for the corruption of artists. In fact, it is up to the artist. In our own time, T. S. Eliot received a lot of abuse from Dr Leavis for attending cocktail parties and having his values corrupted. The truth of the matter was that Eliot, while encouraging Harriet Shaw Weaver to play the role of artistic patron to which she was clearly suited, was pretty good at keeping his values intact. Leavis would have done better to complain about D. H. Lawrence, who was glad enough to accept Lady Ottoline Morrell's hospitality, mean enough to caricature her afterwards, and, in a way that Rilke and Proust would have recognised, was always careful to stay in good with such generous women as Mabel Dodge Luhan. But in Leavis's eyes Lawrence was someone like himself, a man consciously dedicated to creativity and with his face set like flint against temptation. Like many critics, Leavis had trouble realising that artists, far from being consciously dedicated to creativity, are simply born to it, and experience no difficulty in warding off temptation if they have a mind to.

A successful artist, unlike a critic or an academic, is a celebrity. Celebrities are fated to be lionised anyway, so it is no mystery when they choose to have it done by people who know how and won't bore them. The wise cultural hero, however, is always careful to disarm the resentment of his own admirers by keeping a low profile. Picasso was a social lion all his life but took pains to cultivate a reputation as someone who never stopped working.

There is also the question of the artist's attitude to his material, which is best summed up by saying that everything is grist to his mill. Hence the absurdity of condemning a writer for his associations without first assessing what use he puts them to. One of the advantages of an historical perspective, however scrappy, is to dispel the illusion that England is the only country possessing a class system. The whole history of civilisation offers not a single example of a country that doesn't. At any time, anywhere, can be found impeccably humble stay-at-homes who accomplish nothing and frantic bounders who achieve great things. Moralistic criticism based on the social behaviour of the artist is useless and not even moral. Even Professor Carey, the cleverest of reviewers, seems resolutely wedded to provincialism in this matter. Writing a typically brilliant review of a book whose essential foolishness he failed to detect, Professor Carey happily classified Brian Howard and Evelyn Waugh as twin exemplars of a decayed ruling class. Any attitude which can find two such men even remotely similar is worthy of study in itself. It takes no great predictive power to see that in the long term there will be no such thing as a social context in which Evelyn Waugh can be placed. The context will be gone and his work will remain.

To the artists she favoured, Misia Sert was as exciting at the time as they will always be to us. She was the way they felt: she didn't just live, she represented. We should bear this in mind when considering that, of the two redoubtable women bobbing in the gondola, it was Chanel and not Misia who was the practical creator. Fortunate not to be lynched after the Liberation, Chanel had her repellent aspects, but she knew what she was for. She belonged, even if in a small way, to a more robust history than that of chic. The Chanel suit should figure early in any virago's list of artefacts that shook the world. In teaching her the ways of the *beau monde*, Misia was fulfilling the timeless function of the great lady educating the artist born of the people. Chanel knew it and in their later years paid her back with such loyalty as she could summon. On the train south they would cackle scandal at each other and shoot junk. Cocteau dramatised their rancid friendship in *Les Monstres sacrés* but really they were beyond him, and he knew them both well. It would be a brave outsider, at this distance, who presumed to solve the mystery of such an alliance.

The mark Chanel made is still discernible. Misia survives only in the work of others. The authors of this book can be charged with having failed to tell us what she was like, but probably nobody could now, since even the most gifted artists of the day could only partly do so then. Gold and Fizdale have talked to everyone still alive who ever knew her. In doing so, they have assembled an admirable testimony to her personality. But the personality itself has been long gone. In a way that no artist can ever quite understand but nearly all of them find irresistibly attractive, she did nothing with her capacity for beauty except live. Yet the human personality, which dies with the memory of individuals, and the work of art, which lives on in the collective consciousness, are different forms of the same thing – a truth made acutely visible by Misia's portraits, which, if they do not capture her, certainly capture uncapturability. She gave the artists the gift of her sublime ephemerality and they made it last. That true sacred monster the Comtesse Anna de Noailles wrote herself an epitaph which would have done much better for Misia: 'I shall have been useless but irreplaceable.'

(*London Review of Books*, 1980)

Bernard Levin: Book Two

***Taking Sides* by Bernard Levin (Cape, London)**

FOR ALL his faults, the absence of Bernard Levin has been one of the best reasons for missing *The Times* during the months it has been off the streets. His first book since *The Pendulum Years*, and indeed only the second book he has ever published, *Taking Sides* is part compensation for not being able to read his latest opinions in less durable form. The book contains a selection of his strongest pieces from the last decade or so, most of them *Times* columns. One of Levin's best subjects, British politics, has been left out altogether, with a note in the introduction to inform us that the doings of Sir Harold Wilson and his kind are too ephemeral to be worth perpetuating in volume form. The present compilation deals with every subject but that.

There is plenty to be going on with, although perhaps not quite as much as Levin thinks. 'I am afraid,' says Levin, 'that I have a very great deal to say.' Courageous, self-willed and frantically energetic, Levin holds strong views which he enunciates with unambiguous force. He has some reason to be proud of his individuality. The things he says are mainly his, not somebody else's. But he says them over and over. Even when his reams of tireless production are sifted down to this one volume, the effect is still long-winded. The long-windedness is in the style. Bernard Levin is simply a verbose writer. This fact is scarcely enough to disqualify him from consideration in a world where the average journalist is not a writer of any kind, but it suffices to make you wonder if some of the attitudes he strikes are not struck partly so that he might rant without interruption.

Credit, though, where credit is due. Levin's habit of staying with a story too long comes in handy when the story is about what the Gas Board is doing to some poor old darling's kitchen. As the Gas Board goes on and on replacing the wrong part with another wrong part, you can depend upon it that the poor old darling is keeping Levin bang up to date with all the details. The details usually turn out to be funnier than Levin's comments on them, but at least they are there.

Similarly he is good on unions. Levin has been personally active in the free-lance branch of the journalists' union, the NUJ, where by his energies he has done a lot to frustrate the plans of those giftless radicals who wait around at meetings until there is no one left to interfere with a unanimous vote. Levin published lists which helped write-in voters to support sane candidates. He did the same with regard to the actors' union, Equity, thereby materially helping to stop that organisation passing into the control of the zanier members of the Redgrave family. For a writer it is not a very exalted level on which to be politically effective, but it counts, especially when you consider how few writers are politically effective on any level.

Besides, it is good copy: Levin's Trot-busting activities invariably yield rich plunder in the form of the enemy's own verbal communications. Levin is adept at collating such material and letting it speak for itself to a wider world. For a find like the marvellous senior librarian Keith Harrison, we can only be grateful. Keith, it transpires, is a leading light in an outfit called Librarians for Social Change. 'It's books that I'm into,' says Keith.

Keith is so deeply into books that he would like to see all racist, sexist and élitist literature cleared from the library shelves, so as to leave more room for the kind of books he is into. Eliot once said that the translators of the New English Bible were atheists without knowing it. Keith is a censor without knowing it, and Levin is good on censors of any kind. His review of *The Longford Report* is an exemplary job of demolition, made all the more convincing by his generous willingness to regard Lord Longford as something better than a buffoon.

Commendably ready to hold an opinion no matter who

agrees with him, Levin finds himself siding with Lord Longford over the matter of Myra Hindley. 'In this matter,' he says, 'I am of Lord Longford's opinion.' But on those few occasions when one finds one's views congruent with those of the daffy peer it is always advisable to pause for thought. Alas, pausing for thought is not Levin's habit. Once having struck an attitude, he prefers to plug away at it. In the case of Myra Hindley he insists on thinking that the reason the majority of people want her kept in gaol is revenge: even if the Home Secretary thought it safe to release her he would be reluctant to do so because of the public's 'inevitable fury'. 'And the inevitable fury is, of course, based on the theory of punishment that is supposed to have no place in our system, to wit the retributive. Myra Hindley did terrible things to children; therefore, runs the instant but unreasoning answer, she must rot in gaol for the rest of her life.' The whole article takes the same high tone of judicial detachment. He sounds like Solomon, Cato the Elder and Oliver Wendell Holmes all rolled into one. Levin likes nothing better than to hand down a ruling. But although it is probably true that the majority of the public would be furious if Myra Hindley were released, it is unlikely that their desire to keep her locked up has anything to do with revenge. They just don't want her to do it again.

Lord Longford is too fascinated with himself to realise that a woman twisted enough to derive sexual pleasure from torturing a child to death might be capable of duping him into the belief that she has repented. But Levin has set himself up as somebody who is hard to gull. He has no excuse for ignoring the considerable range of reasonable opinion that would prefer it if Myra Hindley were not turned loose, even with Lord Longford's personal guarantee of her future good conduct.

On a larger and more serious scale, Levin spent years loudly ignoring reasonable opinion about the foreign policy of the United States. Much of this reasonable opinion was itself American. But Levin is so fond of Taking Sides that he will back the lesser evil against the greater, as if he himself were a man of action on the international stage. He has always been quite right about the horrors of totalitarianism. Where he has always been wrong is in supposing that reasonable people have no case when they argue that the United States does itself a profound injury by opposing totalitarianism with totalitarian methods. Year after year, Levin wrote as if anybody who doubted the wisdom of Kissinger's policies in South America and South-East Asia was in cahoots with Jane Fonda and possibly the Kremlin.

On the issue of Watergate, Levin went on proclaiming Nixon's innocence when even Rabbi Korff must have been thinking about giving up. Compared to what the Russians got up to, Levin argued, Watergate was nothing. From his position on the bench of the Supreme Court of the Universe, Levin should have been able to see that Nixon had been subverting the Constitution of the United States by attempting to form a Presidential party, and that this was why many patriotic Americans took such exception – because they didn't want the United States to become a country in which such things meant nothing. Levin missed the point.

On all these issues Levin went on and on missing the point, and always at the top of his voice. Having read in the *Reader's Digest* an account of what the Khmer Rouge regime had been doing in Cambodia, he boldly focused his attention on 'that crucified nation of which the world prefers to know nothing'. Always confident in his predictions, Levin warned us that the pseudo-liberal press would from now on have nothing to say about Cambodia. But Levin need not have waited for his subscription copy of the *Reader's Digest* to bring him the story. The *New York Review of Books*, for example, had already carried detailed reports.

Levin still goes on insisting that there has been a conspiracy of silence on the subject of what happened in Cambodia after the Khmer Rouge took over. But in actual fact that very subject has been widely discussed by the very people Levin is castigating – many of whom, indeed, predicted just such an outcome. The true conspiracy of silence was the one maintained by Nixon and Kissinger on the subject of what happened *before* the Khmer Rouge took over. This might seem an elementary point to make, but when you are dealing with Levin's high-and-mighty treatment of world politics you are forced to make elementary points all the time. In matters of the NUJ and the Gas Board Levin's rhetorical posturing may have some result. In matters of global conflict it can have no result at all, apart from the negative one of further distorting the truth.

Levin sees great issues in the form of psychodrama. There are heroes and villains, with nobody in between. For all his passionate advocacy, the net effect is to diminish the truth. Solzhenitsyn is certainly the hero of our time that Levin says he is, but it does no good for Levin to gush over him as if he were Kiri Te Kanawa. Just as Levin's admiration for Kiri Te Kanawa would count for more if he interrupted his praise of her undoubtedly gorgeous voice to point out that in Lieder concerts she has occasionally been known to sing a stanza with its lines in reverse order, so his admiration for Solzhenitsyn would count for more if he could entertain the possibility that Solzhenitsyn's challenging call for a unifying sense of purpose on the part of the free world might be a contradiction in terms. If the free world had a unifying sense of purpose it would not be free.

But merely to raise such a point is to be enrolled by Levin among the ranks of those who are intent on belittling his hero. It never occurs to him that *he* is the one who is belittling his hero, by heaping him with indiscriminate acclaim. An encomium from Levin is a spray of treacle which leaves its object a shapeless mass.

Levin talking about Solzhenitsyn doesn't sound very different from Mrs Thatcher talking about Solzhenitskin, the mysterious Russian writer whose name was so memorably invoked in a Conservative Party Political Broadcast. In other words, he sounds as if he is speaking in the debating chamber. The difference between making debating points and arguing in a true debate is the difference between fantasy and reality. Levin's *Times* column has been a useful clearing house for atrocity stories about the Marxist totalitarian states. He performs a valuable service in keeping his readers up to date about how awful those places are. But you would never learn from Levin that there is a genuine debate going on about how to deal with the Soviet Union, and that the debate is mainly being conducted among the Russian dissidents themselves.

Solzhenitsyn, understandably, wants the Soviet government discredited entirely. Sakharov, even though his own scientific career has by now been ruined by the Soviet authorities, persists in thinking that the Soviet Union might be forced to rejoin the civilised world if it could be persuaded that only a measure of liberalisation will enable it to keep up as a first-rate productive country. Most people who have gone into the matter think that Sakharov is more concrete in his proposals than Solzhenitsyn, but the important point to make is that Levin, abjectly copying Solzhenitsyn's apocalyptic tone, is even less concrete.

Levin's proposal for our salvation is a change of heart. This new *Weltanschauung* has noticeable affinities with the political theories of Arianna Stassinopoulos, of which the best that can be said is that they catch votes in the debating chamber. In the *Spectator*, Christopher Booker has been emitting, by instalments, a speculative pontification which echoes the same uplifting sentiments. Perhaps these philosophers should be thought of as forming a school, like the Vienna Circle. Perhaps sitting in London is, after all, the best way of probing the soul of Western Man. But it seems more likely that they are all simply fanning the air in the usual manner of those who can't live without an Answer, and that Levin, in particular, has a thirst for mystical transcendence which not even regular exposure to the *Ring* cycle can assuage.

Confidently predicting, in 1977, that Brian Inglis's book *Natural and Supernatural* would be greeted by a chorus of rejection from terrified scientists, Levin never noticed that it was greeted by a chorus of indifference. Fantasising flat out, Levin insists that Science is blindly determined to deny the inexplicable: 'That, surely, is why the very distinguished scientist I met soon after I wrote about Brian Inglis's book attacked me and it (he had not read it, of course) in a voice that was shrill and unsteady and with the sweat breaking out on his forehead; not because he knew he was right, but because the most important part of him knew he was wrong.' Possibly so, but there is always the chance that the boffin snapped his wig because Levin had turned out to be just another zombie wanting to bore him about Uri Geller. On this subject, the real story has never been about rational people resisting the inexplicable. It has always been about irrational people resisting the explicable. For some reason they find Occam's razor too frightening an instrument. For them, the world is not enough. Solipsism wants more.

Schopenhauer called style the physiognomy of the soul. Levin's style is essentially self-dramatising. The whole thing is a pose. Often it is an entertaining pose, but it is always bombastic, and the slightest lapse leads to a bad sermon. He can echo the Gibbonian period, although in his case the dignity is hollow; and the Shavian paragraph, although in his case the sprightliness is elephantine; but the main reason he is given to long sentences is that he is not unselfconscious enough to write short ones. He can no more say it short than A. J. P. Taylor can say it long. In the long sentences of Proust you can still hear the aphoristic tradition that started with Pascal. In the long sentences of Levin you can hear a tradition being forgotten.

The English essay grew and flowered in newspapers and magazines. In keeping with its setting, it should be terse. Unfortunately *The Times* seems to have offered Levin a contract by which they must pay him by the word and leave every word untouched. His stint as the *Sunday Times* theatre critic produced better results. With a plenitude of stimuli to choose from, he was able to dismiss what was not worth discussing. Whether what he praised was worth seeing is another question. After hearing him praise Alan Howard's portrayal of Coriolanus, I ran to the Aldwych with my knees high. There I found Alan Howard portraying Coriolanus as a Roman version of Carol Channing. He swivelled his hips and blew kisses at the stalls, which were full of Japanese businessmen and Norwegians in anoraks. As a theatre critic Levin is less dimwitted than most of his colleagues but probably no more reliable.

Levin's jokes leave you straight-faced. He takes an admirable stand on apartheid but weakens his own case by putting it in the form of a laborious revue sketch peppered with funny names which are just like Beachcomber's except that they are not funny. Also he lacks tact. James Agate filled his column with excerpts from Racine but some of his readers could read French. Levin employs Latin tags copiously and almost always leaves them untranslated. I feel pleased at being able to puzzle some of these out, but not as pleased, I fear, as Levin must have felt when he found ways of dragging them in. There is a lot of Greek in Cicero's Latin but there is even more Latin in Levin's English. Who does he think he is?

Victor Hugo was under the impression that he was Victor Hugo. Bernard Levin feels the same way about Bernard Levin. He is never off his plinth. On *Face the Music* he takes a sip of water after getting the right answer. It is meant to look humble but screams conceit. In his prose he is even more given to overstating his own importance. When Beecham said that he would give all the Brandenburg concertos for Massenet's *Manon* he was drawing your attention to Massenet. When Levin said that he would give all Puccini for Gounod's *Faust* he was drawing your attention to Levin. He also once said that he could not see what was so sublime about Bach, evidently supposing that this would lead us to think twice about Bach.

Self-assertion on that scale is fun to watch but it is not quite the same thing as self-assurance. You have only to compare the way Levin comments on the press with the way A. J. Liebling once commented on it to see what Levin lacks. Liebling had the compressed but relaxed colloquial raciness of someone who had a lot to say and genuinely believed that it was more important than he was. Another telling American example is I. F. Stone. With few literary graces except clarity and conversational rhythm, Stone's prose is the embodiment of honesty. Treating a comparable range of interests, Stone has all of Levin's energy with none of his flim-flam.

Stone does his best to see an issue straight. He talks sense even when he is wrong. Truly patriotic and truly democratic, he is a truly independent commentator who has never taken sides with his own government against liberal principles and has consequently always been doubly influential in his condemnations of totalitarian repression. Looking through his books – most of them compiled, like this one, from articles – you can get a good idea of what has actually been going on in the world over the last thirty years. There is a human voice talking. It is the difference between personality and histrionics.

Nevertheless Levin has personality of a kind. Reviewers often scold writers for publishing collections of pieces. Usually the reviewer is peeved because nobody has asked him to do the same. Some writers work best in short forms. Of Chesterton's hundred or so books, his books of pieces rank high among those worth seeking out. Something of a latter-day Chesterton, Levin gets ten pieces out of the same number of ideas that would have served Chesterton for one, but he has a modicum of the same gusto. He pumps hot air into the English language, but at least he is using it, not abusing it. Half the feature writers in Fleet Street can't tell the difference between a paragon and a paradigm. The other half believe you can mitigate against militating circumstances. Levin at least knows how to say what he means. What is hard to believe, sometimes, is that he means what he says. Perhaps he just gets carried away. Most of us would find it hard to deny that there are occasions when we enjoy being carried away with him.

(*London Review of Books*, 1979)

Doubting Castle

God's Apology: A Chronicle of Three Friends by Richard Ingrams (Deutsch, London)

IT SEEMED an unpromising enough idea for a book. Richard Ingrams, inky editor of *Private Eye*, writes about the friendship between three literary journeymen – Hugh Kingsmill, Hesketh Pearson and Malcolm Muggeridge – and in defining their values defines his own. Such as they are. Having been keel-hauled by Ingrams when he reviewed one of my own books, I confess that when I accepted the commission (all right: begged for the opportunity) to review his latest volume my heart was not entirely free of the desire to take revenge. It is with mixed feelings, then, that I find *God's Apology* a substantial and interesting piece of work.

Hugh Kingsmill was an adept at spotting the gap between a writer's real-life personality and the personality which that same writer projected on to the paper. He thought that no writer could successfully put into words more virtue than he practised. Bad character would reveal itself as pretentious writing. This basic critical precept was the main thing which Kingsmill passed on to Hesketh Pearson. They both passed it on to Malcolm Muggeridge. Muggeridge passed it on to Richard Ingrams. An apostolic succession of antipseuds.

Ingrams succeeds Michael Holroyd in helping to complete the process of enrolling Hugh Kingsmill among the most celebrated of neglected modern writers. Holroyd's anthology – and earlier biography – had already demonstrated that Kingsmill's talents lay towards the aphoristic. After respectfully absorbing Holroyd's anthology, you could see no reason for turning to the books from which it was culled. After respectfully absorbing *God's Apology*, you will see no reason for turning to Holroyd's anthology. Ingrams has appended a brief section entitled 'Sayings of Hugh

Kingsmill'. These, coupled to the portrait of their author provided in the body of the book, give you the essence of the man. He was clearly a penetrating moralist. The best of his aphorisms have La Rochefoucauld's realism tempered by La Bruyère's humanity. Some of them even have Santayana's or Lichtenberg's philosophical depth. The aphorism is a revealing form, to the point that anyone who cultivates it deliberately is almost certain to be no good at it. Kingsmill was good at it.

> *Suicide*: The coward's way in. *Spiritualism*: Spiritualism is the mysticism of the materialist. *Talent and Genius*: A man of talent thinks more highly of himself when he has a success, a man of genius thinks more highly of the world. *Shyness*: Shyness is egotism out of its depth. *Fanaticism*: Fanaticism consists in redoubling your effort when you have forgotten your aim.

The last example is from Santayana. I don't see that Kingsmill's efforts are shown up by it, except perhaps for the one about shyness, which has a tinge of Wildean mascara. (Most of the shy people I know suffer from the opposite of egotism.) Kingsmill's place in the short list of valuable aphorists can from now on be regarded as secure. Success, of course, has come late. Ingrams argues forcefully that Kingsmill was a man out of his time. In Britain during the 1930s a literary journalist had to be seen to care about public affairs and politics. Kingsmill, who was indifferent to them, disqualified himself from being in demand even as a hack. Compiling pot-boiling anthologies, spending the derisory advances for books he never got around to writing, he lived the classic pawned existence of the unworldly literatus. His was the Grub Street of George Gissing, writ even smaller. Like Edward Thomas he wore himself out producing books that were successful only in the completeness of their failure to do him justice.

But Ingrams overstates his case by linking Kingsmill's frustration solely to his lack of sympathy with the spirit of the age. There are Kingsmills in every age. On Ingrams's own evidence, Kingsmill was a recognisable literary type. Grub

Street can always boast a quota of hacks ready to erect their own fecklessness into a moral code. Obviously Kingsmill was better than that, but Ingrams might have argued harder to prove it. It is clear that Kingsmill was genuinely unworldly, genuinely hated the will to power, genuinely distrusted success. But he was capable of lapses from his own standards.

Ingrams introduces such lapses as if they were lovable touches of character. Possibly so, but the reader can't help wondering what *Private Eye*'s unforgiving editor might have made of them if his purpose had been demolition instead of hagiography. Kingsmill envied the more successful Pearson and quarrelled with him because of it. After half a lifetime of poking fun at Bernard Shaw's materialism Kingsmill was not above touching the despised sage for ten quid. Even in the Australian school of literary morals, we weren't allowed to slag a man *and* put the bite on him simultaneously: it had to be one or the other.

But on the whole Kingsmill was true to himself. His failings were only human, even though he might have found those same failings ruinous in his enemies, and in *his* enemies Ingrams would be certain to. Kingsmill was against Dawnism – he distrusted any political movement which offered happiness to all mankind. It is easy to say now that he was right. At the time there were still intelligent idealists who needed convincing. Hesketh Pearson was one of them. Kingsmill helped relieve Pearson of his illusions about millenarian prophets such as Bernard Shaw. (It was at a later time, and in even more straitened circumstances, that Kingsmill helped relieve Bernard Shaw of ten pounds.)

The friendship between Kingsmill and Pearson was close, surpassing the love of women. (Again one can only speculate about the tone Ingrams might have taken if his intentions had been hostile: Lord Gnome's clean-living organ has traditionally given poovery short shrift.) Kingsmill idealised his women and usually had a thin time. Pearson, a handsome charmer, suffered from abundance. For nine years he was torn between wife and mistress. For nine years the mistress begged him to ask for a divorce but he couldn't bring himself to hurt his wife. He chose the moment after their son had been killed in the Spanish Civil War to ask his devastated spouse if she would let him go. She let him go. The mistress told him it was too late. The wife agreed to take him back. The best you can say about the hero of such a story is that even if his instincts were right, his timing was off.

Ingrams says that Pearson never forgave himself. What Ingrams doesn't say is whether or not we should examine Pearson's writings in the light of his behaviour. All we are told is that Pearson's unfortunate experience gave him special insight into Hazlitt. Granted, but one would have thought that the main thing raising the author of *Liber Amoris* above the Hesketh Pearsons of this world is the ability to keep failure in mind as well as take it to heart. There is no comment left to make on Hazlitt's foolishness. He said everything himself. It helped him to become wise. In doubting himself, he understood the world.

As transmitted to us in this book, Kingsmill and Pearson doubt the world. Neither is shown to be very good at understanding himself. Actually Kingsmill's aphoristic subtlety suggests a greater degree of self-knowledge than Ingrams allows him. Hampered by parochialism, Ingrams is plainly unaware that in every language and epoch even the most gifted poets have always idealised the object of their love, not because they see less than other men but because they see more. The secret of Kingsmill's critical power lies as much in his receptivity as in his nose for pretension. In this respect Ingrams sells Kingsmill short. But perhaps that was inevitable, since he is so eager to stress the embattled stance these men adopted against the follies of the age, a posture made familiar to the present generation by the youngest and now only living member of the trio, Malcolm Muggeridge.

Ingrams hasn't much to say about Muggeridge, which is lucky, because as an exemplar of selfless utterance Muggeridge can scarcely bear much examination. He fits neatly enough into the line of homespun philosophers, leading from Kingsmill down to Ingrams, who are not gulled by popular enthusiasms. But he does plenty of gulling on his own account. If you accept Kingsmill's distinction between the charlatan and the thinker ('A charlatan makes obscure what is clear, a thinker makes clear what is obscure'), then Muggeridge is a charlatan. He has never raised an issue without leaving it more clouded than it was before. Far from being stimulating even when wrong, he is misleading even when right. His intransigence is really a way of indulging himself.

But all Ingrams allows himself to see is the intransigence. And indeed there is something attractive about the picture he paints of a tiny band of brothers defying the spirit of the age. At its best, this book is an engaging celebration of independent men – sceptics who defended intelligence with humour. But there was something cosy about the way they applied their test of sincerity – which is, though always a necessary, never a sufficient measure of value. It left them scornful of almost everything except each other. *Private Eye* radiates the same cosiness. Contemptuous of the will to power, it misuses its own power without a qualm. The division is in its editor's nature: like his three heroes, he is a reactionary, in the sense that he is sure only of what he is against. He and the *Eye* crew forgive nothing to anyone else and everything to themselves. So it is that Ingrams is able on the one hand to write a book as sensitive as this, and on the other to let one of *Private Eye*'s anonymous gossip columnists fulfil a lifetime's ambition, which is to tell dirty stories about the people he envies, and send their children crying home from school.

(*New Statesman*, 1977)

Only Human

Reaching Judgment at Nuremberg **by Bradley F. Smith (Deutsch, London, and Basic Books, New York)**

NO EXPERT in either international jurisprudence or the formal study of modern history, I can perhaps represent the general reader in welcoming Professor Smith's new book as a substantial contribution to the understanding of the age we live in. *Reaching Judgment at Nuremberg* could easily have been the sort of book that leaves you wondering whether this is an age worth living in at all. It might have brought the horrors to mind without making sense of them, which would have been depressing. Or it might have made sense of all the horrors without bringing them to mind, which would have been more depressing still. But the author has proved himself equal to this most formidable of tasks. He has uncovered new facts without being tempted into unbalanced opinions. The issues are raised and treated without the innocent dead being further dishonoured. Despite its terrible weight of subject, this is one contemporary historical work which leaves you with the encouraging feeling that the form and pressure of modern political tragedy might somehow be transmitted intact to the generations that will succeed us.

If it now seems evident that genocide was the central issue in the Nuremberg trials, we largely have the Nuremberg trials to thank. It was only during the trials themselves that the industrial scale of the Nazi onslaught on innocent people came to be revealed. During the preparation of their case, and indeed during much of their conduct of it, the prosecution lawyers were seldom able to grasp the significance of what they were faced with. Especially on the part of the Americans and the British, there was a striking inability to imagine what everyday life had been like in Nazi Europe.

Fortunately the tribunal itself was quicker on the uptake.

Drawn from all four of the occupying powers, the judges were on the whole able to see the correct import of evidence so overwhelmingly awful that the prosecution scarcely knew how to present it. One of the many services performed by Professor Smith's book is to show that Nuremberg was not a kangaroo court. Even the Russian and the French judges were able to act with some independence from their governments. It is true that some of the defendants were arbitrarily chosen, true that the indictment was questionably framed, and true again that some of the verdicts were anomalous. But by and large justice was done. The idea that at Nuremberg the victors tried the vanquished is a false one.

The vanquished were the millions of guiltless men, women and children already obliterated. Most of the men on trial were victors who would have remained victorious if something had not been done. Whether or not they deserved death in their turn, they certainly had *something* coming to them. The Nuremberg tribunal, in making sure that they got it, went some way towards a squaring of the accounts – and in making sure that they were tried by due process achieved something better than mere revenge. Revenge would have been a raindrop echoing an ocean.

The accused were indicted on four counts. Count One concerned a general conspiracy to wage aggressive war. Count Two concerned substantive crimes in furtherance of that end. Count Three concerned war crimes as defined by the Geneva Convention and similar agreements. Count Four concerned Crimes against Humanity. Although it might seem obvious to us that Count Four is the one that matters most, the prosecution focused most of its efforts on Count One. In retrospect this might seem hard to explain. Conspiracy theories have a bad reputation among lawyers and this particular conspiracy theory is no longer popular even among historians, who have done their best to convince us that Hitler's plan for world conquest was really a sequence of brilliant improvisations. Yet at the time of the Nuremberg trials the climate of opinion dictated that the Nazis should be punished collectively, even if the punishment was only symbolic. As revealed in captured documents, the sheer cynicism with which Hitler had toppled governments shocked the world. Anybody could appreciate that here had been a pack of gangsters on the loose.

Count Four, on the other hand, although it seems of enduring importance to us, was difficult to cope with at the time. Since there were no statutes covering crimes against humanity, law had to be invented *ex post facto* – always a questionable procedure. But, as has since become clear, separating Count Four from Count Three was a crucial move. Even though the fact was not generally accepted at the time, in the matter of ordinary war crimes the Allies were fully as guilty as the Axis powers. It was the extraordinary crimes which made the Nazis special.

Convinced that Count One was the heart of the case, the prosecution presented its evidence on Count Four so unsystematically that Rudolf Hoess, the Auschwitz commandant, was put on the stand only as a *defence* witness, in an attempt to exculpate the party hierarchs by showing that the exterminations had been undertaken on local initiative. (The seed of the David Irving thesis was planted thirty years ago.) But the tribunal was wiser than the prosecution. Most of the evidence was in the form of documents, repetitively presented with a doggedness that bored the court stiff. The testimony of witnesses, which might have made the subject vivid both for the bench and for the watching world, was sparingly employed. Nevertheless the judges quickly educated themselves in Nazi realities. In this department as in most others they showed themselves independent of the prosecution. They might not have been the very top men in their profession but they had legal reputations it was in their interest to keep intact. Beyond that, they simply happened to be a group of reasonably decent men. With access to their papers, Professor Smith is able – and obviously glad – to show that their deliberations were rarely cynical, even when circumstances forced them into absurdity.

Most of the absurdity came from the choice of defendants. Each occupying country wanted to include some of its own captives, with the result that the dock held the obscure as well as the notorious. Alfried Krupp would probably have been there if the prosecution had not mixed him up with his mad father Gustav. On the other hand Fritzsche, who had never done much and whom nobody had ever heard of, *was* there. There was an element of farce. But for the most part the verdicts sorted the defendants out. The small fry were thrown back and the bigger fish were fairly sentenced. Most importantly, they were sentenced as individuals, for substantive crimes. There was not much resort to the conspiracy theory. With the exception of Streicher, men were punished for what they did, and not for what they said they might do.

Granted that hanging was an appropriate punishment, those who were sentenced to it deserved no less. Goering, Ribbentrop, Kaltenbrunner, Rosenberg, Frank, Frick, Sauckel, Jodl, Seyss-Inquart . . . apart from Rosenberg, a batty ideologist whose books not even the Nazis could get through, they all knew what they had been at. Among those executed, Streicher was the only really doubtful case. An awful man who edited an awful newspaper, Streicher was hanged for his bad character rather than substantive crimes. He was a victim of the conspiracy theory if anybody was. There is no reason to waste grief on him, but we can wish that the judges who hesitated might have hesitated harder. The Russian judges, as always, didn't hesitate at all. They wanted the death penalty for everybody and saw no objections to *ex post facto* law. As we now know, Stalin's post-war purge was already rolling at the time of the trials. But the Nuremberg trials can't be written off just because the Russians participated in them. If we now have standards for measuring Soviet history, Nuremberg helped to establish them.

Streicher was hanged and Speer got twenty years. Professor Smith is now able to reveal that some of the judges wanted the rope for Speer. Whatever you think of capital punishment, it is difficult not to hope that Speer has been suffering a slight difficulty in breathing after hearing this news. Speer got away with it. When he sent his demands for forced labour down to Sauckel, he knew what the results would be. His air of civilisation saved him from death. If the Nuremberg trials had dealt out divine justice, Streicher would have been released into the care of an animal trainer and Speer would have been punished to the full extent. But as things were, the tribunal was only human. Speer got the benefit of the doubt. The court had the drawbacks of its virtues, the chief virtue being its moderation. In extending due process, humane treatment and mercy to men who would have liked to have driven those things from the face of the earth, the Nuremberg judges did us a favour we will be a long time repaying. This excellent book is part of their reward.

(*New Statesman*, 1977)

From Log Cabin to Log Cabin

The Memoirs of Richard Nixon (Sidgwick & Jackson, London, and Grosset & Dunlap, New York)

LARGELY deservedly, Richard Nixon is in such low repute that it is hard to give him credit for anything without sounding capricious. Yet it must be said, in the teeth of all expectation, that his *Memoirs* constitute a readable book of no small literary merit and considerable human dignity. Doubtless there are ghost writers in the picture somewhere; in the acknowledgments a large number of secretaries and editors receive thanks; but if a committee wrote this book, it was one of those rare committees which, setting out to design a horse, actually succeed in designing a horse instead of a camel.

Nixon has done many reprehensible things in his career and in a way this book is just one more of them. By internal contradictions alone, quite apart from evidence that can be brought up from outside, it is a book patently full of half-truths and false conclusions. But it is not a mean book. Nixon's faults are all on view, but so is the fact that they are faults in something substantial. His claims to a place in history are shown to be not all that absurd. He will be harder to mock from now on, although perhaps even easier to distrust.

Such a judgment should emerge naturally from any fair reading of the text. A fair reading, however, might well be prejudiced by an initial glance at the copious photographs. Featuring a hero described in the captions as RN, these tend to show Nixon at his most bogusly histrionic. During the Hiss case he profiles like a concave Dick Tracy while examining the 'pumpkin papers' through a magnifying glass. His dog Checkers helps him read the newspaper on a bench in Central Park. There is a supposedly eloquent photograph of construction-union leaders' safety-helmets arranged on a White House table as an endorsement for Nixon's Cambodian adventure, with nothing in the caption to tell you that the union leaders would probably have reacted the same way if he had atom-bombed the Eskimos. Finally there are pictures commemorating his long hamming contest with Brezhnev. The most startling of these shows Brezhnev apparently sticking his tongue in Nixon's right ear. If you get no further than the photographs, your estimate of the book is bound to be wide of the mark.

The text proper is more than a thousand pages long. Most people who tackle it at all will probably start near the end, to find out what the author (for practical reasons I shall assume this to be Nixon himself) says about Watergate. But there are good reasons for beginning at the beginning and reading the whole way through. For one thing, it's a good story. Nixon's anabasis was the classic journey from log cabin to White House, and the early stages of the trip are made no less absorbing by the consideration that he was later obliged to retrace a portion of the itinerary from White House to log cabin.

Nixon's poor-but-honest Quaker background in Depression-era California is celebrated with all-American pride. The scene-setting is like watered-down Steinbeck, but there is a certain gusto in the way the clichés are deployed, and the prose is grammatical. (As, indeed, it is throughout the book: apart from a solitary use of 'credence' for 'credibility' there are no solecisms.) Nixon's father is portrayed as a strong-willed populist, his mother as an exemplar of 'inner peace'. There are deaths in the family. There is no money. But deprivation is material not spiritual. At Whittier High School Nixon plays Aeneas in a production marking the two-thousandth anniversary of Virgil's death. Working his way through Whittier College, in his Junior year he reads Tolstoy. Winning a place at Duke University Law School in North Carolina, he strengthens his mind with the unyielding facts of case law.

The emphasis is always on self-help. The boy Nixon professed liberalism with a populist tinge, but in effect he was already a conservative. He was always for a free economy as opposed to a managed one. He was thus a Republican from the outset. His political beliefs are the most honest things about him and it is doubtful if they ever varied. Since they were hard won, in circumstances which favoured the opposite case – if any family stood to gain from the Democratic Party, the New Deal and the welfare mentality, it was the Nixons – he should be given credit for his independence of mind.

Even when young, Nixon can never have been a charming figure, but he has every right to be proud of his upbringing. Later in life, especially after his defeat by Kennedy, it became an article of liberal belief that Nixon was embittered by resentment of the Eastern establishment and its fancy Ivy League ways. In particular he was supposed to be eaten up by envy of the Kennedys. If any of this was ever true, he has done a thorough job of covering it up in his memoirs. But there is good cause to suppose that Nixon's undoubted vindictiveness was more against liberalism as a philosophy than against the Eastern establishment as an institution. Nixon felt that liberals were fashion-conscious, changeable and unscrupulous. He felt that they would get him if he did not get them. In the end his obsession with this point led to his downfall. But we will fail to understand the strength of Nixon's mind, and the breadth of his political appeal, if we suppose that his fixations were energised by nothing except spite.

It is better to be a poor boy who makes good than a rich man's son. This general truth becomes particularly true when you compare Nixon and Kennedy according to criteria more telling than mere points of style. Nixon knew American society and politics from the ground up. Kennedy had the shallowness of the man who starts at the top. Nixon has his gaucheries, but they have always been part of the whole man. The Kennedy clan thought that Nixon lacked class. It was never strictly true, but even if it had been, there are worse things to lack. In the long view corn looks better than chic. Kennedy pretended to admire Casals. Nixon honestly thought that Richard Rodgers's score for *Victory at Sea* was great music. Nixon was the one who could actually play the piano. Nixon's homely enthusiasms were in fact part of his strength.

Unfortunately for himself, America and the world, Nixon could never see his strength for what it was. He was forever augmenting it with unnecessary cunning. If he had been less clever he might have lasted longer. But he always felt that he needed an edge – he had to get the bulge on the other guy. He claims to have joined the House Committee on Un-American Activities with 'considerable reluctance'. You would think from his account of the Hiss case that he had conducted the prosecution in a temperate manner. He is careful to dissociate himself from McCarthy, whose own juggernaut was soon to get rolling. But on any objective view, Nixon behaved like a demagogue throughout the hearings. Whether Hiss was guilty or not is a separate issue. Nixon tries to make Hiss's guilt a matter of historic importance, but in fact the historic importance has all to do with the way Nixon used the Fifth Amendment to undermine the spirit of the First Amendment. Nixon pioneered the McCarthyite technique of establishing silence as an admission of guilt. It was Nixon who gave McCarthy the courage to be born.

The House Committee was a Star Chamber. Nixon still professes to assume that Hiss invited suspicion by being mistrustful of the Committee. But only a fool would have expected to be tried fairly by such methods. The point recurs awkwardly a thousand pages later, when the author can be heard protesting that his own trial by Senate Committee is a travesty of justice. If Nixon objects to the methods by which his Presidency was destroyed, then he should repudiate the methods by which he destroyed Hiss. They were the same methods. He claims that Sam Ervin and the other Watergate committee members were publicity seekers. But what, on his own admission, did the Hiss case bring him? It brought him 'publicity on a scale that most congressmen only dream of achieving'.

And so he was off and running – running for President. He pretends, characteristically, that such thoughts were not yet in his mind. Quoting Harry Truman's observation that the Vice-Presidency is about as useful as a fifth teat on a cow, he makes out that it was his very innocence of high ambitions which enabled him to take on the job of playing second fiddle to Eisenhower. After all, it was a thankless task. The media applied their double standards, forgiving Adlai Stevenson everything and Nixon nothing. Because Ike was too big to touch, the liberals ganged up on Nixon. Or so Nixon tells it. Certainly the attack over his supposed misuse of campaign funds must have hurt: his first response was the horribly maladroit 'Checkers' speech, and the long-term result was an unquenchable hatred of the press. But he usually forgets to say how indiscriminate he himself was accustomed to being when dishing out abuse. The furthest he will go is to say that he had no choice. 'Some of the rhetoric I used during the campaign was very rough. Perhaps I was unconsciously overreacting to the attacks made against me.' Someone else was always unscrupulous first. Nixon, says Nixon, would have played clean if they had let him.

During Ike's 1956 campaign Nixon tries to fight high-mindedly, but he can feel that people are disappointed. They *want* him to be tough against the ruthless Stevenson. This is Nixon's message throughout: the liberal-dominated media might be against him, but the pulse from the grass-roots is the country's true heart-beat. Nixon could already hear the low roar of the silent majority long before he gave it a name. Its good wishes sustained him in adversity, which arrived in

1960, when he lost the Presidential race to Kennedy. In an act of heroic self-sacrifice, Nixon talked Ike *out* of appearing on his behalf, lest Ike's heart should give way. Nevertheless he came within a whisker of not losing. He might have won on a recount, but patriotism stopped him asking for one.

As everywhere else in the book, Nixon has only good to say of JFK. But he is scornful of the Kennedy machine. 'From this point on I had the wisdom and the wariness of someone who has been burned by the Kennedys and their money and by the licence they were given by the media.' He certainly learned the wariness. One doubts if he learned the wisdom: anger probably exacerbated his natural vindictiveness. It must have been galling for Nixon to see Joe Kennedy's family being indulged by the press while he himself was hounded, right up to the end, for transgressions which often did not even exist. But sympathy should not mislead, although Nixon would like it to: the whole tendency of the book is to suggest that extraordinary persecution justified extraordinary retaliation.

Honourable defeat in the 1960 Presidential race was followed by ignominious disaster in the 1962 California gubernatorial contest and a duly embittered retirement to the wilderness, where the Internal Revenue Service, egged on by the White House, harassed him about his tax returns. (What he did unto others was done unto him first.) Will he run again? On Key Biscayne, Billy Graham and Bebe Rebozo help him decide. Bebe Rebozo is half of a comedy duo, Bebe Rebozo and Bob Abplanalp. It is nowadays fashionable to deride these two as shady characters, although it seems likely that they are just a pair of routinely dreary millionaires. Billy Graham is harder to explain away. Here again we see the real difference between Kennedy and Nixon. Kennedy paid lip-service to the Pope. Nixon really believed in Billy Graham. Kennedy was a high-flying cynic. Nixon was low-rent sincere.

Back from nowhere, Nixon runs and wins. He has the grace to concede that his victory over Humphrey was no more convincing than his loss to Kennedy. But that's war, and here, thrown open, is the White House with all its wonders, including a refrigerator well stocked with butter-brickle ice-cream, left by the Johnson girls so that Tricia and Julie shall not starve. Bliss!

Vietnam spoiled it all in the short term, and Watergate ruined it in the long, but before turning to those issues we ought to concede that Nixon had a lot going for him as President. Without dressing the set too much, he is able to show us in these pages that he could handle the work. Just the way he offers us proof of his political intelligence is proof of his political intelligence. The picture he paints is of a man on top of the job. With Haldeman keeping the side-issues at bay, Nixon deals with the essentials. Whether in the Oval Office, at Camp David, at San Clemente or on Key Biscayne he is at the hub of America. Whether in America, Europe, China or the Soviet Union he is at the spindle of the world.

He obviously revelled in the task and doesn't fail to convey the excitement. He gives you a better idea than anybody else has of why someone should want to take the job on. He even transmits a sense of mission. You can see how he might have thought of himself, without megalomania, as ideal casting for the role. Pat was just right too. She wasn't as flash as Jackie, but she was solid: less up-to-the-minute, but more in tune with the past. She might not have known Andy Warhol personally, but she arranged an exhibition in the White House for Andrew Wyeth. The Nixons were proud to be square. At their best, they showed why squareness is better than sham.

It could have been an idyll. But America was at war, both in South-East Asia and in Nixon's soul. Attaining the Presidency made him feel more victimised than ever. The Democrats had bequeathed him the mess in Vietnam. Now they would attack him however he handled it. They would stop at nothing. 'Therefore I decided that we must begin immediately keeping track of everything the leading Democrats did. Information would be our first line of defence.' He says this on page 357. The thought is supposed to be going through his head in 1968, when he was already looking forward to the 1972 elections. A harmless enough looking statement, until you realise that he is attempting to justify, in advance, the private espionage activities carried out by the slapstick team later to become famous as the Plumbers.

Nixon makes the best possible case for himself. He was certainly in a fix about Vietnam. If he had been the cynic he is often supposed to be, he could have blamed American involvement on Kennedy and Johnson and brought the troops home. We can see now that it would have been the right thing to do, since the North Vietnamese won anyway. Even at the time it was clear to every responsible authority except the Pentagon that Vietnam was a bottomless pit. By staying to fight it out, Nixon was contravening his own idea of a sensible foreign policy. The Nixon Doctrine advocated aiding only independently viable governments and confining the assistance to hardware – roughly the same policy Carter is pursuing now.

Nixon might have got out of Vietnam straight away if he had thought it was the difficult thing to do. But the liberal opposition to the war convinced him that quitting was the easy thing to do, and he made a fetish of doing the difficult thing instead of the easy one. If the whole world begged Nixon to do the easy thing he would do the difficult one, every time. But it would be a mistake to underestimate the strength of Nixon's convictions. He thought he was saving the world from communism. He was probably right to believe that for communists peace is never an end, only a means. He was certainly right to be untrusting. But he never understood that there was such a thing as handing the moral advantage to the other side. He thought that the other side was too immoral for that to be possible.

Kissinger thought the same way. As Nixon's National Security Adviser Kissinger was the man in charge of strategic brainwaves. It would be easy now for Nixon to blame Kissinger. More damagingly for them both, he approves of everything Kissinger did. There are successes to record: détente was probably the right move, which Nixon carried through patiently, without weakness. The Middle East policy was realistic in an area of competing unrealities. But Nixon still seems to think that the toppling of Allende was some kind of triumph, by which the Red Sandwich was undermined. The Red Sandwich was the device by which communism, squeezing inwards from Cuba and Chile, would capture the whole of South America. The Red Sandwich had to be foiled. Innocent Chileans have gone through the torments of the damned because Nixon and Kissinger thought that a sandwich had to be stopped from closing in on a continent.

It would have been better for everyone, capitalists included, if Nixon had burdened Allende with help. The best that can be said for such catastrophic initiatives is that they did not originate with Nixon. Eisenhower turned down Castro's requests for aid. The same sort of mistake goes all the way back to the repudiation of the Dixie Mission. Nixon's proudest boast is that he reopened the doors to China. He forgets to say that he started out as a fervent advocate of the policy which closed them.

So in foreign affairs Nixon didn't show quite the clear vision that he thinks he did. He still seems to think that the invasion of Cambodia was a 'complete success'. Right up to the final débâcle, he and Kissinger understood everything about the war in Vietnam except what mattered. 'As Kissinger saw the situation, we were up against a paradoxical situation in which North Vietnam, which had in effect lost the war, was acting as if it had won; while South Vietnam, which had effectively won the war, was acting as if it had lost.' If that was indeed how Kissinger saw things, then he was seeing them backwards. (Apart from a few such local outbreaks, incidentally, the word 'situation' is kept under tight control.)

Meanwhile, as Nixon tells it, the liberals and radicals were wrecking the country. On page 471 he argues that the depredations of the Weathermen were sufficient reason for stepping up the activities of the intelligence agencies. Reference is made to the FBI's long history of black-bag jobs in defence of liberty. The reasoning is specious, since Nixon is really out to justify the existence of the Plumbers, who were not a government agency but a private army. On page 496 he is to be found 'keeping the pressure on the people around me . . . to get information about what the other side was doing', the other side being the Democrats. He admits that he overstepped the mark, but blurs the importance of the mark he overstepped. He was in fact subverting the Constitution of the United States, which is framed not so much for democracy as against the tyrant, and declares that a Presidential party shall not be formed. 'At least, unlike previous administrations,' he says on page 781, 'we hadn't used the FBI.' But at least the FBI is to some extent accountable for its actions. Nixon's personal fact-gathering unit was accountable to nobody – not even, apparently, to Nixon.

Nixon persuasively argues that he knew nothing about the black-bag jobs in detail. There is no good reason to suppose that he did – what use is power if you can't leave the dirty work to subordinates? But plausibility evaporates when he tries to suggest that his ignorance was genuine rather than wilful. The first unmistakable evasion comes on page 514, when he addresses himself to the matter of the raid on Ellsberg's psychiatrist's office. 'I do not believe I was told about the break-in at the time.' Why isn't he certain? How could he forget?

Credibility slips further on page 638, which records the day – 18 June 1972 – when Nixon, at ease on Key Biscayne, first hears about the Watergate caper. Haldeman tells Nixon that the FBI will have to go further than Miami if it wishes to trace the cash found on the burglars. Nixon tells us nothing of how he reacted to what Haldeman said. An eloquent silence, because what Haldeman was really saying was that the cash was laundered. Why would Nixon accept that information without question, unless he knew that the White House was bankrolling intelligence operations with funds meant to be untraceable even by government agencies?

For the rest of the book, Nixon gives a convincing impersonation of a man standing on a landslide. As his world collapses, his prose attains the authentic poise of deep grief. But the remorse is all about the cover-up, not the crime. Just as Nixon always did the difficult thing instead of the easy thing, so he always accepted the responsibility but refused the blame. He takes the responsibility for the cover-up: his subordinates started it, but in order to protect them he allowed it to go on. He doesn't take the blame. Still less, then, does he take the blame for the crime itself. To the end of the line, the most he will admit to is an error of judgment. His aides sinned through an excess of zeal. His own sin was to let them do it.

'If I had indeed been the knowing Watergate conspirator that I was charged as being,' he says on page 902, 'I would have recognised in 1973 that the tapes contained conversations that would be fatally damaging.' It ought to be a strong point. Unfortunately Nixon has by this time already made it clear that the main reason he considered himself guiltless was that circumstances had made extraordinary measures legitimate. He had done what he thought necessary with such self-righteousness that the possibility of ever being called to account hadn't entered his head.

Nixon's book is one long act of self-justification. To a remarkable degree the attempt succeeds. At the end his enemies are plausibly made to sound hysterical victims of what he calls 'liberal chic'. The House Judiciary Committee produced 7,000 pages of evidence against Nixon, but most people now would have trouble being precise about what he did wrong. The media caught Watergate fever. Rumours that he had lined his pockets assumed the status of common knowledge. He almost certainly didn't. He would never have risked losing the Presidency for the sake of personal enrichment. He lost it because he went on feeling hunted even after he was home and dry.

A House Committee created him and a Senate Committee destroyed him. Under a different system Nixon's talents might have flourished and his drawbacks been nullified. Men just as devious warm the front benches on either side of the House of Commons. The strangest thing is that none of it was necessary. He could have pulled out of the war straight away. Failing that, he could have resisted the liberal opposition by constitutional means. But to a fatal extent he was still the man he had always been. 'The Presidency is not a finishing school,' he says memorably on page 1,078. 'It is a magnifying glass.' Judging by his own case, he is only half right. The job did in fact bring out the best in him. But it also magnified the worst. Even as their President, he still felt that the liberals and intellectuals had an unfair advantage. So he tried to preserve his power by extreme means, and if he had not first resigned he would surely have been impeached for it.

The book is well enough done to establish Nixon as a tragic figure and turn the tide of sympathy. It might even put him on the come-back trail. But we ought to keep our heads. The real tragic figures are all in Chile, Vietnam and Cambodia. It is ridiculous to class Nixon with the great villains of modern history, but not so ridiculous to be more angry with him than with them. He should have known better. Nobody sane expects Russia or China to be bound by scruple. The Russians and Chinese, says Nixon – as if their endorsement supported his case – couldn't understand what the Watergate fuss was all about. Of course they couldn't. They have forgotten what freedom feels like. A state in which power does not perpetuate itself has become unimaginable to them.

In certain crucial respects Nixon forgot what America is supposed to mean. Yet the virtues of this book prove that in other respects he didn't. Even now that he has lost everything, he has difficulty seeing himself from the outside. But whatever havoc he might have played with his country's institutions, in these pages he does not betray its free spirit. The book is like a soap-opera, yet the central character emerges as a human being. They were right to throw him down. Here is proof that they were not entirely wrong to raise him up in the first place.

(*New Statesman*, 1978)

Little Malcolm and His Struggle against the Masses

***Malcolm Muggeridge: A Life* by Ian Hunter (Collins, London, and William Morrow, New York)**

EVEN those of us who don't know Malcolm Muggeridge personally can be certain that the charm to which his friends attest would quickly enslave us too, should we be exposed to it. One would probably soon give up quarrelling with him. But his public persona invites quarrel and not much else. He is not really very illuminating even when he is right. As a writer and television performer he has always had the virtue of embodying the questioning spirit, but he has been even more valuable as an example of what happens to the questioning spirit when it is too easily satisfied with its own answers. Self-regard makes him untrustworthy even in the pursuit of truth. Life has been brighter for his having been around, but for a long time his explanations have not done much more than add to the general confusion. From one who makes so much noise about being hard to fool it is hard to take being fooled further. There he is waiting for you up the garden path, all set to lead you on instead of back.

Ian Hunter, billed as Professor of Law at Western University in London, Canada, was born in 1945, which makes him about half the age of his hero. Blemishes can thus partly be put down to exuberance. Professor Hunter still has time to learn that when you discomfit somebody you do rather more than make him uncomfortable. On page 109 a passage of French has gone wrong and on page 138 'exultation' should be 'exaltation', although it is hard to be sure. Referring to 'the historian David Irving' is like referring to the metallurgist Uri Geller. There were, I think, few ball-point pens in 1940. On page 160 the idea that the USA passed straight from barbarism to decadence is praised as if it had been conceived by Muggeridge, instead of Oscar Wilde. When Professor Hunter finds time to read other philosophers he might discover that such an example of an epigram being borrowed, and muffed in the borrowing, is characteristic of Muggeridge's essentially second-hand intelligence. But on the whole Professor Hunter does not fail to be readable.

What he fails to be is critical. Instead he has allowed himself to be infected by Muggeridge's later manner, so that for much of the time we have to put up with an old fogey's opinions being endorsed by a young fogey. This callow enthusiasm sometimes has the advantage of revealing the fatuity underlying the master's show of rigour, but the reader must work hard to stay patient. When Muggeridge goes on about the futility of liberalism or the gullibility of the masses, you can just about see why he should think such things, but when Professor Hunter does the same, you know it is only because he has been influenced by Muggeridge. Professor Hunter is a born disciple.

Not that Muggeridge, on the face of it anyway, was a born prophet. He made a quiet start, enjoying a sheltered upbringing among Fabians. Early insecurity might have been a better training for life, whose disappointments can easily seem to outweigh its attractions unless one learns in childhood that the dice are rolling all the time. As a young adult, Muggeridge lost one of his brothers in bitterly casual circumstances. Later on he lost a son in a similarly capricious way. These events perhaps changed a tendency to bless fate for being kind into an opposite tendency to curse it for being cruel, but you can never tell. For all I know, solipsism is genetically determined. What is certain is that Professor Hunter drastically under-estimates Muggeridge's capacity for being fascinated with his own personality and its requirements. Our infatuated author honestly thinks he is dealing with a case of self-denial.

But Muggeridge is a clear case of self-indulgence. On his own evidence, he indulged himself in fleshly pleasures while he still could. At the same time, he indulged himself in heated warnings against the frivolity of all earthly passion. These warnings waxed more strident as he became less capable. Finally he was warning the whole world. Professor Hunter has not been at sufficient pains to distinguish this behaviour from ordinary hypocrisy. If he had been, he might have helped Muggeridge to sound less like a Pharisee and more like what he is – a victim of rampant conceit, whose search for humility is doomed to remain as fruitless as Lord Longford's. Like his friends and mentors Hugh Kingsmill and Hesketh Pearson, Muggeridge mocked the world's follies but never learned to be sufficiently humbled by the turmoil within himself. He could detect it, but he blamed the world for that too. Self-indulgence and severity towards others are the same vice. The epigram is La Bruyère's. It could just conceivably have been Kingsmill's. It could never have been Muggeridge's.

Later on, in his memoirs, Muggeridge pretended that Cambridge had been a waste of time. At the time, as Professor Hunter reveals, he thought being up at Selwyn frightfully jolly. All memoirists simplify the past to some extent but Muggeridge tarts it up at the same time. He turns changes of heart into revelations, probably because he has always seen himself as being on the road to Damascus, if not Calvary. It became clear to him that the socialists at whose feet he had once sat had got everything wrong. The world could never be as they wished it, since suffering was inevitable. Professor Hunter gaily sings a descant to these opinions, as if Muggeridge had actually provided a serious commentary on intellectual history, instead of just a cartoon. Celebrating the young Muggeridge's failure to carry out his planned study of economics, Professor Hunter sums up a century of economic debate. 'Fortunately, like so many of his schemes at this time, nothing came of it, and the dismal science was left to Keynes and his contemporaries to wreak their particular brand of havoc through recessions, deficits and inflated, worthless currency on an unsuspecting world.' Students of law at Western University in London, Canada, will be familiar with Professor Hunter's wide sweep, but for those of us in the provinces it is all a bit daunting.

Working for the *Manchester Guardian* in the early 1930s, Muggeridge learned to distrust, not just socialism in particular, but liberal thought in general. No doubt there were good reasons at the time to be contemptuous of a newspaper whose leader columns were always assuring 'moderate men of all shades of opinion' that 'wiser counsels' would 'prevail'. But it was typical of Muggeridge, and went on being typical, to extend his loathing from the cliché to the idea behind it. Professor Hunter enthusiastically backs him up, without pausing to consider the likelihood that without an appropriate supply of moderate men and wiser counsels there would be no stage for Muggeridge to strut his stuff on.

But Muggeridge, before passing on once and for all to the higher realms of spiritual insight, made at least one contribution to moderation and wisdom. He was right about the Soviet Union. Professor Hunter takes it for granted that nobody else was, but once again this can be put down to the demands that the study of law must make on his time. In his memoirs Muggeridge makes himself out to have been, before his visit, completely sold on the Soviet Union's picture of itself. Professor Hunter shows that Muggeridge was in fact less gullible than that, but typically neglects to raise any questions about Muggeridge's habit of reorganising his past into an apocalyptic drama. Muggeridge saw forced collectivisation at first hand, wrote accurate reports of it, and aroused, in the brief time he could get them published, the hatred of fellow-travelling propagandists. Muggeridge fought the good fight and deserves admiration. But he was not alone in it, and would not have been alone even if he had been the only writer to raise his voice on that side of the argument. The liberal reaction against Marxism had already become so deep-seated that the Left intelligentsia was unable to take the centre with it. Muggeridge disdains and disclaims the title of intellectual, but he shares the intellectual's tendency to overestimate the importance of formal intellect in politics. At the time, Muggeridge performed a valuable service in helping to reveal how the majority of the Left intelligentsia worshipped power in one form or another. But in the long run he undid his share of the good work by expanding his contempt for the Soviet Union into an indiscriminate attack on any form of social betterment whatever. The Soviet Union, according to the early Muggeridge, had claimed to be paradise but had turned out to be Hell. Yet the Welfare State, according to the later Muggeridge, was a kind of Hell too. Do-gooding attempts to make the masses happier were misguided at best and at worst were the machinations of those driven crazy by the will to power. In a way, the Welfare State and the New Deal were even worse than the Soviet Union and Nazi Germany, which at least disciplined their citizens. Eleanor Roosevelt was a bigger threat than Hitler. Suffering was man's fate. To pretend otherwise was to defy the natural order. Eventually Muggeridge roped God in, so that the natural order could be backed up by a heavenly dispensation.

There are good arguments to be made against welfare ideology but Muggeridge has always gone out of his way to make bad ones. He succeeded in convincing himself, for example, that if the masses are mollycoddled they become bored. He has always been able to read the collective mind of entire populations. Stalin's example was not enough to teach him that there is no such thing as the masses. Nor was Hitler's. Operating as a spy in Africa, Muggeridge was apparently responsible for the sinking of a German submarine. He was decorated for his achievements but subsequently played them down, preferring to find his clandestine activities farcical. Such reticence would have been admirable on its own but less so was his growing habit of prating about the decline of civilisation, as if the war, instead of saving it, had merely helped seal its doom. For most people of any sense, the combined effect of the Soviet Union and Nazi Germany had been to convince them of the absolute value of free institutions. But for Muggeridge it was somehow impossible to reach this conclusion.

One reason was that Muggeridge finds it either unpalatable or impolitic, or both, to express any opinion that the majority of reasonable people happen to hold. But another reason is more interesting. Muggeridge just doesn't believe that anyone in an official position, even if he has been elected to it, can be acting from any other motive except the will to power. Hence the idea of a free institution has small meaning for him, since it must inevitably express itself in the form of what he sees as manipulation, with the masses at the receiving end. Adherence to this view has always given him ample latitude to play the gadfly, but its flexibility does not make it true. It is, in fact, a lazy man's charter. Muggeridge's critique of modern society is too ill-founded to be very informative. He assumes that things have gone wrong because powerful men have willed it so. There is no suggestion that some things go wrong of their own accord, and often as a direct consequence of other things going right. Muggeridge thinks he is being sophisticated when he rejects the vulgar idea of progress, but really his idea that there is no such thing as progress is equally vulgar. Muggeridge was subject to a hail of abuse when the tabloid press misrepresented him as having attacked the Monarchy. There was a time when the same circumstances would have earned him a slit nose and cropped ears. It might not be much of an advance, but it is an advance, and one brought about by those men of all shades of moderate opinion whose labours Muggeridge finds it convenient to forget. Helping him to forget is his comprehensive lack of a historical view. He has small idea of how civilisation got the way it is, beyond a vague notion that it somehow all depends on Christianity, and must necessarily collapse now that Christianity is no longer generally believed in.

Unable to believe in either the incarnation or the resurrection, Muggeridge can only loosely be described as a Christian himself, yet except in a cantankerously paradoxical mood he would probably be ready to admit that he is fairly civilised. The question of how he got that way would have given him pause long ago if he had ever been any good at self-examination, but the evidence suggests that he can contemplate his navel endlessly without drawing much enlightenment from it. He can read God's mind better than he can read his own. He knows that God regards things like contraception and legal abortion as gross interference. Muggeridge, it will be remembered, could tell which women were on the Pill by the dead look in their eyes. Those nineteenth-century women who had a baby every year until they were worn out doubtless had a dead look in their eyes too, but Muggeridge was not around to see it. Nor has he ever been able to grasp that the alternative to legal abortion is not Christian chastity or even the edifying responsibility of bringing up an illegitimate child. The alternative to legal abortion is illegal abortion. Contraception and legal abortion were brought in to help eradicate manifest injustices. They might have created other injustices on their own account, which leaves us with the not unfamiliar problem of how to stem the excesses that arise from freedom, but only a fool would have expected life to grow less complicated just because fate had been made less capricious.

Dealing in the millennium, Muggeridge never feels obliged to admit that for mankind there is no natural order to go back to, and never has been. Human beings have been interfering with nature since the cave. That's how they got out of it in the first place. Most religions of any sophistication find some way of attributing humanity's meddlesome knack of creativity to a divine impulse, but Muggeridge would rather preach hellfire than allow God the right to move in such mysterious ways. While reading Professor Hunter's book I also happened to be renewing my acquaintance with Darwin's *Voyage of the Beagle*, and was often struck by the superiority not just of Darwin's intellect but of his religious sense. Humbled but not frightened by nature's indifference to our fate, Darwin still marvels at the way purpose works itself out through chance – as if it were trying to discover itself. With due allowance for scale, if our wish is to contemplate reality while staying sane at the same time, then we probably do best to follow Darwin's example and look for harmony outside ourselves. If there is a divine purpose, then our attempts at understanding are perhaps part of it and might even be its most refined expression, but the universe cares little for us as a species and nothing for us as individuals. That much is entirely up to us. Some people will always find this an inspiring thought. Others it will reduce to despair. Muggeridge is plainly among the latter.

These things come down to personal psychology in the end, which means that they are the opposite of simple. One gains little by objecting to a man's mental condition if his mental condition is what gives him his worth. But Muggeridge's career would have been worth more had he not set his hopes on being vouchsafed an Answer. Muggeridge's real quarrel is not with the modern age but with his creator. For all the looseness of its formulation, his concept of the supreme being is painfully narrow. God is not allowed much dignity. When invoked, he seems to resemble a less tormented version of Muggeridge, whose torment arose in the first place from an incompatibility between his spiritual pretensions and the physical material they had been given to work with. 'Fornication,' Professor Hunter quotes Muggeridge, 'I love it so.' Muggeridge struggled heroically, if unsuccessfully, with his baser desires, but apparently without ever quite seeing the joke. There is no point in being shocked that God gave healthy male human beings ten times more lust than they can use. He did the same to healthy male fiddler crabs. He's a deity, not a dietitian.

Muggeridge's seriousness is incomplete. In God's name he is able to react against a popular fallacy, but he can never give the Devil his due. The result is that he is not even good at attacking a specific abuse. He is concerned but irresponsible. 'Shadows, oh shadows.' Thus Muggeridge on the subject of other people. America is full of people 'aimlessly drifting'. Most people look as if they are aimlessly drifting if you don't know what their aims are. Muggeridge rarely stops to find out. In his later phase he has been heard to contend that whereas the West leads nowhere, the Soviet Union might at least lead somewhere. 'The future is being shaped there, not in the lush pastures of the welfare state.' What does he think the Soviet Union has that the West hasn't, apart from a certain neatness? Perhaps he means belief. But what kind of belief? He can't even remember his own lessons. And if he means that the repressed learn the value of life, surely he underestimates how much they would like to be excused their schooling.

If you are talking to aimless drifting shadows you can say anything. Muggeridge canes television for its superficiality but he never seemed to mind being superficial when he appeared on it. 'Television,' opines Professor Hunter, 'a medium that inevitably takes first prize in the fantasy stakes.' On the contrary, the television personality who condescends to his audience soon unmasks himself. Despite his undoubted and much-missed willingness to say irritating things, Muggeridge stood revealed on television as someone who would rather make a splash with a bogus epigram than worry at the truth. Remorse struck only to the extent of making him blame the medium for his own histrionics. Similarly he never drew the appropriate conclusions from the fact that a good number of those old *Manchester Guardian* leading articles about moderate men and wiser counsels had been written by himself. 'Already I find leader writing infinitely wearisome,' he wrote in his diary, 'but it is easy money, and the great thing to do is just not worry about it.' Times were hard and Muggeridge had every excuse to do what paid the bills. It is even possible to imagine George Orwell doing the same – but not to imagine him not worrying about it, or regarding such an injunction as good advice. No real writer can think of his writing as something separated from his essential being. It shouldn't be necessary to state such an obvious truth, but when dealing with Muggeridge you find your values sliding: you have to spell things out for yourself. Like many people who have lost their innocence, he can make you feel stupid for wanting to be elementary. Yet without a firm grasp of the elementary there can be no real subtlety. When Muggeridge tries to make a resonant remark the facts don't fit it.

Muggeridge forgives himself for doing second-rate work in the press and television by calling them second-rate media. This self-exculpatory technique has been found to come in handy by those of his acolytes grouped around *Private Eye*. Already absolved from trying too hard by a public school ethos which exalts gentlemen above players, the *Private Eye* writers are glad to have it on Muggeridge's authority that if a thing is not worth doing then it is not worth doing well. Recently I found myself being praised by Richard Ingrams for my radio quiz performances, which evinced, he said, a properly contemptuous attitude for the job. I have no such attitude, but I have no doubt that Ingrams, despite his notoriously eager availability for such assignments, has. He burns to be on the air and yet he despises the whole business. The conflict would be hard to live with if Muggeridge had not already provided so conspicuous an example of how to become a household name while expressing the utmost contempt for the means by which one attains such a position.

Nevertheless Muggeridge deserves praise for having, while on television, been himself, even if that self is so shot through with falsity. At least he resisted the usual pressure to wheel out a mechanical persona. If he camped it up, he did so in his own manner. As a prose stylist he also deserves some praise, although not quite as much as the doting Professor Hunter thinks. Muggeridge has always overworked the trick of biblical pastiche. Hacks think him a good writer because he writes a refined version of what they write. Nor have his jokes been all that funny. There is some wit to be attained through knowingness but not as much as through self-knowledge. The human comedy begins in the soul but for Muggeridge it begins somewhere outside. In this he is like his mentors Kingsmill and Pearson, just as his *Private Eye* disciples are like him. 'Laughter belongs to the individual, not to the herd,' Professor Hunter explains, 'and is therefore repugnant to the herd and to those whose concern is the welfare of the herd.' But there is no such thing as the herd. There are only people, and until we have made some effort to prove the contrary it is usually wiser to assume that they are like us.

People who will say anything are often the victims of diminished self-esteem, but Muggeridge suffers from the opposite condition. He is stuck on himself. It isn't all that easy to see why. He is, after all, only a literary journalist. Even his obviously heartfelt admiration for Mother Teresa of Calcutta has its component of arrogance. Mother Teresa cares for those who suffer, which fits Muggeridge's idea of God's plan for the world. He would find it hard to express the same admiration for, say, Jonas Salk. Indeed he would probably regard immunisation as part of the modernising process which has led the herd astray. Yet when you think of what polio can do, to forestall such pain seems no lesser an act of mercy than to care for the dying. Preventive medicine is surely a development that the modern age has a right to be proud of, even in the light of some of its unintended consequences.

From the law of unintended consequences no human activity is exempt, not even holiness. Muggeridge has consistently belittled many original people who have brought lasting benefits to mankind. He has been helped in this by the fact that the benefits have brought liabilities in their turn. But benefits always bring liabilities. Christianity is a clear enough proof of that.

Original people do great things. Ordinary people do the world's work. Both kinds of people are apt to lose track of what their efforts add up to. The news they make needs to be made sense of as it happens. If the literary journalist thinks himself too grand to do that, he is unlikely to be much good for anything. The literary journalist keeps faith with himself by saying what is so and betrays himself by saying anything less, however powerful his reasons. Not many writers are prophets, and those who are foretell the future by the accuracy with which they report the present.

(*London Review of Books*, 1981)

Part Two

FACT MEETS FICTION

Hard-core Gore

***Matters of Fact and of Fiction: Essays 1973–1976* by Gore Vidal (Heinemann, London, and Random House, New York)**

NOBODY dissents from marking Gore Vidal high as an essayist, not even those – especially not those – who would like to mark him low as a novelist. His *Collected Essays 1952–1972* was rightly greeted with all the superlatives going. Since one doesn't have to read far in this new volume before realising that the old volume has been fully lived up to and in some respects even surpassed, it becomes necessary either to wheel out the previous superlatives all over again or else to think up some new ones. Rejecting both courses, this reviewer intends to pick nits and make gratuitous observations on the author's character, in the hope of maintaining some measure of critical independence. Gore Vidal is so dauntingly good at the literary essay that he is likely to arouse in other practitioners an inclination to take up a different line of work. That, however, would be an excessive reaction. He isn't omniscient, infallible or effortlessly stylish – he just knows a lot, possesses an unusual amount of common sense and writes scrupulously lucid prose. There is no need to deify the man just because he can string a few thoughts together. As I shall now reveal, he has toenails of clay.

Always courageous about unfolding himself, Vidal sometimes overcooks it. He is without false modesty but not beyond poor-mouthing himself to improve a point. 'The bad movies we made twenty years ago are now regarded in altogether too many circles as important aspects of . . . ' But wait a minute. It might remain a necessary task to point out that the nuttier film-buffs are no more than licensed illiterates: the ability to carry out a semiotic analysis of a Nicholas Ray movie is undoubtedly no compensation for being incapable of parsing a simple sentence. But some of those bad movies were, after all, quite good. Vidal himself had his name writ large on both *The Left-Handed Gun* and *The Best Man*, neither of which is likely to be forgotten. It suits his purposes, however, to pretend that he was a dedicated candy-butcher. He wants to be thought of as part of the hard-bitten Hollywood that produced the adage: 'Shit has its own integrity.'

As a Matter of Fact, Vidal rarely set out to write rubbish: he just got mixed up with a few pretentious projects that went sour. Summarising, in the first of these essays, the Top Ten Best Sellers, Vidal makes trash hilarious. But there is no need for him to pretend that he knows trash from the inside. He was always an outsider in that regard: the point he ought to make about himself is that he never had what it took to be a Hollywood hack. It was belief, not cynicism, that lured him to write screenplays. Even quite recently he was enthusiastically involved in a mammoth project called *Gore Vidal's Caligula*, once again delivering himself into the hands of those commercial forces which would ensure that the script ended up being written by Caligula's Gore Vidal.

Yet you can see what he is getting at. Invention, however fumbling, must always be preferred over aridity, however high-flown. In all the essays dealing with Matters of Fiction, Vidal is constantly to be seen paying unfeigned attention to the stories second-rate writers are trying to tell. His contempt is reserved for the would-be first-raters obsessed with technique. For the less exalted scribes honestly setting about their grinding chores, his sympathy is deep even if his wit is irrepressible. Quoting a passage from Herman Wouk, he adds: 'This is not at all bad, except as prose.' Taken out of context, this might seem a destructive crack, but when you read it in its proper place there is no reason to think that the first half of the sentence has been written for the sole purpose of making the second half funny.

If this were not a nit-picking exercise we would be bound to take notice of Vidal's exemplary industry. He has actually sat down and read, from front to back, the gigantic novels by John Barth and Thomas Pynchon for which the young professors make such claims. Having done so, he is in a position to give a specific voice to the general suspicion which the academic neo-theologians have aroused in the common reader's mind. Against their religious belief in The Novel, Vidal insists that there is no such thing – there are only novels. In this department, as in several others, Vidal is the natural heir of Edmund Wilson, whose *The Fruits of the MLA* was the opening salvo in the long campaign, which we will probably never see the end of, to rescue literature from its institutionalised interpreters.

But Wilson is not Vidal's only ancestor. Several cutting references to Dwight Macdonald are a poor reward for the man whose devastating essay 'By Cozzens Possessed' (collected in *Against the American Grain*) was the immediate forerunner of everything Vidal has done in this particular field. It would be a good thing if Vidal, normally so forthcoming about his personal history, could be frank about where he considers himself to stand in relation to other American critical writers. In his introductory note to this book there is mention of Sainte-Beuve; in a recent interview given to the *New York Times* there was talk about Montaigne; but among recent essayists, now that Wilson is gone, Vidal seems to find the true critical temperament only among 'a few elderly Englishmen'. Yet you have only to think of people like Macdonald or Mary McCarthy or Elizabeth Hardwick to see that if Vidal is *primus* it is only *inter pares*: there is an American critical tradition, going back to Mencken and beyond, which he is foolish to imagine can be disowned. This is the only respect in which Vidal seems shy of being an American, and by no coincidence it is the only respect in which he ever sounds provincial.

Otherwise his faults, like his virtues, are on a world scale. In the Matters of Fact, which occupy the second part of the book, the emphasis is on the corrupting influence of power and money. Born into the American ruling class, Vidal is as well placed as Louis Auchincloss (about whom he writes appreciatively) to criticise its behaviour. He is angrily amusing about West Point, Robert Moses, ITT, the Adams dynasty and the grand families in general. Indeed it is only about Tennessee Williams and Lord Longford that he is *un*angrily funny – for the most part his humour about Matters of Fact is sulphuric. There is no question of Vidal's sincerity in loathing what he calls the Property Party. On the other hand he is a trifle disingenuous in allowing us to suppose that all connections have been severed between himself and the ruling class. Certainly he remains on good terms with the ruling class of Britain – unless Princess Margaret has become as much of an intellectual exile from the British aristocracy as he has from the American.

As a Matter of Fact, Gore Vidal is a Beautiful Person who chooses his drawing-rooms with care. He hobnobs with the rich and powerful. He hobnobs also with the talented, but they tend to be those among the talented who hobnob with the rich and powerful. He likes the rich and powerful as a class. He hates some of them as individuals and attacks them with an invective made all the more lacerating by inside knowledge. For that we can be grateful. But we can also wish that his honesty about his own interior workings might extend to his thirst for glamour. Speaking about Hollywood, he is an outsider who delights to pose as an insider. Speaking about the ruling class, he is an insider who delights to pose as an outsider. In reality he is just as active a social butterfly as his arch-enemy Truman Capote. But in Vidal's case the sin is venial, not mortal, since his writings remain comparatively unruffled by the social whirl, whereas Capote has become a sort of court dwarf, peddling a brand of thinly fictionalised tittle-tattle which is really sycophancy in disguise. Vidal reserves that sort of thing for after hours.

Yet even with these nits picked, it must still be said that Vidal is an outstanding writer on political issues. 'The State of the Union', the last essay in the book, is so clear an account of what has been happening in America that it sounds commonplace, until you realise that every judgment in it has been hard won from personal experience. Only one of its assumptions rings false, and even there you can see his reasons. Vidal still assumes that any heterosexual man is a culturally repressed bisexual. This idea makes a good basis for polemical assault on sexual intolerance, but as a Matter of Fact it is Fiction. As it happens, I have met Gore Vidal in the flesh. The flesh looked immaculately preserved. In a room well supplied with beautiful and brilliant women, he was as beautiful as most and more brilliant than any. I was not impervious to his charm. But I examined myself in vain for any sign of physical excitement. He might say that I was repressing my true nature but the real reason was simpler. It was just that he was not a female.

Not even Gore Vidal is entirely without self-delusion. On the whole, though, he is among the most acute truth-tellers we possess. Certainly he is the most entertaining. The entertainment arises naturally from his style – that perfectly disciplined, perfectly liberated English which constitutes all by itself a decisive answer to the Hacks of Academe. Calling them 'the unlearned learned teachers of English' and 'the new barbarians, serenely restoring the Dark Ages', he has only to quote their prose against his and the case is proved. A pity, then, that on page 260 there is a flagrant (well, all right: barely noticeable) grammatical error. 'Journalists who know quite as much or more than I about American politics . . . ' is not good grammar. There is an 'as' missing. But the other 281 scintillating pages of error-free text go some way towards making up for its loss.

(*New Statesman*, 1977)

Go Back to the Cold!

The Honourable Schoolboy by John le Carré (Hodder & Stoughton, London, and Knopf, New York)

JOHN LE CARRÉ's new novel is about twice as long as it should be. It falls with a dull thud into the second category of his books – those which are greeted as being something more than merely entertaining. Their increasingly obvious lack of mere entertainment is certainly strong evidence that le Carré is out to produce a more respectable breed of novel than those which fell into the first category, the ones which were merely entertaining. But in fact it was the merely entertaining books that had the more intense life.

The books in the first category – and le Carré might still produce more of them, if he can only bring himself to distrust the kind of praise he has grown used to receiving – were written in the early and middle 1960s. They came out at the disreputably brisk rate of one a year. *Call for the Dead* (1961), *A Murder of Quality* (1962), *The Spy Who Came In From the Cold* (1963), and *The Looking Glass War* (1965) were all tightly controlled efforts whose style, characterization, and atmospherics were subordinate to the plot, which was the true hero. Above all, they were brief: *The Spy Who Came In From the Cold* is not even half the length of the ponderous whopper currently under review.

Elephantiasis, of ambition as well as reputation, set in during the late 1960s, when *A Small Town in Germany* (1968) inaugurated the second category. Not only was it more than merely entertaining, but it was, according to the *New Statesman*'s reviewer, 'at least a masterpiece'. After an unpopular but instantly forgiven attempt at a straight novel (*The Naive and Sentimental Lover*), the all-conquering onward march of the more than merely entertaining spy story was resumed with *Tinker Tailor Soldier Spy* (1974) which was routinely hailed as the best thriller le Carré had written up to that time.

The Honourable Schoolboy brings the second sequence to a heavy apotheosis. A few brave reviewers have expressed doubts about whether some of the elements which supposedly enrich le Carré's later manner might not really be a kind of impoverishment, but generally the book has been covered with praise – a response not entirely to be despised, since *The Honourable Schoolboy* is so big that it takes real effort to cover it with anything. At one stage I tried to cover it with a pillow, but there it was, still half visible, insisting, against all the odds posed by its coagulated style, on being read to the last sentence.

The last sentence comes 530 pages after the first, whose tone of myth-making portent is remorselessly adhered to throughout. 'Afterwards, in the dusty little corners where London's secret servants drink together, there was argument about where the Dolphin case history should really begin.' The Dolphin case history, it emerges with stupefying gradualness, is concerned with the Circus (i.e., the British Secret Service) getting back on its feet after the catastrophic effect of its betrayal by Bill Haydon, the Kim Philby figure whose depredations were the subject of *Tinker Tailor Soldier Spy*. The recovery is masterminded by George Smiley, nondescript hero and cuckold genius. From his desk in London, Smiley sets in motion a tirelessly labyrinthine scheme which results in the capture of the Soviet Union's top agent in China. Hong Kong is merely the scene of the action. The repercussions are world-wide. Smiley's success restores the Circus's fortunes and discomfits the KGB. But could it be that the Cousins (i.e., the CIA) are the real winners after all? It is hard to tell. What is easy to tell is that at the end of the story, a man lies dead. Jerry Westerby, the Honourable Schoolboy of the title, has let his passions rule his sense of duty, and has paid the price. He lies face down and lifeless, like someone who has been reading a very tedious novel.

This novel didn't *have* to be tedious. The wily schemes of the Circus have been just as intricate before today. In fact the machinations outlined in *The Spy Who Came In From the Cold* and *The Looking Glass War* far outstrip in subtlety anything Smiley gets up to here. Which is part of the trouble. In those books character and incident attended upon narrative, and were all the more vivid for their subservience. In this book, when you strip away the grandiloquence, the plot is shown to be perfunctory. There is not much of a *story*. Such a lack is one of the defining characteristics of le Carré's more recent work. It comes all the more unpalatably from a writer who gave us, in *The Spy Who Came In From the Cold*, a narrative so remarkable for symmetrical economy that it could be turned into an opera.

Like the Oscar Wilde character who doesn't need the necessary because he has the superfluous, le Carré's later manner is beyond dealing in essentials. The general effect is of inflation. To start with, the prose style is overblown. Incompatible metaphors fight for living space in the same sentence. 'Now at first Smiley tested the water with Sam – and Sam, who liked a poker hand himself, tested the water with Smiley.' Are they playing cards in the bath? Such would-be taciturnity is just garrulousness run short of breath. On the other hand, the would-be eloquence is verbosity run riot. Whole pages are devoted to inventories of what can be found by way of flora and fauna in Hong Kong, Cambodia, Vietnam, and other sectors of the mysterious East. There is no possible question that le Carré has been out there and done his fieldwork. Unfortunately he has brought it all home.

But the really strength-sapping feature of the prose style is its legend-building tone. Half the time le Carré sounds like Tolkien. You get visions of Hobbits sitting around the fire telling tales of Middle Earth.

> Need Jerry have ever gone to Ricardo in the first place? Would the outcome, for himself, have been different if he had not? Or did Jerry, as Smiley's defenders to this day insist, by his pass at Ricardo, supply the last crucial heave which shook the tree and caused the coveted fruit to fall?

Forever asking questions where he ought to be answering them, the narrator is presumably bent on seasoning mythomania with Jamesian ambiguity: *The Lord of the Rings* meets *The Golden Bowl*. Working on the principle that there can be no legends without lacunae, the otherwise omniscient author, threatened by encroaching comprehensibility, takes refuge in a black cloud of question marks. The ultimate secrets are lost in the mists of time and/or the dusty filing cabinets of the Circus.

> Was there really a conspiracy against Smiley, of the scale that Guillam supposed? If so, how was it affected by Westerby's own maverick intervention? No information is available and even those who trust each other well are not disposed to discuss the question. Certainly there was a secret understanding between Enderby and Martello. . . .

And after a paragraph like that, you get another paragraph like that.

> And did Smiley *know* of the conspiracy, deep down? Was he aware of it, and did he secretly even welcome the solution? Peter Guillam, who has since had two good years in exile in Brixton to consider his opinion, insists that the answer to both questions is a firm *yes* . . .

Fatally, the myth-mongering extends to the characterization. The book opens with an interminable scene starring the legendary journalists of Hong Kong. Most legendary of them all is an Australian called Craw. In a foreword le Carré makes it clear that Craw is based on Dick Hughes, legendary Australian journalist. As it happens, Australian journalists of Hughes's stature often *are* the stuff of legend. In the dusty little corners where London's journalists do their drinking, there is often talk of what some Australian journalist has been up to. They cultivate their reputations. After the Six Day War one of them brought a jeep back to London on expenses. But the fact that many Australian journalists are determined to attain the status of legend does not necessarily stop them being the stuff of it. Indeed Hughes has been used as a model before, most notably by Ian Fleming in *You Only Live Twice*. What is notable about le Carré's version, however, is its singular failure to come alive. Craw is meant to be a fountain of humorous invective, but the cumulative effect is tiresome in the extreme.

> 'Your Graces,' said old Craw, with a sigh. 'Pray silence for my son. I fear he would have parley with us. Brother Luke, you have committed several acts of war today and one more will meet with our severe disfavour. Speak clearly and concisely omitting no detail, however slight, and thereafter hold your water, sir.'

Known to be an expert mimic in real life, le Carré for some reason has an anti-talent for comic dialogue. Craw's putatively mirth-provoking high-falutin' is as funny as a copy of *The Honourable Schoolboy* falling on your foot. Nor does Craw do much to justify the build-up le Carré gives him as a master spy. The best you can say for him is that he is more believable than one of his drinking companions, Superintendent 'Rocker' Rockhurst, the legendary Hong Kong policeman. 'Rocker' Rockhurst? There used to be a British comic-strip character called Rockfist Rogan. Perhaps that was the derivation. Anyway, it is 'Rocker' Rockhurst's main task to preserve order among the legendary Hong Kong journalists, who are given to drinking legendary amounts, preparatory to engaging in legendary fist-fights. Everything that is most wearisome about journalism is solemnly presented as the occupation of heroes. No wonder, then, that espionage is presented as the occupation of gods.

Le Carré used to be famous for showing us the bleak, tawdry reality of the spy's career. He still provides plenty of bleak tawdriness, but romanticism comes shining through. Jerry Westerby, it emerges, has that 'watchfulness' which 'the instinct' of 'the very discerning' describes as 'professional'. You would think that if Westerby really gave off these vibrations it would make him useless as a spy. But le Carré does not seem to notice that he is indulging himself in the same kind of transparently silly detail which Mark Twain found so abundant in Fenimore Cooper.

It would not matter so much if the myth-mongering were confined to the minor characters. But in this novel George Smiley completes his rise to legendary status. Smiley has been present, on the sidelines or at the centre, but more often at the centre, in most of le Carré's novels since the very beginning. In Britain he has been called the most representative character in modern fiction. In the sense that he has been inflating almost as fast as the currency, perhaps he is. His latest appearance should make it clear to all but the most dewy-eyed that Smiley is essentially a dream.

It could be, of course, that he is a useful dream. Awkward, scruffy, and impotent on the outside, he is graceful, elegant, and powerful within. An impoverished country could be forgiven for thinking that such a man embodies its true condition. But to be a useful dream Smiley needs to be credible. In previous novels le Carré has kept his hero's legendary omniscience within bounds, but here it springs loose. 'Then Smiley disappeared for three days.' Sherlock Holmes, it will be recalled, was always making similarly unexplained disappearances, to the awed consternation of Watson. Smiley's interest in the minor German poets recalls some of Holmes's enthusiasms. But at least the interest in the minor German poets was there from the start (*vide* 'A Brief History of George Smiley' in *Call for the Dead*) and was not tacked on later *à la* Conan Doyle, who constantly supplied Holmes with hitherto unhinted-at areas of erudition. Conan Doyle wasn't bothered that the net effect of such lily-gilding was to make his hero more vaporous instead of less. Le Carré, though, ought to be bothered. When Smiley, in his latest incarnation, suddenly turns out, at the opportune moment, to be an expert on Chinese naval engineering, his subordinates might be wide-eyed in worship, but the reader is unable to resist blowing a discreet raspberry.

It was Smiley, we now learn, who buried Control, his spiritual father. (And Control, we now learn, had two marriages going at once. It is a moot point whether or not learning more about the master plotter of *The Spy Who Came In From the Cold* leaves us caring less.) We get the sense, and I fear are meant to get the sense, of Camelot, with the king dead but the quest continuing. Unfortunately the pace is more like Bresson than like Malory.

Smiley's fitting opponent is Karla, the KGB's chief of operations. Smiley has Karla's photograph hanging in his office, just as Montgomery had Rommel's photograph hanging in his caravan. Karla, who made a fleeting physical appearance in the previous novel, is kept offstage in this one – a sound move, since like Moriarty he is too abstract a figure to survive examination. But the tone of voice in which le Carré talks about the epic mental battle between Smiley and Karla is too sublime to be anything but ridiculous. 'For nobody, not even Martello, quite dared to challenge Smiley's authority.' In just such a way T. E. Lawrence used to write about himself. As he entered the tent, sheiks fell silent, stunned by his charisma.

There was a day when Smiley generated less of a nimbus. But that was a day when le Carré was more concerned with stripping down the mystique of his subject than with building it up. In his early novels le Carré told the truth about Britain's declining influence. In the later novels, the influence having declined even further, his impulse has altered. The slide into destitution has become a planned retreat, with Smiley masterfully in charge. On le Carré's own admission, Smiley has always been the author's fantasy about himself – a Billy Batson who never has to say 'Shazam!' because inside he never stops being Captain Marvel. But lately Smiley has also become the author's fantasy about his beleaguered homeland.

The Honourable Schoolboy makes a great show of being realistic about Britain's plight and the consequently restricted scope of Circus activities. Hong Kong, the one remaining colony, is the only forward base of operations left. There is no money to spend. Nevertheless the Circus can hope to make up in cunning – Smiley's cunning – for what it lacks in physical resources. A comforting thought, but probably deceptive.

In the previous novel the Philby affair was portrayed as a battle of wits between the KGB and the Circus. It was the Great Game: Mrs Philby's little boy Kim had obvious affinities with Kipling's child prodigy. But the facts of the matter, as far as we know them, suggest that whatever the degree of Philby's wit, it was the Secret Service's witlessness which allowed him to last so long. Similarly, in the latest book, the reader is bound to be wryly amused by the marathon scenes in which the legendary codebreaker Connie (back to bore us again) works wonders of deduction among her dusty filing cabinets. It has only been a few months since it was revealed that the real-life Secret Service, faced with the problem of sorting out two different political figures who happened to share the same name, busily compiled an enormous dossier on the wrong one.

There is always the possibility that in those of its activities which do not come to light the Secret Service functions with devilish efficiency. But those activities which do come to light seem usually on a par with the CIA's schemes to assassinate Castro by poisoning his cap or setting fire to his beard. *Our Man in Havana* was probably the book which came closest to the truth.

This novel still displays enough of le Carré's earlier virtues to remind us that he is not summarily to be written off. There is an absorbing meeting in a sound-proof room, with Smiley plausibly outwitting the civil servants and politicians. Such internecine warfare, to which most of the energy of any secret organization must necessarily be devoted, is le Carré's best subject: he is as good at it as Nigel Balchin, whose own early books – especially *The Small Back Room* and *Darkness Falls From the Air* – so precisely adumbrated the disillusioned analytical skill of le Carré's best efforts.

But lately disillusion has given way to illusion. Outwardly aspiring to the status of literature, le Carré's novels have inwardly declined to the level of pulp romance. He is praised for sacrificing action to character, but ought to be dispraised, since by concentrating on personalities he succeeds only in overdrawing them, while eroding the context which used to give them their desperate authenticity. Raising le Carré to the plane of literature has helped rob him of his more enviable role as a popular writer who could take you unawares. Already working under an assumed name, le Carré ought to assume another one, sink out of sight, and run for the border of his reputation. There might still be time to get away.

(*New York Review of Books*, 1977)

In Our Graham Greenery

***The Human Factor* by Graham Greene (Bodley Head, London)**

THE FICTIONS of Graham Greene never really divided into serious novels and 'entertainments', whatever the author might once have insisted. Even the best of his serious novels have always been entertainments and even the slightest of his entertainments have always been serious novels. His latest effort is very serious indeed – one of his best books, in fact. It is also an outstanding entertainment, which means that the reviewer is hard pressed, since it would be bad form to give away too much of the story. The book is a lot more than just a spy novel, but it is still a spy novel in the first instance, with a satisfactorily intricate plot. The reader should not be deprived of the chance to exercise his deductive powers, although if he does not rumble the significance of the hero's purchasing *two* copies of the Aylmer Maude translation of *War and Peace* on page 50 then he is either a dull dog or else he has never read *Our Man In Havana*.

As so often happens with Greene's later work, knowledge of his earlier work can only increase the reader's admiration. Familiarity breeds respect. As time has gone on, Greene's life-long preoccupations have come back again and again, more thoroughly explored, more subtly interwoven, so that everything comes up looking new even when it is most recognisable. Self-parody threatens only when his grip on likelihood momentarily goes slack – as it does, for example, towards the end of *The Honorary Consul*, when the dialogue between Eduardo and León is a bit too wonderfully concentrated for men due to be hanged in the morning. But generally Greene's touch has seldom ceased to grow more asssured, which means that all his characteristic themes, relationships, personalities, atmospheric effects, plot twists, gimmicks and props can safely be brought around for another airing.

At this point a clear line should be drawn between fandom and appreciation, even though both processes may be going on within the same reader. It is fandom to be unduly delighted by spotting a standard piece of Greenery recurring in compressed form. Fans open each new novel with a head full of ready-made expectations. Who's got the birthmark? Will there be a chess game? Who's going to be the whisky priest, the wise policeman, the ethnic love-partner? The fan's needs are usually satisfied. But appreciation depends on remembering that the author is making things more difficult for himself instead of less: he goes back over the same ground in order to dig deeper, and he can dig deeper because he has lived longer. It may well be true that Greene has never again written anything as perfect as *The Heart of the Matter*, but he knows more of life now than he knew then. The same themes of moral responsibility have been more profoundly gone into even in those subsequent books which most conspicuously lack the fearful symmetry of his masterpiece. *The Heart of the Matter* is evidence that in a master's work the apex of his craft can arrive relatively early yet need not necessarily represent the height of his interest.

But to business. Greene's latest hero, Maurice Castle, is another in the series of morally exhausted protagonists that nominally started with Querry in *A Burnt-Out Case*, although really the tradition stretches back to Scobie and beyond. Greene's central theme has always been partly about the impossibility of making a separate peace – nobody can escape responsibility by doing nothing, since the world will always catch up. Castle is a Secret Service officer stationed in London. Before the novel started he was a field-man who fell in love with one of his own black African agents. To get her safely away, he had to pay a price. What the price consists of emerges during the course of the action, which is all set in England. You can't hide even in England. In the last analysis even England is a foreign country.

This is the first time since *The End of the Affair* (an artistic catastrophe which has become in retrospect steadily more interesting) that Greene has made a full-scale attempt to set a novel in his homeland. He has succeeded in the most extraordinary way. You feel that he is seeing it as a foreign country. In the same way that he so carefully gets the details right about all those African, South American and Far Eastern trouble-spots, you can hear him being careful to get the details right about England. The protagonist has been a long time away and the narrator who writes about him has been away even longer – so long that the return is like a fresh beginning. There is a tight, nervous focus on such minor items of local colour as Maltesers and Smarties. The geographical features of inner London have not just been thought out, they have practically been paced out: you could walk all the distances in the right times and find all the named buildings. The topography is so neurotically accurate that it might have been seen by the self-exiled writer somewhere along one of his lawless roads, on the journey without maps.

Still straining every nerve to avoid giving away the plot, I can perhaps reveal that once again a joke figure gets caught in the firing line. The same thing happened in *Our Man in Havana* and *The Comedians*. The idea reached its fullest elaboration in *The Honorary Consul*, where Charley Fortnum pretended to be what he wasn't, got kidnapped instead of someone else, and turned the tables on everybody by knowing how to die. In this novel the role is taken by Castle's colleague Davis, a comic figure right up to the moment when he is mistakenly bumped off by his own side. As so often happens in the later Greene – and the later Greene is mainly the earlier Greene consciously exploiting his own preoccupations – the comic figure is not the true comedian. The true comedian is the poised sophisticate who succumbs to the ultimate folly of hoping to remain uninvolved.

Is there a wise policeman? Yes, there is a wise policeman. Or in this case a wise Secret Service officer, named Daintry. He and Castle end up on opposite sides of the fence, but there is a kinship between them. The kinship goes back to at least *The Power and the Glory*; in *Our Man in Havana* they played chess with miniature bottles of spirits and liqueurs; in *The Honorary Consul* they were in Argentina. (Castle is slow to emerge as a reincarnation of the whisky priest, by the way, but fans will be pleased to note that when he finally gets to the bottle he pours himself a quadruple.) Daintry comes even closer than his predecessors to being the good man in a bad job. Estranged from his bitchy wife, he dines alone on sardines and yesterday's Camembert. As usual, however, seediness has a sharpening effect on the moral sense. Daintry is the one who is most disgusted by Davis's death – more so, indeed, than Castle, which leaves you wondering if the author hasn't repressed his hero's sensibilities in order to safeguard the plot.

If the book has a serious flaw, it lies in the fact that Castle is too complacent about the fate of Davis. Faced with such indifference, we are bound to care less than we should about his love for his wife and child. It might be, of course, that Castle *can't* care about Davis – because he is a burnt-out case. But even at his most elliptical Greene would be sure to make such a point explicitly, if he were making it at all. I think that the point is not made, and that the book is somewhat weakened by having a central character less interesting than his dilemma warrants. In fact Castle is almost put in the shade by Daintry, who shows signs of wanting to break free and start a novel of his own.

Daintry, like his creator, seems to be experiencing England as a strange land. The eye for exotic fauna is never more sharp than when Daintry is at large among the upper classes to whom he is supposed to belong but among whom he never loses the heightened consciousness engendered by discomfort. The huntin'-shootin'-and-fishin' high-echelon Secret Servicemen are observed with the kind of sardonic penetration that Evelyn Waugh partly lost after he moved into his latter-day romanticism. As with Greene, so with

Waugh, Catholicism was a guarantee against the supposition – crippling to any artist – that paradise can be attained on earth. But Waugh eventually reneged to the extent of romanticising the vanishing English social order: *Sword of Honour*, like Ford's *Parade's End*, is in many ways a self-serving fantasy. Greene has never allowed himself to lapse. He is not as inventive as Waugh but in the long run he has proved himself tougher. Here is the final proof, if proof were needed: an England treated not as home but as a far country, in which evil forces are operating uncomprehended.

Greene's Catholicism is the real answer to the question, still often posed, about whether or not he has the gift of prescience. He moves into a country, writes a novel about its inner tensions, and straight afterwards the novel happens in real life. He does have a gift, but it is not for clairvoyance. It is not that he sees ahead. He just sees straight. In South-East Asia, for example, he simply saw what was actually happening: *The Quiet American* succeeded in foretelling the future by reporting the present, at a time when others, for the best of reasons, couldn't see realities for ideals. Since Greene's ideals are not of this earth, he is free to see realities. The spiritual component of his religion must necessarily remain mostly private, but it is possible to say that the intellectual component has been a boon to him as an artist. His natural talent for political analysis has been able to flourish unswayed by any temporal allegiance.

Whether his Catholicism is of much help in the analysis of personality is a moot point. He would as soon explore non-believers as believers – perhaps, nowadays, even sooner. For the record, Castle, although not a Catholic, gravitates into a confessional box on page 233. Even if he had not felt the need, his remorse would have remained the same: no more and no less. If Castle is insufficiently realised, it is not because he is an apostate but because the story got in the road, leaving him neither fish, fowl nor good red Philby.

But the story is absorbing enough to justify the intrusion. Quibbling for a moment, I can't see why Castle couldn't get the details of Operation Uncle Remus back to his superiors without blowing his cover – all he would have had to do would have been to warn his control that there was a defector in place. Apart from that one slip, however, the plot is both plausible and engrossing from start to finish. It is like one of those good, solid, early le Carré novels, plus the moral overtones which the later le Carré vainly tries to add by cramming on hundreds of extra pages, but which Greene can't help generating from the first sentence, simply because he views life in a certain way. We can only be grateful that his unique vision has gone on intensifying for so long, time after time choosing the right issue to clarify at the right moment in the right place. Which is to say, on this occasion: apartheid, now and England.

(*New Statesman*, 1978)

Pensée Persons

Kalki by Gore Vidal (Heinemann, London, and Random House, New York)

THE NARRATOR of Gore Vidal's new novel, Teddy Ottinger, is a surgically revamped bisexual beauty sharing many characteristics with one of his previous heroines. The hero she does most of her narrating about, James J. Kelly, alias Kalki, has come to announce the end of the world. Not to put too fine a point on it, in *Kalki* Myra Breckenridge meets Messiah.

But just because two of Vidal's long-term preoccupations can here be seen snuggling up to each other is no reason to be snooty. Their coupling is punctiliously discreet, intromission occurring with a minimum of fanfare ('I shall not describe Kalki's genitals') somewhere in the vicinity of page 79. Salaciousness is never permitted to intrude. However famous it has helped to make him, social satire is the most minor vein in Vidal's work. *Kalki*, lacking even the sensationalism of *Myra Breckenridge*, ought logically to be minorissimo. Yet it somehow manages to be a very enjoyable literature invention – a term I borrow gladly from the publicity handout accompanying my proof copy. *Kalki* might not be the full thing as literature, but it is undeniably some kind of invention, even if several components of the mechanism are recognisable from earlier devices patented by the same busy man.

The main reason for the enjoyability of this new literature invention is the piercing sibilance with which Vidal's obsessions come hissing through the seams. In his essays he has given us a body of sane comment for which it is difficult to be sufficiently grateful – few contemporary writers have told us so much about the world. But in his essays he does not really tell us a lot about himself, least of all when he makes a show of frankness. You would think, for example, that he despised power, wealth, privilege, and glamour without being drawn to them. But his literature inventions invariably demonstrate that he is very strongly drawn to these things. And it is valuable to find this out, since the knowledge lends his criticisms even more force. He would be a less impressive moralist if we thought him invulnerable to the passions he attacks.

Unlike Myra, Teddy is no movie buff. She is an aviation buff instead. It quickly becomes obvious that Vidal has less interest in aeroplanes than in the movies. Teddy's enthusiasm is consequently a bit abstract. She worships the memory of Amelia Earhart. (Significantly, this particular idea comes most intensely to life when Teddy speculates about the possibility of ousting Shirley MacLaine from the title role in the projected bio-pic: Myra rides again.) There is a fleeting obeisance to Jacqueline Cochrane. Mention of these lady fliers sorts well enough with Teddy's feminism, but it is not enough in itself to convince the reader that she finds liberation in the wild blue yonder. The only thing that would do that would be a vividly transmitted sense of what it feels like to be mad about flying.

But the author doesn't possess, and can't convincingly

simulate, any real feeling for the nuts and bolts of the matter. As a consequence, the promising theme of a ballsy woman who can outfly any man in the house ends up going for nearly nothing. Teddy hardly begins to embody the real spirit of American aviation, which has usually been based on a practicality so self-sufficient that even the most beautiful machines are given numbers instead of names. When Teddy waxes poetical about flying, she invokes the ghost of St-Exupéry. Wind, sand, and stars. The Frenchified reference fits the author (who made favourable mention of St-Exupéry in an essay on Richard Hillary in 1951) better than it fits the character. St-Exupéry actually wasn't all that hot as a pilot. He kept getting lost all the time, and crashed for silly reasons, such as running out of gas. It was his writing that made him exceptional.

Teddy is a writer too. She is meant to be more flier than writer, but she comes over as more writer than flier. She has so scrupulous a regard for correct English usage that she almost reminds you of Gore Vidal. It appears that her previous, bestselling book was ghosted by a hack, but that the book she is writing now – i.e., *Kalki* – is all her own work.

The reader is bound to conclude that for a flier Teddy has almost supernatural literary gifts. She knows all about what Norman Mailer once called the Talent in the Room. She is scornful about Erica Jong. She is apprehensive about what even lesser scribes are doing to the English language. Above all, she is sensitive to cliché. She is quick to spot clichés in other people and would obviously rather be caught dead than perpetrate one herself. Instead of writing 'by hook or by crook' she writes 'by crook or by hook'. Instead of writing 'part and parcel' she writes 'parcel and part'. She gets you down, rather.

Vidal must be well aware that these are the concerns of a professional artist with his antennae tuned to the limit. In Teddy Ottinger, girl test pilot, they are scarely credible: she is supposed to have taken her degree in engineering, not English lit. But as usually happens in his social satires, Vidal can't resist using the central character to put himself over in a manner untrammelled by modesty. 'I am considered beautiful,' purrs Teddy. It might almost be Vidal talking. 'I have always wanted to know everything.' It *is* Vidal talking – he said that very thing in his last *New York Times* interview. Speaking through the character, he can let his cornier impulses rip. Bitchy gossip is suddenly legit. Newsmakers and stylesetters pop up everywhere throughout the book. *Per media* Teddy's all-American success hunger, Vidal can be almost as concerned with the insubstantial pageant as Truman Capote.

Here they come, in no particular order, just as they leap to the reader's eye. Ed Griffin, Clay Felker, Joan Didion, Renata Adler, Rupert Murdoch (how did *he* get in?), Oriana Fallaci, Paul Ehrlich, Barry Commoner, Norman Mailer, Barbara Walters, George Harrison, Walter Cronkite, Grace Kelly, Jackie O., Harold Rosenberg, Milton Friedman, Germaine Greer, Kate Millett, Eva Figes, Noam Chomsky, Joni Mitchell, Evel Knievel. . . . Teddy sounds as if the doctors who cut out her tubes plugged her brain into the same computer that writes the captions for *W*.

But Teddy, for a blessing, is a bit more than just Vidal's way of succumbing on the sly to the heady attractions of the fame market. He is right to keep tabs on such things, of course: there is certainly something interesting about a culture in which a magazine like *Rolling Stone*, say, can start off as the voice of iconoclastic youth and within ten years be running a full-length article by Lally Weymouth about Diana Vreeland. If Vidal were to miss out on that kind of stuff he would be missing out on part of America. But such matters are interesting only up to a point. Luckily Teddy's scope of attention ranges well beyond the things of this world.

Teddy has mystical leanings. A great eschewer of gurus, she is nevertheless deeply into Pascal, who haunts this book the way Plotinus haunted *Julian*. When taxed on the subject of Julian's powerful yearning for a vision of the One, Vidal has been known to assert the autonomy of his created character and disown all involvement. He could do the same here, but none the less the reader will find himself wondering if Teddy's thirst for revelation is all hers. '*Console-toi*,' she quotes Pascal, '*tu ne me chercherais pas si tu ne m'avais trouvé*'. (Once again notable is the uncanny cultivation of Teddy's literary sensibility. Never once does she drop a pearl from Kahlil Gibran or ask for your sign. She's a *pensée* person.)

But whom has she found? Kalki, the nominal prime mover of this literature invention, proclaims himself to be the Avatar, Vishnu, highest of the high, the bee's knees. He looks with pity upon mere mankind's innumerable busy littlenesses. He is a golden boy with thick legs. Teddy tries hard to be sceptical but soon caves in. So does all the world. Messiah-style, Kalki sweeps to fame with his apocalyptic message.

The new wrinkle is that the apocalypse really happens, wiping out the whole population of the world except for Kalki and his immediate entourage. It turns out that Kalki cheated. Does that make him a fake? Teddy can't seem to decide. You could be forgiven for suspecting that Vidal can't either. Aren't Kalki and Teddy really just megaton versions of Charles Manson and Squeaky Fromm? No answer. The novel drifts elegantly to an end in a world empty of people. The last few human beings while away their time by dressing up in classic gowns looted from the Smithsonian and throwing dinner parties for each other. With a free choice from the great galleries, they assemble ideal personal art collections. Teddy goes for the Impressionists. So, given the same opportunities, did Goering, but Vidal forgets to mention it.

Eventually even the charms of high fashion fade. The last human beings die off, leaving the monkeys to take over. (They have done a good job of publishing Teddy's testament, incidentally: apart from a fleeting appearance put in by someone called Noah Chomsky the text is as clean as a whistle.) But the one question we can't help asking is why Vidal – not Teddy: Vidal – gives Kalki so much numinous energy. Are people fools to believe in him, or are they fools not to? On this evidence, fools not to.

The book has many subsidiary pleasures. Arlene Wagstaff, Teddy's steady date, is a fully reconstructed television pitchperson brimming over with what Vidal, referring to Barbara Walters, is given to calling the Vivacity; there are a pair of knockabout narcs straight out of the Fabulous Furry Freak Brothers; there are cleverly detailed freeze-frame visions of the unpeopled planet. These things help to offset a certain lack of humour – caught between two personalities, Vidal in this kind of writing seldom generates the same sort of laughter that he so easily arouses when he is just being himself.

But even if the grimness were entirely unmitigated, this would still be a considerable book. Vidal's literature inventions have the virtue of blowing some of the cool which as a public figure he is so notoriously well able to keep. As soul and body begin to fall asunder, his fictional works must inevitably reveal more and more about what he really wants, feels, and is. It will be a boon but no surprise: so clear an intelligence was bound to be powered by dark fires. One of the most interesting of contemporary American writers, Vidal is almost alone in becoming more interesting all the time.

(*New York Review of Books*, 1978)

Look Forward in Mild Irritation

1985 by Anthony Burgess (Hutchinson, London, and Little Brown, Boston)

ANTHONY BURGESS has words the way the be-bop saxophonists used to have notes – in scads. With him as with them, you have to hear something slow before you can make up your mind. *Nothing Like the Sun* and the Enderby books prove that Burgess is as clever as he seems. His utopian satires, of which *1985* is yet another, mainly just seem clever. At a generous estimate there are half a dozen ideas in each of them.

1985 avowedly exaggerates trends already visible in present-day Britain. The unions are in control, everyone is on strike, children learn nothing in school, and the whole place is overrun with Arabs. Readers will have no trouble recognising the reality behind the exaggeration. Britain is certainly a bit like that. So why exaggerate? To point out the obvious? A better reason for concocting this kind of fantasy is to expose what is not obvious – in a word, to analyse. Burgess himself is given to saying that this is one of the things serious writers can do that science fiction writers cannot do.

A good case can be made for Zamyatin, Huxley and Orwell as having struck deeper than the science fiction writers. The case does not look quite so strong to anyone who has actually read reasonably widely among the science fiction writers, but let us suppose for the moment that it is watertight. The question remains whether Burgess can be enrolled along with Zamyatin, Huxley and Orwell. *The Wanting Seed*, for example, hammers its theme – overpopulation – with no more subtlety than the best science fiction writers of the 1950s were wont to employ, and a good deal less invention. The world is short of food; England is urbanised from end to end; infanticide is officially encouraged; wars are arranged in order to kill people off.

All these ideas were handled at least as vigorously by science fiction writers. Frederik Pohl and C. M. Kornbluth, in *The Space Merchants*, showed a world so crowded that whole families in New York were sleeping on the stairs of skyscrapers. The main source of food was an enormous hunk of protein called Chicken Little, who could be kept from engulfing her attendants only by an ultrasonic whistle. Most of the other effects in the book were comparably striking.

Pohl and Kornbluth come to mind again when you consider *A Clockwork Orange*, the book for which Burgess – to his understandable dismay – is best known. A handy transitional primer for anyone learning Russian, in other respects it is a bit thin. Burgess makes a good ethical point when he says that the state has no right to extirpate the impulse towards violence. But it is hard to see why he is so determined to link the impulse towards violence with the aesthetic impulse, unless he suffers, as so many other writers do, from the delusion that the arts are really rather a dangerous occupation. Presumably the connection in the hero's head between mayhem and music was what led Stanley Kubrick to find the text such an inspiration. Hence the world was regaled with profound images of Malcolm McDowell jumping up and down on people's chests to the accompaniment of an invisible orchestra.

It is a moot point whether Burgess is saying much about human psychology when he so connects the destructive element with the creative. What is certain is that he is not saying much about politics. Nothing in *A Clockwork Orange* is very fully worked out. There is only half a paragraph of blurred hints to tell you why the young marauders speak a mixture of English and Russian. Has Britain been invaded recently? Apparently not. Something called 'propaganda', presumably of the left-wing variety, is vaguely gestured towards as being responsible for this hybrid speech. But even when we leave the possible causes aside, and just examine the language itself, how could so basic a word as 'thing' have been replaced by the Russian word without other, equally basic, words being replaced as well?

In *Gladiator at Law*, which ranks alongside *The Space Merchants* among the novels they collaborated on during the 1950s, Pohl and Kornbluth treated some of the same themes that cropped up later in *A Clockwork Orange*. There were even squads of marauding children talking a special language. But the important point is that the authors did their best to cut deep. Pohl and Kornbluth weren't just the American version of Ilf and Petrov. They were far more dissatisfied with capitalism than Ilf and Petrov ever were with communism. *Gladiator at Law* still stands today as a sharp reminder of what modern society can be like for those who run out of credit. At the time it was prophetic.

Compared with an artist like Burgess, of course, none of the science fiction scriveners could write at all. In science fiction circles the standard of literary style was set by Ray Bradbury. But science fiction still achieved better results in the line of utopian satire than is commonly assumed, and often precisely because it was obliged to eschew, or could not attain to, such literary luxuries as character and atmosphere. Kurt Vonnegut's *Player Piano* is a better book than anything he wrote in his later incarnation as a serious writer. First-rate science fiction was, and remains, more interesting than second-rate art. Burgess is right to think that Zamyatin, Huxley and Orwell go deeper than science fiction, but his opinion ought not to receive automatic assent. It is far from certain that he knows quite why they do.

The first half of *1985*, before the fiction starts, is a long factual essay about *Nineteen Eighty-Four*, in which Burgess establishes with marvellous thoroughness that he has misunderstood Orwell. Burgess knows all there is to know about Britain in 1948, when *Nineteen Eighty-Four* was completed. He evokes the country's atmosphere of rationing and frustration in all its pathetic detail. He also knows a lot about Orwell's personal circumstances at that time. But he knows very little about Orwell's mind if he thinks that *Nineteen Eighty-Four* is mainly concerned with Britain in 1948.

By now it is a critical commonplace that the canteen of the Ministry of Truth in *Nineteen Eighty-Four* was modelled on the BBC's. But Burgess, with his strangely obtuse conviction that novels are more about 'sense data' than about ideas (as if, in any kind of developed art, there could be any real difference), follows the same tack to absurd lengths, finding 1948 equivalents for almost everything in *Nineteen Eighty-Four*. He makes some useful points, but he just doesn't seem to notice that he ends up sounding like one of those terrible academics who tell you that generations of readers have got it all wrong, and that such-and-such a book was really about something else all the time.

If Burgess needs reminding, perhaps we all need reminding. *Nineteen Eighty-Four* is not concerned with the sense data of Britain in 1948, but with totalitarianism in the twentieth century. Orwell is trying to show what a totalitarian state is like in its essence. The nightmare had already come true, in the form of the Soviet Union, but it had been widely misunderstood. Orwell's main aim was to make the nightmare intelligible and hand on an instructive myth. The totalitarian state and its mind and language – to analyse, characterise and combat these things were the main tasks of Orwell's life.

In the 1930s Orwell had been pre-eminently the man who saw that it wasn't enough to be antifascist, you had to be antitotalitarian. Saying so, he put himself beyond the pale of the British left and indeed the left the world over. *Animal Farm* and *Nineteen Eighty-Four* were books written to help change world opinion. To a large extent they did. Orwell was thus a writer and thinker of global consequence. He had his weaknesses, but it makes no sense to belittle his range of concern. Yet that is exactly what Burgess seems bent on doing.

Perhaps Burgess just doesn't get it. His introductory essay, well argued though it sometimes is, reinforces the impression one had formed some time ago that for Burgess the world's ills are conceived of as a set of irritants aimed principally at his own person. Burgess sees himself, no doubt rightly, as an individualist. He thinks that if there were less government there would be fewer bureaucratic agencies devoting themselves to making his life less bearable by introducing such soulless novelties as decimal coinage. A few years ago, when he was still living in Italy, Burgess wrote articles for British newspapers saying that the British ought to be more like the Italians, who had learned how to live with chaos. This was before the sudden popularity of kidnapping and terrorism suggested that Italy needed a lot less chaos than it was getting.

The novel *1985* itself chugs along determinedly enough, although you could hardly call its progress inexorable. The hero's name is Bev Jones. 'Bev' stems from such names as Beveridge, Bevin, and Bevan – all of them denoting left-wing collectivism of one shade or another. 'Jones' is probably there as a conscious substitute for Orwell's Smith, with the additional consideration that Jack Jones is currently the most famous of the British trades union leaders, and a powerfully boring man he is too. Britain's other name is Tucland, from TUC: Trades Union Congress. I only wish that Burgess's handling of these details could have been less tedious than my summary of them.

The firemen being on strike, Bev's wife burns to death. He goes on the vengeance trail – a variation on the standard exploratory voyage common to most utopian satires. On the way he meets the same breed of cultivated muggers already made familiar to us by *A Clockwork Orange*. This idea is no more convincing now than it was then, but at least it retains something of its original verve. The muggers are the liveliest characters in the book. They sit at the back of the class reading bootleg copies of Latin classics while their dumber contemporaries lap up the daily doses of sociology and WE (Workers' English, plus a nod to Zamyatin). There is something touching about the way Burgess goes on being convinced that this is a point worth making.

Daring to work when he should be on strike (the films *The Angry Silence* and *I'm All Right Jack* were based on the same idea), Bev is stripped of his union card and descends to the lower depths. Eventually he is sent away for re-education. Sex is allowed at the rehabilitation centre, as in *We* – another bow to Zamyatin. The publishers' names allocated to some of the minor characters perhaps constitute a nod to Bulgakov, who used composers' names in *Master and Margarita*. Bing Crosby is several times referred to as 'Saint Bing' – a weak idea. In *Brave New World* it makes some kind of sense that Henry Ford is remembered as Our Ford. But why would Tucland canonise Bing Crosby? Or, granted that it would canonise him, why would it not canonise a lot of other entertainers along with him? If the point is not worth following up, it was not worth raising in the first place.

Burgess would probably like *1985* to be thought of as a teeming grab-bag of ideas. In fact it is a scrap heap. The first requirement of any fantasy is that it should hang together. If the questions you ask of it yield contradictory answers, it evaporates. Burgess extrapolates current left-wing tendencies without extrapolating current right-wing tendencies, or even mentioning them. If all those Arabs came in, what happened to the National Front? One is forced to the conclusion that the fiction is fragmentary because, for Burgess, reality is fragmentary. He doesn't see politics as anything coherent. Instead he sees it as a lot of different inconveniences ganging up on him.

In the introductory essay there is a revealing remark about Zamyatin. Burgess says that *We* was not written about any contemporary state. But it was. *We* was a prophetic book not because Zamyatin gazed into a crystal ball but because he saw the likely consequences of what people were thinking in the first years of the Soviet Union. That is why we think Zamyatin, Huxley and Orwell better than the science fiction writers – because they trace conditions back to sources in the mind. For all their direct engagement, they are contemplative writers, capable, at their best, of bringing reason to bear even on their own instincts. Burgess is less like them, and more like the science fiction writers, than he might be willing to allow.

The science fiction writers, no matter how brilliantly inventive, were never strong on self-examination. Like most second-rate artists, they wrote to express their prejudices, not to explore them. Stories by Pohl and Kornbluth usually came out right in the end. After however prolonged a struggle, the hero emerged healthy out of the rotten system, ready to reform it or start afresh on another planet. Among the science fiction writers there was no real difference between the satirists and the celebrants, so there was no good reason for preferring the former to the latter. Indeed the science fiction writer Robert Heinlein, whose politics were largely indistinguishable from those of John Wayne, attacked the consumer society more effectively from the right than the satirists from the left. His *Starship Troopers* and *The Puppet Masters*, quite apart from their unarguable virtues as adventure stories, have the additional quality of representing the authoritarian instinct in its purest form and thereby helping us to comprehend it.

But it rarely occurred to Heinlein, or to any other science fiction writer, that his instincts should *be* his subject. Zamyatin, Huxley and Orwell all knew, to varying degrees, that the nightmare state had its embryonic counterpart in the impulse to order within their own souls. They were worried men. Without calling Burgess conceited, it is still fair to say that he has few such doubts. Perhaps his surging abundance of verbal talent gives him too great a reason to feel unique. He is an individualist by instinct – a valuable trait in a personality, but a limited viewpoint from which to criticise a whole society.

1985 sounds like the same union-bashing gone in for by all those members of the British managerial class who are convinced that their entrepreneurial flair is being stifled. It seldom crosses their minds that they, too, are part of the problem. Solipsistic without being self-searching, Burgess shares the same irritable conviction that he knows how things should be. *1985* is a yelp of annoyance, already out of date before it is published. *Nineteen Eighty-Four*, a minatory illumination of the darkest propensities in human nature, will be pertinent forever.

(*New York Review of Books*, 1978)

A Blizzard of Tiny Kisses

Princess Daisy by Judith Krantz
(Sidgwick and Jackson, London, and Crown, New York)

TO BE a really lousy writer takes energy. The average novelist remains unread not because he is bad but because he is flat. On the evidence of *Princess Daisy*, Judith Krantz deserves her high place in the best-seller lists. This is the second time she has been up there. The first time was for a book called *Scruples*, which I will probably never get around to reading. But I don't begrudge the time I have put into reading *Princess Daisy*. As a work of art it has the same status as a long conversation between two not very bright drunks, but as best-sellers go it argues for a reassuringly robust connection between fiction and the reading public. If cheap dreams get no worse than this, there will not be much for the cultural analyst to complain about. *Princess Daisy* is a terrible book only in the sense that it is almost totally inept. Frightening it isn't.

In fact, it wouldn't even be particularly boring if only Mrs Krantz could quell her artistic urge. 'Above all,' said Conrad, 'to make you see.' Mrs Krantz strains every nerve to make you see. She pops her valves in the unrelenting effort to bring it all alive. Unfortunately she has the opposite of a pictorial talent. The more detail she piles on, the less clear things become. Take the meeting of Stash and Francesca. Mrs Krantz defines Prince Alexander Vassilivitch Valensky, alias Stash, as 'the great war hero and incomparable polo-player'. Stash is Daisy's father. Francesca Vernon, the film star, is her mother. Francesca possesses 'a combination of tranquillity and pure sensuality in the composition of the essential triangle of eyes and mouth'. Not just essential but well-nigh indispensable, one would have thought. Or perhaps that's what she means.

This, however, is to quibble, because before Stash and Francesca can generate Daisy they first have to meet, and theirs is a meeting of transfigurative force, as of Apollo catching up with Daphne. The scene is Deauville, 1952. Francesca the film star, she of the pure sensuality, is a reluctant spectator at a polo game – reluctant, that is, until she claps eyes on Stash. Here is a description of her eyes, together with the remaining component of the essential triangle, namely her mouth. 'Her black eyes were long and widely spaced, her mouth, even in repose, was made meaningful by the grace of its shape: the gentle arc of her upper lip dipped in the centre to meet the lovely pillow of her lower lip in a line that had the power of an embrace.'

And this is Stash, the great war hero and incomparable polo-player: 'Valensky had the physical presence of a great athlete who has punished his body without pity throughout his life and the watchful, fighting eyes of a natural predator. His glance was bold and his thick brows were many shades darker than his blonde hair, cropped short and as coarse as the coat of a hastily brushed dog . . . His nose, broken many times, gave him the air of a roughneck . . . Not only did Valensky never employ unnecessary force on the bit and reins but he had been born, as some men are, with an instinct for establishing a communication between himself and his pony which made it seem as if the animal was merely an extension of his mind, rather than a beast with a will of its own.'

Dog-haired, horse-brained and with a bashed conk, Stash is too much for Francesca's equilibrium. Her hat flies off.

> 'Oh no!' she exclaimed in dismay, but as she spoke, Stash Valensky leaned down from his pony and scooped her up in one arm. Holding her easily, across his chest, he urged his mount after the wayward hat. It had come to rest two hundred yards away, and Valensky, leaving Francesca mounted, jumped down from his saddle, picked the hat up by its ribbons and carefully replaced it on her head. The stands rang with laughter and applause.
>
> Francesca heard nothing of the noise the spectators made. Time, as she knew it, had stopped. By instinct, she remained silent and waiting, passive against Stash's soaking-wet polo shirt. She could smell his sweat and it confounded her with desire. Her mouth filled with saliva. She wanted to sink her teeth into his tan neck, to bite him until she could taste his blood, to lick up the rivulets of sweat which ran down to his open collar. She wanted him to fall to the ground with her in his arms, just as he was, flushed, steaming, still breathing heavily from the game, and grind himself into her.

But this is the first of many points at which Mrs Krantz's minus capability for evocation leaves you puzzled. How did Stash get the hat back on Francesca's head? Did he remount, or is he just very tall? If he did remount, couldn't that have been specified? Mrs Krantz gives you all the details you don't need to form a mental picture, while carefully withholding those you do. Half the trick of pictorial writing is to give only the indispensable points and let the reader's imagination do the rest. Writers who not only give the indispensable points but supply all the concrete details as well can leave you feeling bored with their brilliance – Wyndham Lewis is an outstanding example. But a writer who supplies the concrete details and leaves out the indispensable points can only exhaust you. Mrs Krantz is right to pride herself on the accuracy of her research into every department of the high life. What she says is rarely inaccurate, as far as I can tell. It is, however, almost invariably irrelevant.

Anyway, the book starts with a picture of Daisy ('Her dark eyes, not quite black, but the colour of the innermost heart of a giant purple pansy, caught the late afternoon light and held it fast . . .') and then goes on to describe the meeting of her parents. It then goes on to tell you a lot about what her parents got up to before they met. Then it goes on to tell you about *their* parents. The book is continually going backwards instead of forwards, a canny insurance against the reader's impulse to skip. At one stage I tried skipping a chapter and missed out on about a century. From the upper West Side of New York I was suddenly in the Russian Revolution. That's where Stash gets his fiery temperament from – Russia.

'At Chez Mahu they found that they were able only to talk of unimportant things. Stash tried to explain polo to Francesca but she scarcely listened, mesmerised as she was with the abrupt movements of his tanned hands on which light blonde hair grew, the hands of a great male animal.' A bison? Typically, Mrs Krantz has failed to be specific at the exact moment when specificity would be a virtue. Perhaps Stash is like a horse not just in brain but in body. This would account for his tendency to view Francesca as a creature of equine provenance. 'Francesca listened to Valensky's low voice, which had traces of an English accent, a brutal man's voice which seemed to vibrate with an underlying tenderness, as if he were talking to a newborn foal . . . '

There is a lot more about Stash and Francesca before the reader can get to Daisy. Indeed, the writer herself might never have got to Daisy if she (i.e. Mrs Krantz) had not first wiped out Stash and Francesca. But before they can be killed, Mrs Krantz must expend about a hundred and fifty pages on various desperate attempts to bring them alive. In World War Two the incomparable polo-player becomes the great war hero. Those keen to see Stash crash, however, are doomed to disappointment, since before Stash can win medals in his Hurricane we must hear about his first love affair. Stash is fourteen years old and the Marquise Clair de Champery is a sex-pot of a certain age. 'She felt the congestion of blood rushing between her primly pressed together thighs, proof positive that she had been right to provoke the boy.' Stash, meanwhile, shows his customary tendency to metamorphose into an indeterminate life-form. 'He took her hand and put it on his penis. The hot sticky organ was already beginning to rise and fill. It moved under her touch like an animal.' A field mouse? A boa constrictor?

Receiving the benefit of Stash's extensive sexual education, Francesca conceives twins. One of the twins turns out to be Daisy and the other her retarded sister, Danielle. But first Stash has to get to the clinic. 'As soon as the doctor telephoned, Stash raced to the clinic at 95 miles an hour.' Miserly as always with the essentials, Mrs Krantz trusts the reader to supply the information that Stash is attaining this speed by some form of motorised transport.

Stash rejects Danielle, Francesca flees with Danielle and Daisy. Stash consoles himself with his collection of jet aircraft. Mrs Krantz has done a lot of research in this area but it is transparently research, which is not the same thing as knowledge. Calling a Junkers 88 a Junker 88 might be a misprint, but her rhapsody about Stash's prize purchase of 1953 is a dead giveaway. 'He tracked down and bought the most recent model available of the Lockheed XP-80, known as the Shooting Star, a jet which for many years could out-manoeuvre and outperform almost every other aircraft in the world.' USAF fighter aircraft carried 'X' numbers only before being accepted for service. By 1953 the Shooting Star was known as the F-80, had been in service for years, and was practically the slowest thing of its type in the sky. But Mrs Krantz is too fascinated by that 'X' to let it go. She deserves marks, however, for her determination to catch up on the arcane nomenclature of boys' toys.

Stash finally buys a farm during a flying display in 1967. An old Spitfire packs up on him. 'The undercarriage of the 27-year-old plane stuck and the landing gear could not be released.' Undercarriage and landing gear are the same thing – her vocabularies have collided over the Atlantic. Also an airworthy 27-year-old Spitfire in 1967 would have been a very rare bird indeed: no wonder the undercarriage got in the road of the landing gear. But Mrs Krantz goes some way towards capturing the excitement of machines and should not be mocked for her efforts. Francesca, incidentally, dies in a car crash, with the make of car unspecified.

One trusts that Mrs Krantz's documentation of less particularly masculine activities is as meticulous as it is undoubtedly exhaustive, although even in such straightforward matters as food and drink she can sometimes be caught making the elementary mistake of piling on the fatal few details too many. Before Stash gets killed he takes Daisy to lunch every Sunday at the Connaught. After he gets killed he is forced to give up this practice, although there is no real reason why he should not have continued, since he is no more animated before his prang than after. Mrs Krantz has researched the Connaught so heavily that she must have made herself part of the furniture. It is duly noted that the menu has a brown and gold border. It is unduly noted that the menu has the date printed at the bottom. Admittedly such a thing would not happen at the nearest branch of the Golden Egg, but it is not necessarily the mark of a great restaurant. Mrs Krantz would probably hate to hear it said, but she gives the impression of having been included late amongst the exclusiveness she so admires. There is nothing wrong with gusto, but when easy familiarity is what you are trying to convey, gush is to be avoided.

Full of grand meals served and consumed at chapter length, *Princess Daisy* reads like *Buddenbrooks* without the talent. Food is important to Mrs Krantz: so important that her characters keep turning into it, when they are not turning into animals. Daisy has a half-brother called Ram, who rapes her, arouses her sexually, beats her up, rapes her again, and does his best to wreck her life because she rejects his love. His passion is understandable, when you consider Daisy's high nutritional value. 'He gave up the struggle and devoured her lips with his own, kissing her as if he were dying of thirst and her mouth were a moist fruit.' A mango? Daisy fears Ram but goes for what he dishes out. 'Deep within her something sounded, as if the string of a great cello had been plucked, a note of remote, mysterious but unmistakable warning.' Boing.

Daisy heeds the warning and lights out for the USA, where she becomes a producer of television commercials in order to pay Danielle's hospital bills. She pals up with a patrician girl called Kiki, whose breasts quiver in indignation – the first breasts to have done that for a long, long time. At such moments one is reminded of Mrs Krantz's true literary ancestry, which stretches all the way back to Elinor Glyn, E. M. Hull and Gertrude Atherton. She is wasting a lot of her time and too much of ours trying to be John O'Hara. At the slightest surge of congested blood between her primly pressed together thighs, all Mrs Krantz's carefully garnered social detail gives way to eyes like twin dark stars, mouths like moist fruit and breasts quivering with indignation.

There is also the warm curve of Daisy's neck where the jaw joins the throat. Inheriting this topographical feature from her mother, Daisy carries it around throughout the novel waiting for the right man to kiss it *tutto tremante*. Ram will definitely not do. A disconsolate rapist, he searches hopelessly among the eligible young English ladies – Jane Bonham-Carter and Sabrina Guinness are both considered – before choosing the almost inconceivably well-connected Sarah Fane. Having violated Sarah in his by now standard manner, Ram is left with nothing to do except blow Daisy's secret and commit suicide. As Ram bites the dust, the world learns that the famous Princess Daisy, star of a multi-million-dollar perfume promotion, has a retarded sister. Will this put the kibosh on the promotion, not to mention Daisy's love for the man in charge, the wheeler-dealer head of Supracorp, Pat Shannon ('larky bandit', 'freebooter' etc.)?

Daisy's libido, dimmed at first by Ram's rape, has already been reawakened by the director of her commercials, a ruthless but prodigiously creative character referred to as North. Yet North finally lacks what it takes to reach the warm curve of Daisy's neck. Success in that area is reserved for Shannon. He it is who undoes all the damage and fully arouses her hot blood. 'It seemed a long time before Shannon began to imprint a blizzard of tiny kisses at the point where Daisy's jaw joined her throat, that particularly warm curve, spendthrift with beauty, that he had not allowed himself to realise had haunted him for weeks. Daisy felt fragile and warm to Shannon, as if he'd trapped a young unicorn [horses again – C.J.], some strange, mythological creature. Her hair was the most intense source of light in the room, since it reflected the moonlight creeping through the windows, and by its light he saw her eyes, open, rapt and glowing; twin dark stars.'

Shannon might think he's got hold of some kind of horse, but as far as Daisy's concerned she's a species of cetacean. 'It was she who guided his hands down the length of her body, she who touched him wherever she could reach, as playfully as a dolphin, until he realised that her fragility was strength, and that she wanted him without reserve.'

Daisy is so moved by this belated but shatteringly complete experience that she can be forgiven for what she does next. 'Afterward, as they lay together, half asleep, but unwilling to drift apart into unconsciousness, Daisy farted, in a tiny series of absolutely irrepressible little pops that seemed to her to go on for a minute.' It takes bad art to teach us how good art gets done. Knowing that the dithyrambs have gone on long enough, Mrs Krantz has tried to undercut them with something earthy. Her tone goes wrong, but her intention is worthy of respect. It is like one of those clumsy attempts at naturalism in a late-medieval painting – less pathetic than portentous, since it adumbrates the great age to come. Mrs Krantz will never be much of an artist but she has more than a touch of the artist's ambition.

Princess Daisy is not to be despised. Nor should it be deplored for its concern with aristocracy, glamour, status, success and things like that. On the evidence of her prose, Mrs Krantz has not enough humour to write tongue-in-cheek, but other people are perfectly capable of reading that way. People don't get their morality from their reading matter: they bring their morality to it. The assumption that ordinary people's lives could be controlled and limited by what entertained them was always too condescending to be anything but fatuous.

Mrs Krantz, having dined at Mark's Club, insists that it is exclusive. There would not have been much point to her dining there if she did not think that. An even bigger snob than she is might point out that the best reason for not dining at Mark's Club is the chance of finding Mrs Krantz there. It takes only common sense, though, to tell you that on those terms exclusiveness is not just chimerical but plain tedious. You would keep better company eating Kentucky Fried Chicken in a launderette. But if some of this book's readers find themselves day-dreaming of the high life, let us be grateful that Mrs Krantz exists to help give their vague aspirations a local habitation and a name. They would dream anyway, and without Mrs Krantz they would dream unaided.

To pour abuse on a book like this makes no more sense than to kick a powder-puff. *Princess Daisy* is not even reprehensible for the three million dollars its author was paid for it in advance. It would probably have made most of the money back without a dime spent on publicity. The only bad thing is the effect on Mrs Krantz's personality. Until lately she was a nice Jewish lady harbouring the usual bourgeois fancies about the aristocracy. But now she gives interviews extolling her own hard head. 'Like so many of us,' she told the *Daily Mail* on 28 April, 'I happen to believe that being young, beautiful and rich is more desirable than being old, ugly and destitute.' Mrs Krantz is fifty years old, but to judge from the photograph on the back of the book she is engaged in a series of hard-fought delaying actions against time. This, I believe, is one dream that intelligent people ought not to connive at, since the inevitable result of any attempt to prolong youth is a graceless old age.

(*London Review of Books*, 1980)

Waugh's Last Stand

The Letters of Evelyn Waugh edited by Mark Amory (Weidenfeld & Nicolson, London, and Ticknor and Fields, New Haven, Connecticut)

UNLESS the telephone is uninvented, this will probably be the last collection of letters by a great writer to be also a great collection of letters. It could be argued that the book should have been either much shorter, so as to be easily assimilable, or else much larger, so as to take in all of the vast number of letters Waugh wrote, but even at this awkward length it is a wonderfully entertaining volume – even more so, in fact, than the *Diaries*. Here is yet one more reason to thank Evelyn Waugh for his hatred of the modern world. If he had not loathed the telephone, he might have talked all this away.

'Would you say I was a very ill-tempered and self-infatuated man?' he asked Nancy Mitford in 1947, and added answering his own question: 'It hurts.' Waugh was unhappy about himself, and on this evidence he had every right to be. People who want to emphasise his repellent aspects will find plenty to help them here. For one thing, he revelled in his contempt for Jews. In his correspondence he usually spelled the word Jew with a small 'j' unless he was being polite to one of them for some professional reason. In a 1946 letter to Robert Henriques he asks for information about the Wandering Jew to help him in writing *Helena*. 'Please forgive me for pestering you in this way. You are the only religious Jew of my acquaintance.' In the letter to Nancy Mitford printed immediately afterwards, the Jews are back in lower case. 'I have just read an essay by a jew [Arthur Koestler] which explains the Mitford sobriety and other very peculiar manifestations of the family.' If there was ever anything playfully outrageous about this behaviour the charm has long since fled.

But when your stomach has finished turning over it is worth considering that Waugh was equally nasty about any other social, racial, or ethnic group except what he considered to be pure-bred, strait-laced, upper-class Catholic English. In addition to yids, the book is stiff with frogs, dagoes, Huns, coons, chinks, niggers, and buggers. Of necessity Waugh numbered not a few homosexuals among his acquaintances, but it should also be remembered that he knew some Jews too, and that they, like the homosexuals, seem to have been willing enough to put up with his jibes. In other words they drew a line between the essential Evelyn Waugh and the Evelyn Waugh who was a hotbed of prejudice. It wouldn't hurt us to do the same. Waugh was far too conservative to be an anti-Semite of the Nazi stamp. When he carried on as if the Holocaust had never happened, he wasn't ignoring its significance, he was ignoring it altogether. He wasn't about to modify his opinions just because the Huns had wiped out a few yids.

At the end of the *Sword of Honour* trilogy anti-Semitism is specifically identified as a scourge. The whole closing scene of the third book can confidently be recommended for perusal by anyone who doubts Waugh's emotional range. Anti-Semitism is also one of the things that Gilbert Pinfold finds poisonous about his own mind. Waugh was perfectly capable of seeing that to go on indulging himself in anti-Semitism even after World War Two was tantamount to endorsing a ruinously irrational historical force. But Waugh, with a sort of cantankerous heroism, refused to let the modern era define him. He retained his creative right to interpret events in terms of past principles nobody else considered relevant. When the facts refused to sit, they were simply ignored. (It is remarkable, however, how many of them *did* sit. Rereading his work, one is continually struck by how much he got right. He guessed well in advance, for example, that the Jews would not necessarily be much better liked by the communists than they had been by the Nazis.)

Behaving as if recent history wasn't actually happening

was one of Waugh's abiding characteristics. It is the main reason why his books always seem so fresh. Since he never fell for any transient political belief, he never dates. In the 1930s, far from not having been a communist, he wasn't even a democrat. He believed in a stratified social order and a universal Church, the one nourishing the other. The stratified social order was already crumbling before he was born and the universal Church had disappeared during the reign of Henry VIII. His ideal was largely a fantasy. But it was a rich fantasy, traditionally based. Sustained by it, he could see modern life not just sharply but in perspective. When people say that Waugh was more than just a satirist, they really mean that his satire was coherent. It takes detachment to be so comprehensive.

Waugh seems to have been born with his world view already intact. Even for an English public school boy he sounds unusually mature. The social side of his personality was all set to go. What he had to do was make the facts fit it, since he was neither well off nor particularly well born. In view of these circumstances it is remarkable that he rarely sounds like a parvenu – just like someone waiting to come into his inheritance. If he had not been a writer he might never have made it, but there was no doubt about that side of his personality either. While still at school he was interested in the technicalities of writing and already capable of the first-class practical criticism which he lavished free of charge on his friends' manuscripts throughout his life. At Oxford he was awarded a gentleman's Third but this should not be taken to mean that he was a bad student. He was merely an original one, who absorbed a wide knowledge of history, literature, and the fine arts without appearing to try. As he told Nancy Mitford a long time later, it takes a knowledge of anatomy to draw a clothed figure. Waugh's mind was well stocked.

'I liked the rich people parts less than the poor,' he wrote to Henry Yorke ('Henry Green') about Yorke's early novel *Living*. This was probably a comment about accuracy, or the lack of it. Waugh's preference for the upper classes did not preclude his noting how the lower orders behaved and spoke.

Falling for the Plunket Greenes and the Lygon sisters, Waugh was soon able to satisfy his craving for smart company. It would be easy to paint him as an *arriviste*, but really the success he enjoyed at one level of society seems to have sharpened his response to all the other levels. He didn't shut himself off. One of the enduringly daunting things about Waugh's early satirical novels is the completeness with which they reproduce the social setting. Those rural types at the end of *Scoop*, for example, are not caricatures. Waugh took a lot in. His pop eyes missed nothing. He narrowed his mind in order to widen his gaze.

The misery he was plunged into when his first wife left him still comes through. In the pit of despair he finished writing *Vile Bodies*, which remains one of the funniest books in the world. The connection between work and life is not to be glibly analysed in the case of any artist and least of all in Waugh's. 'It has been infinitely difficult,' he told Henry Yorke, 'and is certainly the last time I shall try to make a book about sophisticated people.' This is a salutary reminder that he didn't necessarily *like* the Bright Young Things – he just found them interesting.

Asking whether Evelyn Waugh was a snob is like asking whether Genghis Khan was an authoritarian. The question turns on what kind of snob, and the first answer is – open and dedicated. During the war he was horrified to find himself sharing the mess with officers of plebeian background, 'like young corporals'. (In the *Sword of Honour* trilogy Guy Crouchback puts up stoically with such affronts. In real life Waugh was probably less patient.) He was under the impression that no Australian, however well educated, would be able to tell a real Tudor building from a false one. (Lack of background.) He doubted whether Proust ('Very poor stuff. I think he was mentally defective') ever really penetrated to the inner circles of French society: as a Jew, or jew, all Proust could have met was 'the looser aristocracy'.

In a 1952 letter to Nancy Mitford, Waugh is to be heard complaining about the unsmart company he had been forced to keep at dinner the previous evening. The guests had included Sir Laurence Olivier (as he then was) and Sir

Frederick Ashton (as he later became). Apparently Waugh had complained to his hostess that 'the upper classes had all left London'. Ashton was referred to as 'a most unarmigerous dancer called Ashton'. Waugh had started off being pretty unarmigerous himself, but by dint of genealogical research had managed to come up with a few quarterings – a feat which he was untypically bashful enough to dismiss as having been performed 'for the children'. Unlike Ashton's, Waugh's own knighthood was destined never to come through, probably because he turned down the CBE. In Britain, if you want high honours, it is wise to accept the low ones when they are offered.

Such a blunder helps to demonstrate that Waugh, if he calculated, did not calculate very well. In this he differed from the true climber, whose whole ability is never to put a foot wrong. Waugh put a foot wrong every day of the week. Quite often he put the foot in his mouth. He was always offending his high-class acquaintances by being more royalist than the King. The best of them forgave him because they thought he was an important artist and because they liked him better than he liked himself. Most of them belonged to that looser aristocracy which Waugh mistakenly believed Proust had been confined to. In Britain, those aristocrats with genuine artistic interests form a very particular stratum. Waugh idealised the philistine landed gentry but his friends, many of whom came from just such a background, did not make the same mistake. In a 1945 letter quoted here in a footnote, Lady Pansy Lamb told Waugh that *Brideshead Revisited* was a fantasy. 'You see English Society of the 20s as something baroque and magnificent on its last legs . . . I fled from it because it seemed prosperous, bourgeois and practical and I believe it still is . . .'

But for Waugh it was a necessary fantasy. He thought that with no social order there could be no moral order. People had to know their place before they could see their duty. In both life and art he needed a coherent social system. His version of *noblesse oblige* was positively chivalric. Because Sir Cosmo and Lady Duff-Gordon escaped from the *Titanic* in an underloaded boat, Waugh was still jeering at them a quarter of a century later. In *Sword of Honour* the fact that Ivor has behaved badly on Crete is one of the longest and strongest moral threads in the story. Mrs Stitch is brought back from the early novels for the specific purpose of taking pity on him in his shame.

Waugh himself had a disappointing time in the army. The head of the special force in which he hoped to distinguish himself in battle regarded him as unemployable and left him behind. In *Sword of Honour* Waugh presents himself, through Guy Crouchback, as a man misunderstood. Ford Madox Ford performed the same service for himself through Christopher Tietjens in *Parade's End*. In fact Waugh, like Ford, had probably been understood. He was simply too fantastic to have around. But the code of conduct which he so intractably expressed in real life lives on in his books as a permanently illuminating ethical vision. There is something to it, after all.

Snobbery was also Waugh's way of being humble about his art. His paragons were Mrs Stitch and Lady Circumference, both of whom could do the right thing through sheer breeding. Lady Circumference's unswerving philistinism he explicitly regarded as a virtue rather than a vice. He thought more of aristocrats than of artists. This viewpoint had its limitations but at least it saved him from the folly of imagining that behaviour could be much influenced by intellectual fashions and left him free to spot the inevitable gap between people's characters and their political beliefs.

His Catholicism was another thing that kept him humble: saints, he pointed out, attach no importance to art. Not that he ever took a utilitarian view of his faith. Waugh believed that Sir John Betjeman's Anglicanism was essentially self-serving and took frequent opportunities to tell him so, with the result that their friendship was almost ruined. For Waugh, Catholicism's uncompromising theology was an enticement. Just as he was more royalist than the king, he was more Catholic than the pope. He was a convert who berated born Catholics for their moral lapses. When Clarissa Churchill married Sir Anthony Eden, Waugh abused her for her apostasy – Eden was a divorced man. The Church's eternal strictness was Waugh's comfort. On the Church's behalf he welcomed new converts among his friends with the promise of a bed turned down and a place at the eternal table. Even more than the English social hierarchy, which in his heart of hearts he knew was a shifting structure, the Church was his bulwark against the modern world. Hence his unfeigned despair at the introduction of a vernacular liturgy. 'The Vatican Council', he wrote to Lady Mosley in 1966, a month before his death, 'has knocked the guts out of me.'

In real life Waugh's fight to hold back the present had the same chance as Canute's to hold back the sea. In his books his lone last stand seems more inspired than absurd. The progressive voices are mainly forgotten. Waugh, the arch reactionary, still sounds contemporary. As an artist he was not moulded by his times and hence neither failed to see them clearly nor vanished with them when they were over. As an ordinary man he was no doubt impossibly rude but there were a lot of intelligent people who forgave him for it, as this book proves.

Mark Amory has edited these letters with a fine touch, occasionally calling in an independent witness when Waugh's delightful capacity for wild exaggeration threatens to distort the historical record. It is hard on the late S. J. Simon that the books he wrote in collaboration with Caryl Brahms, which Waugh enjoyed, should be ascribed only to Caryl Brahms, but apart from that I can't see many important slips, although John Kenneth Galbraith, giving this book an appropriately laudatory review in the *Washington Post*, has pointed out that Father Feeny was an unfrocked priest, not 'the Chaplain at Harvard'. What counts is Mr Amory's sensitivity to the nuances of the English class system. For finding his way around in that self-renewing maze he has the same kind of antennae as Waugh had, with the difference that they are attached to a cooler head. The result is an unobtrusively knowledgeable job of editing.

High-handedly rebuking his wife for writing dull letters, Waugh told her that a good correspondence should be like a conversation. He most easily met his own standard when writing to Nancy Mitford but really there was nobody he short-changed. Even the shortest note to the most obscure correspondent is vibrant with both his irascible temperament and his penetrating stare. Above all he was funny – the first thing to say about him. Writing to his wife in May 1942, he described what happened when a company of commandos set out to blow up a tree stump on the estate of Lord Glasgow. The account can be found on page 161 of this book. Anyone who has never read Evelyn Waugh could begin with that page and become immediately enthralled.

But by this time there is no argument about his stature. While academic studies have gone on being preoccupied with the relative and absolute merits of Joyce and Lawrence, Waugh's characters have inexorably established themselves among the enduring fictions to which his countrymen traditionally refer as if they were living beings. In this respect Waugh is in a direct line with Shakespeare and Dickens. Since he was public property from the beginning, a critical consensus, when it arrives, can only endorse popular opinion. The consensus has been delayed because many critics were rightly proud of the Welfare State and regarded Waugh's hatred of it as mean-minded. He was paid out for his rancour by his own unhappiness. For the happiness he can still give us it is difficult to know how to reward him, beyond saying that he has helped make tolerable the modern age he so abominated.

(*New York Review of Books*, 1980)

Fannikins' Cunnikin

***Fanny: Being the True History of the Adventures of Fanny Hackabout-Jones*, by Erica Jong, (NAL Books, New York, and Granada, London)**

NOT LONG ago there was a popular novelist called Jeffery Farnol, who is now entirely forgotten – which, when you think about it, is as long ago as you can get. Farnol wrote period novels in a narrative style full of e'ens, dosts, 'tises, and 'twases. Men wearing slashed doublets said things like 'Gadzooks!' in order to indicate that the action was taking place in days of yore. Farnol was manifestly shaky on the subject of when yore actually was, but he had a certain naïve energy and his books were too short to bore you. His masterpiece *The Jade of Destiny*, starring a lethal swordsman called Dinwiddie, can still be consumed in a single evening by anyone who has nothing better to do.

Erica Jong knows a lot more than Farnol ever did about our literary heritage and its social background. Her new book, which purports to be the true story, told in the first person, of the girl John Cleland made famous as Fanny Hill, draws on an extensive knowledge of eighteenth-century England. This is definitely meant to be a high-class caper. Nevertheless Jeffery Farnol would recognise a fellow practitioner. There is something Gadzooks about the whole enterprise. On top of that it is intolerably long. Where Farnol's Dinwiddie, after skewering the heavies, would have made his bow and split, Jong's Fanny hangs around for hours.

Jong's Fanny, it turns out, would have been a writer if circumstances had not dictated otherwise. Circumstances are to be congratulated. Left to herself, Jong's Fanny would have covered more paper than Ruskin. There is something self-generating about her style.

> I wrote Tragedies in Verse and Noble Epicks, Romances in the French Style and Maxims modell'd upon La Rochefoucauld's. I wrote Satyres and Sonnets, Odes and Pastorals, Eclogues and Epistles. But nothing satisfied my most exalted Standards (which had been bred upon the Classicks), and at length I committed all my Efforts to the Fire. I wrote and burnt and wrote and burnt! I would pen a Pastoral thro'out three sleepless Nights only to commit it to the Flames! And yet were my Words not wasted, for ev'ry budding Poet, I discover'd, must spend a thousand Words for evr'y one he saves, and Words are hardly wasted if, thro' one's Profligacy with 'em, one learns true Wit and true Expression of it.

Five hundred pages of that add up to a lot of apostrophes, i'faith. But the fault lies not with the 'tises and 'twases. A historical novel can survive any amount of inept decoration if it has some architecture underneath. Take, for example, Merezhkovsky's *The Romance of Leonardo da Vinci*, in the learned but stylistically frolicsome translation by Bernard Guilbert Guerney.

> 'Nay, nay, God forfend, – whatever art thou saying, Lucrezia! Come out to meet her? Thou knowest not what a woman this is! Oh, Lord 'tis a fearful thing to think of the possible outcome of all this! Why, she is pregnant! . . . But do thou hide me – hide me! . . . '
>
> 'Really, I know not where . . . '
>
> ''Tis all one, wherever thou wilt, – but with all speed!'

As transmitted to us by the industrious Guerney, Merezhkovsky's Leonardo is every bit as noisy as Jong's Fanny. But *The Romance of Leonardo da Vinci* is a good novel in the ordinary sense and as a historical novel ranks among the greatest ever written. The characters and the action help you to penetrate history – they light up the past. Jong's Fanny makes the past darker. By the end of the book you know less about the eighteenth century than you did when you started.

Jong deserves some credit for trying to bring back yesterday, but what she is really doing, inadvertently, is helping to make you feel even worse about today. She uses pornography to preach a feminist message. This is a peculiarly modern confusion of motives. At least Cleland had the grace to leave out the philosophising, although it should be remembered that those few general remarks which he put in were more pertinent in every way than anything which his successor has to offer. Here is Cleland's Fanny at a critical moment.

> And now! now I felt it to the heart of me! I felt the prodigious keen edge with which love, presiding over this act, points the pleasure: love! that may be styled the Attic salt of enjoyment; and indeed, without it, the joy, great as it is, is still a vulgar one, whether in a king or a beggar; for it is, undoubtedly, love alone that refines, ennobles and exalts it.

Admittedly Cleland's prose has been somewhat neatened up for modern publication, but you can still see that even in its original state it must have been a less strained instrument than that wielded by Jong's Fanny. Cleland has other points of superiority too. For one thing, his pornographic scenes are actually quite effective. Indeed they are too effective, since pornography exceeds requirements if it makes you want to know the girl. Cleland's *Fanny Hill* might not strike women as a book written from the woman's viewpoint, but it can easily strike men that way. The book's concern is with women's pleasure, not men's. Cleland's Fanny does a powerfully affecting job of evoking what a woman's pleasure is like, or at any rate what a man who likes women would like to think a woman's pleasure is like. She leaves a man sorry for not having met her.

For Jong's Fanny, whose full name is Fanny Hackabout-Jones ('Fannikins to lovers besotted with her charms'), the same cannot be said. She is a bore from page one. Even in moments of alleged transport she has one eye on her literary prospects. You just know that she will one day write *Fear of Flying*. One of her early encounters is with Alexander Pope.

Erica – Fanny, sorry – tries to interest Pope in her verses, but he is interested only in her breasts. Pope is but the first of several famous men who make themselves ridiculous by pursuing Jong's Fanny. (Swift involves her in a threesome with a horse.) All they see, you see, is Fannikins' cunnikin. Passion blinds them to her attainments as a philosopher.

> And yet, clearly, 'twas not the Best of all Possible Worlds for Women – unless, as Mr. Pope had argu'd, there was a hidden Justice behind this Veil of seeming Injustice. . . . Fie on't! 'Twas not possible that God should approve such goings-on! A Pox on the Third Earl of Shaftesbury and his damnable Optimism!

Running away from home, Jong's Fanny falls in with a coven of witches. The witches, you will not be surprised to learn, are prototype feminists. They are given names like Isobel and Joan in order to allay your suspicions that they are really called Germaine and Kate.

> 'Fanny, my Dear,' says Isobel, 'let me tell you my Opinion concerning Witchcraft and then Joan can tell you hers. 'Tis my Belief that in Ancient Times, in the Pagan Albion of Old, Women were not as they are now, subservient to Men in evr'y Respect. . . .'
>
> 'E'en the very word "Witch," ' Joan interrupted, 'derives from our Ancestors' Word "Wicca," meaning only "Wise Woman." '
>
> Isobel looked cross. 'Are you quite finish'd, Joan?' says she. 'Will you hold your Tongue now and let me speak?'

An oppressive male chauvinist society makes sure that these pioneer women's liberationists are appropriately raped and tortured, but meanwhile Jong's Fanny has become installed in a London brothel, where she shows an unusual talent for the trade. Colly Cibber's son ties her to the bed. ('Now I am truly trapp'd in my own Snares, my Arms and Legs spread wide upon the Bed so I can make no Resistance, my Ankles and Wrists chafing 'gainst the Silver Cords.') Then he enters her. (' . . . Theo's Privy Member makes its

Presence felt near my not quite unsullied Altar of Love.') Then he does something I can't quite figure out. ('He sinks upon me with all his Weight and wraps his bandy Legs 'round my own . . . ') How bandy can a man be?

Jong seems to take it for granted that a woman's lust can be aroused against her will, if only her assailant presses the right buttons – a very male chauvinist assumption, one would have thought. Cleland's Fanny was more discriminating. But then, Cleland's Fanny knew her own feelings. Jong makes Cleland one of her Fanny's literary lovers. Jong's Cleland is interested in role swapping and has a propensity for climbing into drag. Thus Jong lays the ghost of Cleland's commendable success in fleshing out a feminine character. She says that *he* had a feminine character. Perhaps so, but what he mainly had was imagination.

Jong's Fanny is meant to be an edifying joke, but the joke is not funny and the edification is not instructive, although it is frequently revealing. Setting out to show up Cleland, Jong unintentionally declares herself his inferior. As to the pornography, Cleland knew when to stop: his Fanny always concedes, while describing the moment of ecstasy, that beyond a certain point words fail her. Words fail Jong's Fanny at all times, but she never stops pouring them out. Finally the sheer disproportion of the enterprise is the hardest thing to forgive.

I quite liked *Fear of Flying*: there was the promise of humour in it, if not the actuality. But in this book, which sets out to be light, comic, and picaresque, everything is undone by an utter inability to compress, allude or elide. Is Peter de Vries to be the last author in America of short serious books that make you laugh? Joseph Heller's *Good as Gold* is at least twice as long as it should be. By the time you get down to Erica there seems to be no awareness at all of the mark to aim at. If Max Beerbohm couldn't sustain *Zuleika Dobson*, how did Erica expect to keep Fanny going for triple the distance on a tenth the talent? I'faith, 'tis a Puzzle beyond my Comprehension.

(*New York Review of Books*, 1980)

In Their Flying Machines

Fighter by Len Deighton
(Cape, London, and Knopf, New York)

The Last Chance by Johannes Steinhoff
(Hutchinson, London)

AFTER *Bomber*, which was mainly about bombers, comes *Fighter*, which is mainly about fighters. Deighton's monomial titles ought not to mislead the reader into thinking that the man who dreams them up is simple-minded. *Bomber* was, and is, an excellent book. It strikes a difficult balance between moral outrage at what men did and enthralled interest in the machines with which they did it. Deighton's bump for advanced technology was already apparent from his spy novels, while even the otherwise unspeakable *Close-Up* was interesting on the nuts and bolts of a film star's career. But *Bomber* was the clearest proof that Deighton possessed an unmatched gift for analysing complex systems. How the RAF went about the sad business of burning Germany by night, and how the Germans tried to stop them doing it, formed an elaborate, interlocking, technology-intensive closed system which nobody before Deighton had ever succeeded in bringing back to life. The sinister poetic force of the original events had not been captured by the official historians, while the full facts were either abridged or distorted in the pop memoirs. Deighton got everything in. I can remember reading the book in a single night, marvelling at the intensity of detail. He even knew what colour flashes the bombs made when they went off. (Like most members of the generation growing up after the war, I had always assumed – because of news reels – that the bombs had exploded in black and white.)

The weakness of *Bomber* lay in its characters. Deighton

invented a representative battle and staffed it with what he fancied were representative types. Actually they weren't as clumsily drawn as you might think. Deighton is not quite as bad at character as the critics say, just as John le Carré is not quite as good. A book like *Yesterday's Spy*, one of Deighton's recent fictions, is not only stronger on action than le Carré's later work, but features more believable people. The cast-list of *Close-Up* is indeed hopelessly makeshift, but the characters flying around in *Bomber*, though divided up and labelled in what looks like a rough-and-ready way, are deployed with some cunning to bring out the relevant tensions. You could be excused, however, for not connecting them to the real world. In *Fighter* there is no way out of it. The Battle of Britain really happened. Not just the machines, but the people too, really existed. And Deighton has managed to give the whole event a clarity which it lacked even at – especially at – the time.

According to Deighton (and he is very likely right) the Battle of Britain was never won, but there was sufficient reason for triumph in the fact that it was not lost. Dowding's whole effort was to ensure that Fighter Command should survive as a force. He could not realistically hope to destroy the Luftwaffe, but on the other hand he could hope to go on denying it command of the air, thereby rendering invasion impossible. Dowding was a percentage player. He was under relentless pressure – especially from one of his own immediate subordinates, Leigh-Mallory – to gamble his strength in mass actions. He resisted the pressure, guarded his resources, and fought a protracted battle with great patience as well as consummate skill and daring.

Deighton takes the full measure of Dowding's superior mind. As conceived of by Dowding, full-scale warfare in the sky was not just chess, but that version of chess proposed by Brecht, in which the pieces change value according to how long they remain on a given square. Dowding balanced all, brought all to mind. The Germans would probably have beaten him if they had concentrated on attacking his radar stations and airfields. But in failing to do that, they were left in the position of matching their own limited supply of men and machines against his. Dowding understood his limitations better than they understood theirs. He kept his nerve while the stakes mounted. Their nerve cracked first.

Fighter would be valuable if it did nothing more than help correct the popular impression that Leigh-Mallory's 'big wing' theory was a possible alternative to Dowding's penny-packet tactics. The big wing theory was widely publicised after the war in Paul Brickhill's best-selling biography of Douglas Bader, *Reach for the Sky*. Even retrospectively it is an appealing notion, and at the time must have seemed like simple common sense to the pilots of Leigh-Mallory's 12 Group, kept in reserve by Dowding's order until the battle was almost over. Bitterly frustrated, they could be forgiven for thinking that if they swooped *en masse* and shot down a whole raid the Germans would throw in the sponge. But Deighton has the facts and figures to prove that Dowding couldn't take the risk. If his number of trained pilots fell below a certain point, there could be no making up the loss. So he set his face like flint against the rage of his own young heroes. In the long run (or, rather, the disgracefully short run) that was probably one of the things which cost him his job.

Eventually the British staved off defeat because they were better led and organised. The German fighter and bomber formations were well commanded at operational level but the generalship in the higher echelons was suspect and at the very top there was no firm control apart from Goering's caprice. Deighton persuasively analyses the contending systems. He is good on the personalities but is well aware that the impersonal mattered at least as much. Above all, the machines mattered, and on those he is tremendous.

Each type of aircraft is traced through its full history. You are told what they were like to fly. There are diagrams to show how they compared in performance. The Messerschmitt Bf 109 could turn inside the Hurricane, which could turn inside the Spitfire. You will find out why dogfights always moved downwards. There is almost no end to what you will find out: even small boys who thought they were clued-up will be open-mouthed.

Deighton can do all this because he looks upon aircraft as works of art as well as articles to serve a purpose. After the Futurist movement's embarrassing enthusiasm it became unfashionable to take an aesthetic interest in machines, but Deighton is independent enough to respond to them with his whole soul. Among the results is that he is able to set new standards for this type of book. A pity that the printers could not do the same: the typeface is miserable and literals are frequent.

Sub-titled 'The Pilots' Plot Against Goering', Johannes Steinhoff's interesting book is the pop war memoir in its more traditional form, complete with vile editing (B-29s are shown bombing Germany). Apart from the few unquestioningly gung-ho efforts like Rudel's *Stuka Pilot* (in which the fighting was described in terms of how many Russian tanks Rudel could destroy before Hitler grounded him under the weight of increasingly elaborate awards for valour) the German fliers, from Galland on down, have usually been bent on telling us how much they could have achieved if they had not been saddled with a Nazi government. They were almost certainly correct. It might have been mere chance that the Allies could come up with leaders like Dowding but with the Germans there was no chance at all. Hitler was too erratic ever to grasp a strategic pattern and Goering simply didn't understand modern aircraft: his mind, like his heart, was still with the Richthofen Circus. The Me 262 jet fighter might not have been able to stop the RAF at night but it could certainly have devastated the US 8th Air Force by day. As we know from the official histories, even with conventional fighters the Luftwaffe made the Schweinfurt raids so expensive that the Americans thought of calling a halt. The jets could have ruled the sky if they had been ready in time. But Hitler's intuitive genius put a stop to that. When they *were* ready, Goering was too far gone to know how to use them. It is doubtful if the pilots ever really hatched much of a 'plot against Goering' but they certainly had every reason to despise him.

As it was, Steinhoff flew Me 262s in some of the last sorties of the war. Too late to affect the picture (which had already been transformed by the P-51 Mustang long-range escort fighter) the jets flew in a world of their own – the future. Steinhoff tells us what they were like to fly. He also tells us what they were like to crash. His face was burned off. There is a portrait of him as he was in 1942, a handsome young ace with the Knight's Cross at his neck. There is also a photo of him taken in 1945, after the bandages were removed. The comparison should help destroy any lingering illusions about the romance of aerial combat.

(*New Statesman*, 1977)

Part Three

POETRY, CRITICISM AND AESTHETICS

The Examined Life of Kingsley Amis

***Collected Poems 1944–79* by Kingsley Amis (Hutchinson, London)**

KINGSLEY AMIS has had to go on and on proving that he is as interesting a poet as he is a novelist. It was inevitable. He is a very interesting novelist. That he should be equally good at the other thing seems unjust. But this volume, which collects all of his verse that he wishes to preserve, should finally be proof positive. Accomplished, literate and entertaining, it is a richly various expression of a moral personality coming to terms with the world.

Since the arrangement of poems is chronological, the personality can be heard discovering its own voice in the opening pages. To become himself, Amis had first of all to absorb the bewitching influence of Auden, whose tones pervade his early poems just as thoroughly as the tones of Yeats pervade the early poems of Philip Larkin. Here are some sample lines, taken from various poems.

> Still flows your northern river like a pulse . . .
> Meanwhile the radiation sprang from the
> tentative rod . . .
> So, stranger, when you come here to unpack . . .

But almost everybody parroted Auden to the extent of turning out lines that sounded like his. To turn out whole stanzas that sounded like his, however, needed a high degree of technical ability, which Amis had:

> But there are people here, unable to understand,
> Randy for cigarettes, moving hands too
> Jerky to move in love; their women matrons, their
> daughters
> Fanatically guarded or whores with lovely teeth;

The sons come from somewhere else, fair of skin;
The children have thick white socks and an English
  laugh,
Bearers of flowers, quiet and pointlessly clean,
Showing their parents up, not easily amused.

Amis has done us a double service by not suppressing these early poems. In the first place, they give us an object lesson in what a gifted young poet finds fascinating about an older master: clearly it was the way Auden made the *prosaic* sound poetic that Amis wanted to steal the secret of. In the second place, they are substantial poems in their own right. He wasn't just scrambling a few borrowed effects together in order to conjure up an air of meaning. He actually had clear themes, even when the themes were callow.

When he discovered what he really wanted to say, he quickly began sounding like himself. This process is usually known as 'finding your own voice'. There is nothing automatic about it. Most poets never find their own voice. Instead they employ quirks to give their anonymity identity. To speak naturally and still be immediately recognisable is a rare thing. In 'Dirty Story', one of the first of his fully individual poems, it can only be Amis talking.

To-morrow, in what shrines gaily excreting,
Will you, our champion even if defeated,
Bring down a solemn edifice with one swing?

Disapproved of and envied, this priapic hero ('Your you-know-what in fabulous readiness') is destined to be one of the poet's perennial characters. Preoccupations begin early. So, in Amis's case, did the ability to discipline a principal strength. It would have been easy for him to indulge his capacity for comic invention. But he used it sparingly from the start. Comedy was always subordinated to argument. Amis's tone has never been less than densely serious, so it was no surprise that Dr Leavis found him frivolous.

Half-shut, our eye dawdles down the page
Seeing the word love, the word death, the word life,
Rhyme-words of poets in a silver age:
Silver of the bauble, not of the knife.

Knives, not baubles, are what poems should be like: a very rigorous aesthetic, which Amis had begun holding to long before he got round to formulating it. Poets find their guiding principles by assessing the implication of what they have done already. Similarly, they increase their range of vision by gazing within. By comically dramatising his own introspection, Amis found a way of taking the conceit out of self-regard. In 'A Dream of Fair Women', the 'squadron of draped nudes' who mob him in his sexual fantasy are banal enough to be flying around in ours too.

> Speech fails them, amorous, but each one's look,
> Endorsed in other ways, begs me to sign
> Her body's autograph-book;
> 'Me first, Kingsley; I'm cleverest' each declares . . .

The poet goes on to admit the sad triteness of that imaginary harem; to contend that if it were real then only 'the best' would settle for anything else; and to regret the fact that everyone else would come along with him to seek 'the halls of theoretical delight'. It is notable that he does not include himself among 'the best', even though the mere ability to analyse the problem would give him some justification to place himself above it. But Amis's insistence on his own propensity for all moral failings is based on deep conviction, quite apart from its being a useful creative device. In Amis's view, we all have similar impulses. What we do about them is a matter of choice. The callous and the stupid have *chosen* to be that way.

Not to be swept up by feelings but to control them – both ethically and aesthetically it is an anti-romantic standpoint. In 'Against Romanticism' he made the connection explicit. Admitting that it does not seem quite enough to be a 'traveller who walks a temperate zone', nevertheless he distrusts the irrepressible hunger for 'a grand meaning' that

> . . . sets the brain raging with prophecy,
> Raging to discard real time and place . . .

It is true that there must be visions, but they should be visions that do not leave the real world out. They should not be

Raging to build a better time and place
Than the ones which give prophecy its field
To work, the calm material for its rage,
And the context which makes it prophecy.

The poet is ready to call such a vision 'pallid', but in fact it is the secret of his peculiar vividness. The aim is not to be disenchanted, but never to be enchanted in the first place: to see things as they are and must be. If we could think the illusion through, we wouldn't have to have it, and would thus avoid the suffering of becoming disillusioned afterwards. The point is argued out in 'The Value of Suffering', a cautionary tale about a princeling who had everything and had to lose it all before he attained wisdom. The last stanza sums up.

What a shame that a regal house must founder,
Its menials die, its favourites undergo
Unheard-of-rape, to emphasise a contrast,
To point one thing out to one person;
Especially since the person could have seen
What it was all about by not laughing
After his father's joke – watching instead,
By changing places with his groom,
By sixty seconds' thought.

Amis is not now, nor has he ever been, a true right-winger. He is a liberal appalled by the left. Nor is he a Philistine: he is an artist sickened by the arty, as is evinced in 'After Goliath'.

The first shot out of that sling
Was enough to finish the thing:
The champion laid out cold
Before half the programmes were sold.

The top Philistine is easily felled. But then whom does David find cheering at his back?

Academics, actors who lecture,
Apostles of architecture,
Ancient-gods-of-the-abdomen men,
Angst-pushers, adherents of Zen . . .

David is undecided whether to keep Goliath's sword as a trophy or use it on his own fans. He shrugs and leaves, 'resigned to a new battle, fought in the mind', the same battle in which Amis himself takes such an active part – and, one suspects, such delight.

Those of us who are always re-reading Amis's novels have grown used to finding his later themes presaged in early works. The same applies to his poetry, where his later setpiece struggles with Eros and Thanatos are merely the culmination of a string of skirmishes that go back to the very beginning.

As I was waiting for the bus
A girl came up the street,
Detectable as double-plus
At seven hundred feet.

Only the fabled travelling salesman of 'A Song of Experience' ('And so he knew, where we can only fumble') can unthinkingly do the right thing about sex. Amis's own conclusion – that at the moment of being overwhelmed by our strongest instinct we are obliged to turn our brains on instead of off – is once again an anti-romantic one. The best we can hope for is to go through life with our eyes open. Those who take short cuts have nothing to tell us: a stricture from which Jesus Christ is not excluded.

Should you revisit us,
Stay a little longer,
And get to know the place . . .

Nor does God himself escape reproof, as in 'The Huge Artifice', where some intractable conditions of existence are quite legitimately complained of.

That the habit of indifference is less
Destructive than the embrace of love, that crimes
Are paid for never or a thousand times,
That the gentle come to grief . . .

Dai Evans is the final development of the travelling salesman. The Evans Country is the land of heart's desire – a version of Wales less stridently fabulous than Llaregubb, yet still mythical, because in it life acts itself out without an inward look. Evans firmly quells all intimations of mortality. Staging a bonfire of his second-rate pornography, he still keeps the first-rate stuff upstairs. Amis was moved to grieved reflection by his father's death:

> I'm sorry you had to die
> To make me sorry
> You're not here now.

Evans's reaction to a similar event is less complicated.

> 'Hallo, pet. Alone? Good. It's me.
> Ah now, who did you think it was?
> Well, come down the Bush and find out.
> You'll know me easy, because
> I'm wearing a black tie, love.'

Amis does not withhold his admiration from this most indefatigable of all stick-men. Yet it is made clear that the void which awaits Evans already has its counterpart in his head: by not noticing he has solved nothing. Facing reality has its own value. That is the sole, but strong, affirmation underlying Amis's later poems. Some of these are merrily contemptuous of what modern life has become:

> So bloody good luck to you, mate,
> That you weren't born too late
> For at least a chance of happiness,
> Before unchangeable crappiness
> Spreads all over the land.

Others tragically accept the brute facts about what life has always been. 'A Reunion', for example, though some of it sounds like Amis and Conquest organising a Kingers 'n' Conkers contribution to the next Black Paper ('A nitwit not fit to shift shit', etc.), is really an extended and painful encounter with the truth about how we grow apart from and forget each other. Two things lie between such a poem and despair. The first is the perfection of the poet's craft, which in Amis as in any other true artist is essentially a moral property. The second is the unspoken corollary of Socrates' insistence that the unexamined life is not worth living. The examined life *is* worth living. Only the fact that he is so marvellously readable can now stop Kingsley Amis from being placed in the front rank of contemporary poets. He has attained his grand meaning after all.

(*New Statesman*, 1979)

On Larkin's Wit

***Larkin at Sixty* edited by Anthony Thwaite (Faber, London)**

THERE is no phrase in Philip Larkin's poetry which has not been turned, but then any poet tries to avoid flat writing, even at the cost of producing overwrought banality. Larkin's dedication to compressed resonance is best studied, in the first instance, through his prose. The prefaces to the re-issues of *Jill* and *The North Ship* are full of sentences that make you smile at their neat richness even when they are not meant to be jokes, and that when they are meant to be jokes – as in the evocation of the young Kingsley Amis at Oxford in the preface to *Jill* – make you wish that the article went on as long as the book. But there is a whole book which does just that: *All What Jazz*, the collection of Larkin's *Daily Telegraph* jazz record review columns which was published in 1970. Having brought the book out, Faber seemed nervous about what to do with it next. I bought two copies marked down to 75p each in a Cardiff newsagent's and wish now that I had bought ten. I thought at the time that *All What Jazz* was the best available expression by the author himself of what he believed art to be. I still think so, and would contend in addition that no wittier book of criticism has ever been written.

To be witty does not necessarily mean to crack wise. In fact it usually means the opposite: wits rarely tell jokes. Larkin's prose flatters the reader by giving him as much as he can take in one time. The delight caused has to do with collusion. Writer and reader are in cahoots. Larkin has the knack of donning cap and bells while still keeping his dignity. For years he feigned desperation before the task of conveying the real desperation induced in him by the saxophone playing of John Coltrane. The metaphors can be pursued through the book – they constitute by themselves a kind of extended solo, of which the summary sentence in the book's introductory essay should be regarded as the coda. 'With John Coltrane metallic and passionless nullity gave way to exercises in gigantic absurdity, great boring excursions on not-especially-attractive themes during which all possible changes were rung, extended investigations of oriental tedium, long-winded and portentous demonstrations of religiosity.' This final grandiose flourish was uttered in 1968.

But the opening note was blown in 1961, when Larkin, while yet prepared (cravenly, by his own later insistence) to praise Coltrane as a hard-thinking experimenter, referred to 'the vinegary drizzle of his tone'. In 1962 he was still in two minds, but you could already guess which mind was winning. 'Coltrane's records are, paradoxically, nearly always both interesting and boring, and I certainly find myself listening to them in preference to many a less adventurous set.' Notable at this stage is that he did not risk a metaphor, in which the truth would have more saliently protruded. In May 1963 there is only one mind left talking. To the eighth track of a Thelonius Monk album, 'John Coltrane contributes a solo of characteristic dreariness.'

By December of that same year Larkin's line on this topic has not only lost all its qualifications but acquired metaphorical force. Coltrane is referred to as 'the master of the thinly disagreeable' who 'sounds as if he is playing for an audience of cobras'. This squares up well with the critic's known disgust that the joyous voicing of the old jazz should have so completely given way to 'the cobra-coaxing cacophonies of Calcutta'. In 1965 Larkin was gratified to discover that his opinion of Coltrane's achievement was shared by the great blues-shouter Jimmy Rushing. 'I don't think he can play his instrument' said Rushing. 'This', Larkin observed, 'accords very well with my own opinion that Coltrane sounds like nothing so much as a club bore who has been metamorphosed by a fellow-member of magical powers into a pair of bagpipes.' (Note Larkin's comic timing, incidentally: a less witty writer would have put 'metamorphosed into a pair of bagpipes by a fellow-member of magical powers', and so halved the effect.) Later in the same piece he expanded the attack into one of those generally pertinent critical disquisitions in which *All What Jazz* is so wealthy. 'His solos seem to me to bear the same relation to proper jazz solos as those drawings of running dogs, showing their legs in all positions so that they appear to have about fifty of them, have to real drawings. Once, they are amusing and even instructive. But the whole point of drawing is to choose the right line, not drawing fifty alternatives. Again, Coltrane's choice and treatment of themes is hypnotic, repetitive, monotonous: he will rock backwards and forwards between two chords for five minutes, or pull a tune to pieces like someone subtracting petals from a flower.' Later in the piece there is an atavistic gesture towards giving the Devil his due, but by the vividness of his chosen figures of speech the critic has already shown what he really thinks.

'I can thoroughly endorse', wrote Larkin in July 1966, 'the sleeve of John Coltrane's "Ascension" (HMV), which says "This record cannot be loved or understood in one sitting."' In November of the same year he greeted Coltrane's religious suite 'Meditations' as 'the most astounding piece of ugliness I have ever heard'. After Coltrane's death in 1977 Larkin summed up the departed hero's career. '. . . I do not remember ever suggesting that his music was anything but a pain between the ears . . . Was I wrong?' In fact, as we have seen, Larkin had once allowed himself to suggest that the noises Coltrane made might at least be interesting, but by now tentativeness had long given way to a kind of fury, as of someone defending a principle against his own past weakness. 'That reedy, catarrhal tone . . . that insolent egotism, leading to 45-minute versions of "My Favourite Things" until, at any rate in Britain, the audience walked out, no doubt wondering why they had ever walked in . . . pretension as a way of life . . . wilful and hideous distortion of tone that offered squeals, squeaks, Bronx cheers and throttled slate-pencil noises for serious consideration . . . dervish-like heights of hysteria.' It should be remembered, if this sounds like a grave being danced on, that Larkin's was virtually the sole dissenting critical voice. Coltrane died in triumph and Larkin had every right to think at the time that to express any doubts about the stature of the deceased genius was to whistle against the wind.

The whole of *All What Jazz* is a losing battle. Larkin is arguing in support of entertainment at a time when entertainment was steadily yielding ground to portentous significance. His raillery against the saxophonists is merely the most strident expression of a general argument which he goes on elaborating as its truth becomes more clear to himself. In a quieter way he became progressively disillusioned with Miles Davis. In January 1962 it was allowed that in an informal atmosphere Davis could produce music 'very far from the egg-walking hushedness' he was given to in the studio. In October of the same year Larkin gave him points for bonhomie. 'According to the sleeve, Davis actually smiled twice at the audience during the evening and there is indeed a warmth about the entire proceedings that makes this a most enjoyable LP.' But by the time of 'Seven Steps to Heaven' a year later, Davis has either lost what little attraction he had or else Larkin has acquired the courage of his convictions. ' . . . his lifeless muted tone, at once hollow and unresonant, creeps along only just in tempo, the ends of the notes hanging down like Dali watches . . .' In 1964, Larkin begged to dissent from the enthusiastic applause recorded on the live album 'Miles Davis in Europe'. ' . . . the fact that he can spend seven or eight minutes playing "Autumn Leaves" without my recognising or liking the tune confirms my view of him as a master of rebarbative boredom.' A year later he was reaching for the metaphors. 'I freely confess that there have been times recently, when almost anything – the shape of a patch on the ceiling, a recipe for rhubarb jam read upside down in the paper – has seemed to me more interesting than the passionless creep of a Miles Davis trumpet solo'. But in this case the opening blast was followed by a climb-down. 'Davis is his usual bleak self, his notes wilting at the edges as if with frost, spiky at up-tempos, and while he is still not my ideal of comfortable listening his talent is clearly undiminished.' This has the cracked chime of a compromise. The notes, though wilting as if with frost instead of like Dali watches, are nevertheless still wilting, and it is clear from the whole drift of Larkin's criticism that he places no value on uncomfortable listening as such. A 1966 review sounds more straightforward. ' . . . for me it was an experience in pure duration. Some of it must have been quite hard to do.'

But in Larkin's prose the invective which implies values is always matched by the encomium which states them plainly. He jokes less when praising than when attacking but the attention he pays to evocation is even more concentrated. The poem 'For Sidney Bechet' ('On me your voice falls as they say love should,/Like an enormous yes') can be matched for unforced reverence in the critical prose: ' . . . the marvellous "Blue Horizon", six choruses of slow blues in which Bechet climbs without interruption or hurry from lower to upper register, his clarinet tone at first thick and throbbing, then soaring like Melba in an extraordinary blend of lyricism and power that constituted the unique Bechet voice, commanding attention the instant it sounded.' He is similarly eloquent about the 'fire and shimmer' of Bix Beiderbecke and of the similes he attaches to Pee Wee Russell there is no end – Russell's clarinet seems to function in Larkin's imagination as a kind of magic flute.

The emphasis, in Larkin's admiration for all these artists, is on the simplicity at the heart of their creative endeavour. What they do would not have its infinite implications if it did not spring from elementary emotion. It can be argued that Larkin is needlessly dismissive of Duke Ellington and Charlie Parker. There is plenty of evidence to warrant including him in the school of thought known among modern jazz buffs as 'mouldy fig'. But there is nothing retrograde about the aesthetic underlying his irascibility. The same aesthetic underlies his literary criticism and everything else he writes. Especially it underlies his poetry. Indeed it is not even an aesthetic: it is a world view, of the kind which invariably forms the basis of any great artistic personality. Modernism, according to Larkin, 'helps us neither to enjoy nor endure'. He defines modernism as intellectualised art. Against intellectualism he proposes, not anti-intellectualism – which would be just another coldly willed programme – but trust in the validity of emotion. What the true artist says from instinct, the true critic will hear by the same instinct. There may be more than instinct involved, but nothing real will be involved without it.

> The danger, therefore, of assuming that everything played today in jazz has a seed of solid worth stems from the fact that so much of it is tentative, experimental, private . . . And for this reason one has to fall back on the old dictum that a critic is only as good as his ear. His ear will tell him instantly whether a piece of music is vital, musical, exciting, or cerebral, mock-academic, dead, long before he can read Don DeMichael on the subject, or learn that it is written in inverted nineteenths, or in the Stygian mode, or recorded at the NAACP Festival at Little Rock. He must hold on to the principle that the only reason for praising a work is that it pleases, and the way to develop his critical sense is to be more acutely aware of whether he is being pleased or not.

What Larkin might have said on his own behalf is that critical prose can be subjected to the same test. His own criticism appeals so directly to the ear that he puts himself in danger of being thought trivial, especially by the mock-academic. Like Amis's, Larkin's readability seems so effortless that it tends to be thought of as something separate from his intelligence. But readability *is* intelligence. The vividness of Larkin's critical style is not just a token of his seriousness but the embodiment of it. His wit is there not only in the cutting jokes but in the steady work of registering his interest. It is easy to see that he is being witty when he says that Miles Davis and Ornette Coleman stand in evolutionary relationship to each other 'like green apples and stomach-ache'. But he is being equally witty when he mentions Ruby Braff's 'peach-fed' cornet. A critic's language is not incidental to him: its intensity is a sure measure of his engagement and a persuasive hint at the importance of what he is engaged with.

A critical engagement with music is one of the several happy coincidences which unite Larkin's career with Montale's. If Larkin's *Listen* articles on poetry were to be reprinted the field of comparison would be even more instructive, since there are good reasons for thinking that these two poets come up with remarkably similar conclusions when thinking about the art they practise. On music they often sound like the same man talking. Montale began his artistic career as a trained opera singer and his main area of musical criticism has always been classical music, but he writes about it the same way Larkin writes about jazz, with unfaltering intelligibility, a complete trust in his own ear, and a deep suspicion of any work which draws inspiration from its own technique. In Italy his collected music criticism is an eagerly awaited book, but then in Italy nobody is surprised that a great poet should have written a critical column for so many years of his life. Every educated Italian knows that Montale's music notices are all of a piece with the marvellous body of literary criticism collected in *Auto da fé* and *Sulla poesia*, and that his whole critical corpus is the natural complement to his poetry. In Britain the same connection is harder to make, even though Larkin has deservedly attained a comparable position as a national poet. In Britain the simultaneous pursuit of poetry and regular critical journalism is regarded as versatility at best. The essential unity of Larkin's various activities is not much remarked.

But if we do not remark it we miss half of his secret. While maintaining an exalted idea of the art he practises, Larkin never thinks of it as an inherently separate activity from the affairs of everyday. He has no special poetic voice. What he brings out is the poetry that is already in the world. He has cherished the purity of his own first responses. Like all great artists he has never lost touch with the child in his own nature. The language of even the most intricately wrought Larkin poem is already present in recognisable embryo when he describes the first jazz musicians ever to capture his devotion. 'It was the drummer I concentrated on, sitting as he did on a raised platform behind a battery of cowbells, temple blocks, cymbals, tomtoms and (usually) a chinese gong, his drums picked out in flashing crimson or ultramarine brilliants.' There are good grounds for calling Larkin a pessimist, but it should never be forgotten that the most depressing details in the poetry are seen with the same eye that loved those drums. The proof is in the unstinting vitality of language.

As in the criticism, so in the poetry, wit can be divided usefully into two kinds, humorous and plain. There is not much need to rehearse the first kind. Most of us have scores of Larkin's lines, hemistiches and phrases in our heads, to make us smile whenever we think of them, which is as often as the day changes. I can remember the day in 1962 when I first opened *The Less Deceived* and was snared by a line in the first poem, 'Lines on a Young Lady's Photograph Album'. 'Not quite your class, I'd say, dear, on the whole.' What a perfectly timed pentameter! How subtly and yet how unmistakably it defined the jealousy of the speaker! Who on earth was Philip Larkin? Dozens of subsequent lines in the same volume made it clearer: he was a supreme master of language levels, snapping into and out of a tone of voice as fast as it could be done without losing the reader. Bringing the reader in on it – the deep secret of popular seriousness. Larkin brought the reader in on it even at the level of prosodic technique.

> Flagged, and the figurehead with golden tits
> Arching our way, it never anchors; it's . . .

He got you smiling at a rhyme. 'Church Going' had the ruin-bibber, randy for antique, 'Toads' had the pun on Shakespeare, 'Stuff your pension!' being the stuff dreams are made on. You couldn't get half way through the book without questioning, and in many cases revising, your long-nursed notions about poetic language. Here was a disciplined yet unlimited variety of tone, a scrupulosity that could contain anything, an all-inclusive decorum.

In *The Whitsun Weddings*, 'Mr Bleaney' has the Bodies and 'Naturally The Foundation Will Bear Your Expenses' has the ineffable Mr Lal. 'Sunny Prestatyn' features Titch Thomas and in 'Wild Oats' a girl painfully reminiscent of Margaret in *Lucky Jim* is finally shaken loose 'after about five rehearsals'. In 'Essential Beauty' 'the trite untransferable/Truss-advertisement, truth' takes you back to the cobra-coaxing cacophonies of Calcutta, not to mention forward to Amis's nitwit not fit to shift shit. Even *High Windows*, the bleakest of Larkin's slim volumes, has things to make you laugh aloud. In 'The Card-Players' Jan van Hogspeuw and Old Prijck perhaps verge on the coarse but Jake Balakowsky, the hero of 'Posterity', has already entered the gallery of timeless academic portraits, along with Professor Welch and the History Man. 'Vers de Société' has the bitch/Who's read nothing but *Which*. In Larkin's three major volumes of poetry the jokes on their own would be enough to tell you that wit is alive and working.

But it is working far more pervasively than that. Larkin's poetry is *all* witty – which is to say that there is none of his language which does not confidently rely on the intelligent reader's capacity to apprehend its play of tone. On top of the scores of fragments that make us laugh, there are the hundreds which we constantly recall with a welcome sense of communion, as if our own best thoughts had been given their most concise possible expression. If Auden was right about the test of successful writing being how often the reader thinks of it, Larkin passed long ago. To quote even the best examples would be to fill half this book, but perhaps it will bear saying again, this time in the context of his poetry, that between Larkin's humorous wit and his plain wit there is no discontinuity. Only the man who invented the golden tits could evoke the black-sailed unfamiliar. To be able to make fun of the randy ruin-bibber is the necessary qualification for writing the magnificent last stanza of 'Church Going'. You need to have been playfully alliterative with the trite untransferable truss-advertisement before you can be lyrically alliterative with the supine stationary voyage of the dead lovers in 'An Arundel Tomb'. There is a level of seriousness which only those capable of humour can reach.

Similarly there is a level of maturity which only those capable of childishness can reach. The lucent comb of 'The Building' can be seen by us only because it has been so intensely seen by Larkin, and it has been so intensely seen by him only because his eyes, behind those thick glasses, retain the naïve curiosity which alone makes the adult gaze truly penetrating. Larkin's poetry draws a bitterly sad picture of modern life but it is full of saving graces, and they are invariably as disarmingly recorded as in a child's diary. The paddling at the seaside, the steamer in the afternoon, the ponies at Show Saturday – they are all done with crayons and coloured pencils. He did not put away childish things and it made him more of a man. It did the same for Montale: those who have ever read about the amulet in 'Dora Markus' or the children with tin swords in *Caffè a Rapallo* are unlikely to forget them when they read Larkin. A third name could be added: Mandelstam. When Mandelstam forecast his own death he willed that his spirit should be resurrected in the form of children's games. All three poets represent, for their respective countrymen, the distilled lyricism of common speech. With all three poets the formal element is highly developed – in the cases of Larkin and Mandelstam to the uppermost limit possible – and yet none of them fails to reassure his readers, even during the most intricately extended flight of verbal music, that the tongue they speak is the essential material of his rhythmic and melodic resource.

In Philip Larkin's non-poetic poetic language, the language of extremely well-written prose, despair is expressed through beauty and becomes beautiful too. His argument is with himself and he is bound to lose. He can call up death more powerfully than almost any other poet ever has, but he does so in the commanding voice of life. His linguistic exuberance is the heart of him. Joseph Brodsky, writing about Mandelstam, called lyricism the ethics of language.

Larkin's wit is the ethics of his poetry. It brings his distress under our control. It makes his personal unhappiness our universal exultation. Armed with his wit, he faces the worst on our behalf, and brings it to order. A romantic sensibility classically disciplined, he is, in the only sense of the word likely to last, modern after all. By rebuilding the ruined bridge between poetry and the general reading public he has given his art a future, and you can't get more modern than that.

(1981)

Catacomb Graffiti

Poems and Journeys by Charles Johnston (Bodley Head, London)

Eugene Onegin by Alexander Pushkin, translated by Charles Johnston (Penguin Classic, Harmondsworth, and Viking Press, New York)

APPEARING unannounced in 1977, Charles Johnston's verse rendering of *Eugene Onegin* established itself immediately as the best English translation of Pushkin's great poem there had yet been. It was an impressive performance even to those who could not read the original. To those who could, it was simply astonishing, not least from the technical angle: Johnston had cast his *Onegin* in the *Onegin* stanza, a form almost impossibly difficult in English, and had got away with it. Only an accomplished poet could think of trying such a feat. Yet as a poet Charles Johnston was scarcely known. Indeed, his profile was not all that high even as Sir Charles Johnston, career diplomat and quondam High Commissioner for Australia. All the signs pointed to gentlemanly dilettantism – all, that is, except the plain fact that anyone who can convey even a fraction of Pushkin's inventive vitality must have a profoundly schooled talent on his own account.

Now a small volume of Johnston's own creations, called *Poems and Journeys*, has quietly materialised, in the unheralded manner which is obviously characteristic of its author. It seems that most of the poems it contains previously appeared in one or other of two even smaller volumes, *Towards Mozambique* (1947) and *Estuary in Scotland* (1974), the second of which was printed privately and the first of which, though published by the Cresset Press, certainly created no lasting impression in the literary world. The poems were written at various times between the late 1930s and now. There are not very many of them. Nor does the Bodley Head seem to be acting in any more forthcoming capacity than that of jobbing printer. 'Published for Charles Johnston by the Bodley Head' sounds only one degree less bashful than issuing a pamphlet under your own imprint.

But this time Johnston will not find it so easy to be ignored. *Poems and Journeys* is unmistakably an important book. Leafing through it, you are struck by its assured displays of formal discipline, but really, from the translator of *Onegin*, that is not so surprising. Hard on the heels of this first impression, however, comes the further realisation that through the austerely demanding formal attributes of Johnston's verse a rich interior life is being expressed. Johnston's literary personality is not just old-fashioned: it is determinedly old-fashioned. He has set up the standards of the clubbable English gentry as a bulwark against encroaching chaos. Even those of us whose sympathies are all in the other direction will find it hard not to be swayed by his laconic evocation of the secret garden. It doesn't do, we are led to assume, to go on about one's predicament. Yet somehow a stiff upper lip makes eloquence all the more arresting.

Johnston's diplomatic duties took him to Japan before the war. After Pearl Harbor he was interned for eight months. After being released in an exchange of diplomatic agents, he was sent to the Middle East. After the war there were various other appointments before he took up his post in Australia. Clearly the accent has always been on uncomplaining service. Nor do the poems in any way question the idea of dutiful sacrifice: on the contrary, they underline it. Trying to identify that strangely identifiable voice, you finally recognise it as the voice of someone who has not talked before, but who has been so amply described that you think you know him. Johnston is the sort of man who has been written about under so many names that when he writes something himself he sounds like a legend come to life. He is the faithful servant of Empire, who now emerges, unexpected but entirely familiar, as its last poet.

By an act of imagination, without dramatising himself, Johnston has made poetry out of his own background. The same background has produced poetry before but most of it has been bad, mainly because of an ineluctable cosiness. Johnston, however, is blessed with a distancing wit. He has the intensity of gift which makes facts emblematic without having to change them. It is the classical vision, which he seems to have possessed from the start, as the first two lines of an early poem about Japan clearly show:

> Over the rockbed, over the waterfall,
> Tense as a brushstroke tumbles the cataract.

The visual element is so striking it is bound to seem preponderant, but there is more at work here than just an unusual capacity to see. To choose a Greek classical measure, alcaics, is an inspired response to the inherent discipline of a Japanese landscape subject: the native poets and painters have already tamed their panorama to the point that their decorum has become part of it, so to match their formality with an equivalent procedure from the poet's own cultural stock is an imaginative coup. Then there is the subtle control of sonic effects, with the word 'tense' creating stillness and the word 'tumbles' releasing it into motion. He sees something; he finds the appropriate form; and then he exploits technical opportunities to elaborate his perception. The classic artist identifies himself.

But everything he was saying was said from under a

plumed hat. The Lake Chuzéji of his early poems was the playground of the foreign diplomats. They raced their boats on it, giving way to each other in such elaborate order of precedence that only a *Chef de Protocole* knew how to steer a perfect race. They committed genteel adultery around its edges. A man of Johnston's mentality, no matter how well he fitted in by breeding, must sometimes have doubted the validity of his role. He was, after all, a double agent, both loyal functionary and universal observer. But he had not yet conceived of his complicated position as his one true subject – hence a tendency, in these early efforts, towards a Georgian crepuscularity, which even affects his otherwise scrupulously alert diction. Locutions like 'when day is gone' crop up with their tone unqualified: something which would not happen again once his manner was fully developed.

Internment helped develop it. The work commemorating this experience is called 'Towards Mozambique' and is one of the three original long poems in the book. Datelined 'Tokyo 1942 – London 1946', it should now be seen, I think, as one of the outstanding poems of the war, even though it is less concerned with fighting than with just sitting around waiting. Exiles traditionally eat bitter bread, but the narrator is more concerned to reflect than to rail against fate. The poem has something of Ovid's sadness in the *Epistolae ex ponto*, except that Johnston is not being sorry just for himself. He is bent on understanding misunderstanding – the tragedy of incomprehension which has brought Japan to war against the West.

The personal element of the tragedy comes not just from the feeling of his own life being wasted (and anyway, much of the poem seems to have been written after the internment was over) but from regret for the years that were wasted before, when diplomacy was being pursued to no effect. He reflects on what led up to this. A lot did, so he chooses a form which leaves room to lay out an argument – the Spenserian stanza whose clinching alexandrine both Byron and Shelley, in their different ways, found so seductive:

Wakening, I watched a bundle tightly packed
That scaled with clockwork jerks a nearby staff.
Hoist to the top, I saw it twitched and racked
And shrugged and swigged, until the twists of chaff
That held it to the halyard broke, and half
Released the packet, then a sharper tease
Tore something loose, and with its smacking laugh
The Jack was thrashing furiously down breeze,
Mocking the feeble stops that lately cramped its ease.

Ripping, what? (The ambiguity in the third line, incidentally, is less a grammatical error than a mark of class. Osbert Lancaster and Anthony Powell have both always let their participles dangle with abandon, and Evelyn Waugh, in the same chapter of his autobiography which tells us that only those who have studied Latin can write English, perpetrates at least one sentence whose past participle is so firmly attached to the wrong subject that there is no prising it loose. This habit has something to do, I suspect, with a confusion between the English past participle and the Latin ablative absolute.) But some of the young diplomats were not content to shelter behind Britannia's skirts. Greatly daring, they took what opportunities they could to mingle with the locals – to penetrate, as it were, the membranes of inscrutable reserve:

> Climbing with shoeless feet the polished stairs,
> Gay were the evenings in that house I'd known.
> The mats are swept, the cushions that are chairs
> Surround the table like a lacquer throne.
> The geisha have been booked by telephone,
> The whisky brought, the raw fish on the ice,
> The green tea boiled, the saké in its stone
> Warmed to a turn, and seaweed, root and spice
> Await their last repose, the tub of nutcrisp rice.
>
> The scene is set, and soon a wall will slide,
> And in will run, professional as hell,
> Our geisha team, brisk as a soccer side,
> We'll ask the ones we like, if all goes well,
> To luncheon at a suitable hotel . . .

Everything in the diplomatic colony is ordered, decorous and unreal. The unreality becomes most apparent during periods of leave in Shanghai, where a phoney aristocrat rules society:

> 'Le tennis, ce jeu tellement middle-class,'
> Drawls the duchesse, whose European start,
> Whose Deauville background manages to pass
> For all that's feudal in this distant part.
> The locals thought she couldn't be more smart,
> And prized admission to her little fêtes,
> And searched through Gotha with a beating heart,
> But vainly, for the names of her estates,
> And for the strange device emblazoned on her plates.

But only in the enforced idleness of internment is there time to see all this in perspective. Long months of contemplation yield no grand might-have-beens or if-onlys. Nor, on the other hand, do they bring nihilistic resignation. Britain's imperial role is not repudiated. Neither is its inevitable passing particularly regretted. Instead, there is redemption in the moment:

> Time passed. A tramcar screaming in the dark
> Of total blackout down the Kudan hill
> Strikes, out of wire, spark on cascading spark,
> Lights from below the cherry swags that spill,
> In all the thickness of the rich April,
> Their pink festoons of flower above the street,
> Creamy as paint new-slapped. I looked my fill,
> Amazed to find our world was so complete.
> Such moments, in the nick, are strange and sharply
> sweet.

A stanza MacNeice would have been proud to have written. Even in these few examples you can see how Johnston is beginning to realise the lexical freedom that strict forms offer. Up to the point where restriction cramps style, the more demanding the stanza, the greater the range of tone it can contain. Slang phrases like 'professional as hell' and 'in the nick' sound all the more colloquial for being pieced into a tight scheme.

The second long poem in the book, 'Elegy', is written in memory of Johnston's brother Duncan, 'killed leading a Royal Marine Commando raid on the Burma Coast, on the night of February 22nd 1945'. This, too, ranks high among poems of the war. On its own it would be enough to class Johnston with Henry Reed, Bernard Spencer, F. T. Prince and Norman Cameron. It is a high-quality example of what can by now be seen to be a particular school of Virgilian plangency, the poetry of the broken-hearted fields. But it is probably not one of Johnston's best things.

It loses nothing by its air of doomed gentility. The narrator could be Guy Crouchback talking: there was a seductive glamour about the squires going off to war, and a potent sorrow when they did not come home. But though Johnston can be impersonal about himself, he cannot be that way about his brother. The poem tries to find outlets for grief in several different formal schemes, including blank verse. The stiff upper lip relaxes, leaving eloquence unchastened. There is no gush, but there is too much vague suggestion towards feeling, made all the more unsatisfactory by your sense that the feeling aimed at is real, harsh, and unblunted even by time. A first-hand experience has aroused a second-hand artistic response. The air is of an Owenesque regret, of the dark barge passing unto Avalon in agony, of a drawing-down of blinds. The few details given of the lost, shared childhood leave you wanting more, but the author is caught between his forte and an ambition foreign to it: he is a poet of controlled emotion who can give way to anguish only at the cost of sapping his own energy:

> Only through the hard
> Shaft-face of self-esteem parsimonious tears
> Are oozing, sour distillate from the core
> Of iron shame, the shame of private failure
> Shown up by the completeness of the dead.
> I wrote in the fierce hope of bursting loose
> From this regime, cracking its discipline . . .

> I wrote, but my intense assertion found
> No substance and no echo, and all I did
> Was raise an empty monument to grief.

'Elegy' is something better than an empty monument, but it is tentative beside its predecessor 'Towards Mozambique', and scarcely begins to suggest the abundant assurance of its successor, the third long poem in the book, 'In Praise of Gusto'. This contains some of Johnston's best work and instantly takes its place as one of the most variously impressive long poems since Auden and MacNeice were at their peak. It is not as long as either 'Letter to Lord Byron' or *Autumn Journal* but it has much of their verve and genial bravura. It embodies the quality to which it is dedicated.

'In Praise of Gusto' returns to some of the same subject-matter dealt with in earlier works, but this time it is all brought fully within the purview of what can now be seen to be his natural tone, a tone which taps its power from the vivacity of experience. His dead brother is again mentioned. This time all the emphasis is on the life they enjoyed together when young. Nevertheless the effect of loss is more striking than it is in 'Elegy', where death is the direct subject. One concludes, aided by hindsight, that Johnston loses nothing, and gains everything, by giving his high spirits free rein. It might have taken him a long time completely to realise the best way of being at ease with his gift, but with consciously formal artists that is often the case. The last thing they learn to do is relax.

The poem is written in two different measures, the *Onegin* stanza and the stanza which Johnston insists on referring to as *Childe Harold*, although really Spenser has the prior title. Johnston's mastery of the latter form was already proven. But by this time he could read fluent Russian and had obviously become fascinated with the breakneck measure in which *Eugene Onegin* unfolds its story. The *Onegin* stanzas of 'In Praise of Gusto' give every indication that their author will one day be Pushkin's ideal translator. As well as that, they serve the author's present purpose. The *Onegin* stanza is a born entertainer. As Johnston points out in his Author's

Note, 'it has an inner momentum, a sort of infectious vitality of its own'. It packs itself tight and then springs loose like a self-loading jack-in-the-box. Comic timing is crucial to it:

> Beauties who manage the conjunction
> Of glamour and fireside repose
> Pack what I call without compunction
> The deadliest of knockout blows.
> Japan bewitched me. Half forgotten
> Were home and faith. The really rotten
> Part of it all, which, when it came
> Back later, made me sweat with shame,
> Was that our worlds were fast dividing
> And that my fondness must ignore
> The headlong chute direct to war
> Down which Japan was quickly gliding
> With all its ravishingly queer
> Compound of sensual and austere.

The rapacious hostesses of pre-war Shanghai and wartime Alexandria now find their perfectly appropriate rhythmic setting. One of the many things that attracted Johnston to his Russian exemplar must have been the way Pushkin gives full value to the glamour of imperial court life without romanticising its meretriciousness. Nobody who admires both will ever tire of counting the ways in which Pushkin and Mozart are like each other. Each could see all the world as it was yet neither could reshape it in any way except by making masterpieces. Even their own disasters lifted their hearts. (Pushkin said that trials and tribulations were included in his family budget.) Everything that happened belonged. Johnston has something of the same defiant exuberance:

> How Egypt's hostesses detested
> The victories in our campaign:
> 'Assez de progrès,' they protested,
> 'Vous étiez bien à Alamein';
> And then they'd stress in full italics
> The point of being close to Alex,
> The races and the gay weekends

Of bathing parties with one's friends.
They saw no merit in advancing
Far from the nightclub and the beach
Out beyond invitation's reach
To worlds remote from cards and dancing
With absolutely not a face
They'd ever seen in the whole place.

But the *Onegin* stanza enforces epigrammatic terseness. As a countervailing force, Johnston employs the Spenserian stanza to luxuriate in his visual memories. Without sinning against cogency, they amply exploit this traditionally expansive form's magically self-renewing supply of pentameter – a copiousness of rhetorical space which is symbolised, as well as sealed, by the long sweep of the alexandrine at the end:

Mersa Matruh. A fathom down, the sun
Lights on the faintest ripple of the sand
And, underseas, decyphers one by one
The cursive words imprinted on the strand
In the Mediterranean's fluent hand;
For eastern waters have the graceful trick,
By way of compliment from sea to land,
Of signing their imprint, with curl and flick
Of the vernacular, in floweriest Arabic.

An extended metaphysical conceit has been matched up to a rigorous physical form: two kinds of intellectual strictness, yet the effect is of a single, uncalculated sensory celebration.

The essence of classical composition is that no department of it gets out of hand. After aberrations in artistic history the classic principle reasserts itself as a balancing of forces. In 'In Praise of Gusto' Johnston uses his Spenserian stanzas to specify his remembered visions, but he uses them also to unfold an argument. The same contrast and balance of perception and rhetoric was demonstrated by Shelley – a romantic with irrepressible classic tendencies – when he used the same stanza in 'Adonais'. Shelley obtains some of his most gravid poetic effects by deploying what sounds like, at first hearing, a prose argument. The same applies, *mutatis mutandis*, to Johnston, when he remembers what the Western Desert looked like after the battles:

> Such scenes have potency, a strange effect,
> Contagion with an undefined disease.
> They throw a chill on all whom they infect,
> Touch them with sadness, set them ill at ease.
> The sense that friends now dead, or overseas,
> Fought here and suffered, hoped here and despaired,
> Transports us outside time and its degrees.
> Here is a new antique, already paired
> With the most classic sites that scholar's trowel has
>   bared.

The poem begins in the *Onegin* stanza, takes a long excursion in the Spenserian, and returns to the *Onegin*. Though tipping its plumed hat to a younger version of the author – a satirical youth who 'shot down other people's fun' – it conveys a whole-hearted acceptance of the good life, which apparently includes plenty of foie gras, champagne and personally slain partridges. If Dr Leavis were still with us it would be hard to imagine him appreciating any of this, especially when he noted the book's dedication to Sacheverell Sitwell, familiarly addressed as Sachie. Yet the spine of the poem's argument is that prepared pleasures, though it is churlish to eschew them, are not what inspires gusto, which is

> Immediately sustained delight,
> Short-lived, unhoped for, yet conclusive,
> A sovereign power in its own right.
> It lends itself to recognition
> More aptly than to definition . . .

The reason it can't easily be defined is that it is something more all-pervading even than a view of life. It is a way of being alive. Those gifted with it, if they have artistic gifts as well, can tell the rest of us what it is like. Reviewing his own life in search of its traces, Johnston now becomes one of those who have done so. The poem ends in a clear-eyed exultation.

The fourth long poem in the book is a translation of 'Onegin's Journey' which was originally designed to go between the present chapters seven and eight of *Eugene Onegin*. Pushkin eventually decided to leave it out, but it remains a logical subject for the translator of *Eugene Onegin* to tackle. He makes the accomplished job of it that you would expect, revelling in the inspiration engendered by the physical obstacles of the tetrameter and the rhyme that continually looms too soon. They help contain his prolific knack – so appropriate in a translator of Pushkin – for sonic effects.

Throughout his work Johnston is to be found exploiting prosodic conventions (such as eliding 'the' into the initial vowel of the next word) for all they are worth. Sometimes he overcooks it, so that you have to read a line twice to pick out the rhythm. Sometimes the conversational stress and the metrical stress separate to the point where the reader must strain to put them back in touch with each other. Usually, though, Johnston maintains the old rules only in order to increase the number of ways he can speak freely. All those ways are on view in his rendition of 'Onegin's Journey'. But anyone wanting to acquaint himself with Pushkin would be advised to turn in the first instance to the *Eugene Onegin* translation itself, which Penguin has now brought out.

The appearance of this great translation in a popular format is made even more significant by the fact that it carries a twenty-page introduction specially written by John Bayley. The author of the most distinguished book on Pushkin in any language, Bayley here gives the essence of his thoughts on Pushkin in general and *Eugene Onegin* in particular. Bayley's book has always been the best full-length introduction to Pushkin, but until now Edmund Wilson's essay in *The Triple Thinkers* (backed up by two further pieces in *A Window on Russia*) has been the best short one. Now Bayley has captured the second title as well as the first. I recommend this essay without hesitation as the first thing to read on Pushkin.

As for the translation itself, it is what it was hailed as when it came out, and what it will go on being for the foreseeable future. Johnston knows better than I do what it lacks of the original. When, in Chapter Eight, he makes Tatyana tell Onegin, 'Today it's turn and turn about,' he is well aware that there is an element of artificiality. In the original, Tatyana says just, 'Today it is my turn,' and it is one of the mightiest lines in all poetry. There is endless artifice in Pushkin but no artificiality. Yet by patient craft Johnston has kept to a minimum those necessarily frequent occasions when the painfully demanding form of the stanza forces an awkward phrase. Much more often he hits off the correct blend of intricate contrivance and easily colloquial expression. He catches the spirit of the thing, and a large part of the spirit of the thing is the *formal* spirit of the thing.

To a remarkable extent, Johnston possesses, not just the same sort of temperament as his model, but the same sort of talent. We had no right to expect that any English poet who combined these attributes would make translating Pushkin the object of his life. But as *Poems and Journeys* shows, Johnston has done a few things of his own. He has recently finished a translation of Lermontov's *The Demon*. There are other Russian poems one can think of that he would be ideally fitted to give us, among them the last and most intensely organised of Pushkin's tetrametric creations, *The Bronze Horseman*. But on the strength of this volume it might also be wished that Johnston would go on to compose a long original work which would go even further than 'In Praise of Gusto' towards transforming the age he has lived through into art.

One of the things art does is to civilise the recent past. In *Poems and Journeys* there are poems, both long and short, which add significantly to the small stock of works that have helped make sense of the British Empire's passing and of Britain's part in the Second World War. Johnston's voice might have been more often heard in this respect, but he chose perfection of the life rather than of the work. As Auden noted, some artists have everything required for high distinction except the desire to come forward.

If Johnston had come forward earlier and more assertively, there can be no doubt that he would have received a hearing. In some of his short pieces he makes fun of the

'Trend Police' and describes the poems turned out by himself and his fellow gifted amateurs as 'catacomb graffiti'. In fact, the Trend Police would not have stood much chance of shouting down work done to this standard. The *locus classicus* is in no more danger of being obscured than the privileged orders are in danger of losing their privileges, although Johnston would have you think, in his more predictable moments, that the contrary was true in each case.

The best reason for Johnston to think of himself as a part-time poet was that as a full-time diplomat he was well placed to write the kind of poetry which is necessarily always in short supply – the poetry of the man who spends most of his day being fully professional at something else, the poetry for which the young Johnston so admired Marvell.

> Yours to restore the wasted field
> And in distress to health
> To serve the Commonwealth;
>
> Yet with a wider-sweeping eye
> To range above the land, and spy
> The virtue and defect
> Of empires, to detect
>
> In vanquished causes, and in kings
> Dethroned, the tragedy of things,
> And know what joys reside
> Where the Bermudas ride.

In recent times we have grown used to the externally formless epic – Berryman's *Dream Songs*, Lowell's *History* – and striven to convince ourselves that it possesses an internal form which makes up for its lack of shape. But this pious belief has become harder and harder to sustain. The virtues of the informal epic are prose virtues, not poetic ones. Only discipline can give rise to the full freedom of mature art. Charles Johnston has given us a better idea than we had any right to hope for of what Pushkin's epic sounds like. But his long poems suggest that he has it in him to write an epic of his own. Even if he does not, his small but weighty output of original work, now that we have at last come to know it, enriches the poetic legacy of his generation and helps clarify that nebulous, nearby area of literary history where uninspired innovation creates its permanent disturbance.

(*London Review of Books*, 1980)

Grigson's Satirical Tradition

The Oxford Book of Satirical Verse chosen by Geoffrey Grigson (Oxford University Press, London and New York)

THERE ARE several glaring omissions, but otherwise *The Oxford Book of Satirical Verse* is one of the best anthologies by the best modern anthologist. Geoffrey Grigson has always had a way of picking plums. His famous anthology of the 1930s, *New Verse*, remains a good introduction to the poetry of that time. He has continued making anthologies ever since. Some of them are anthologies of prose, others are chrestomathies of everything interesting from a given period, but they are all useful. A good anthology gives the reader the sense that he has stumbled on new outcrops of high-grade ore, even in poets whose work he thought he knew. The latest of Grigson's efforts fulfils that condition pretty well.

The selection runs from Skelton all the way through to, well, me. It could have stopped a bit earlier but I won't pretend to be disappointed it didn't. It might have started, however, a *lot* earlier. There are plenty of satirical passages in Chaucer and anyway it is important to include him for technical reasons, since he, to all intents and purposes, invented the couplet, which provides the formal spine of satire in English even when it is elaborated into other measures.

In his short preface, Grigson doesn't waste much time on trying to define satire but he does say that it postulates an ideal of human conduct which it then finds wanting, and takes delight in doing so. He points out that the delight is taken by technical means – rhythm, vocabulary, rhyme, surprise. He might also have pointed out that the form is the embodiment of the ideal: the more the poet can show us proportion, balance, and harmony in his form, the more effectively he can use it to say that the world has gone awry. The contrast between the symmetry of the vehicle and its forensic verve marks out the best satire for what it is. There are such things as formless satirical poems – this book includes a few – but they are almost invariably of the second rank. The licence to speak allowed by its own strict form gives satire the wide intellectual range which permits it to claim the title of embodying the intelligence of English poetry, just as lyric poetry embodies the emotion. The wide intellectual range was staked out by Chaucer, so it is a pity he is not here.

Enough of the quibbles: here comes the parade. John Skelton is only the first of many to be very satirical about the Scots, who were to remain anybody's meat until Culloden, after which it took bad taste to continue the joke.

O ye wretched Scots,
Ye puant pisspots,
It shall be your lots
To be knit up with knots
Of halters and ropes
About your traitors' throats.

'Puant' meant smelly. Skelton is usually put forward as a model of economy but really he is full of wind: those two-beat lines give the illusion of speed but it takes time to get anything complicated said in them, since the rhyme continually arrives too early. For this reason the dimeter had no future in satirical poetry, which has always been most commonly written in tetrameters and pentameters.

Following Skelton, an Anonymous of the early sixteenth century was likewise extremely satirical about the Scots.

Sanct Peter said to God
In a sport word,
Can ye not mak a Hielandman
Of this horse turd?

Wyatt satirised court life with unremarkable invention, but he did it in pentameters, which meant that Chaucer's forgotten accomplishments were beginning to be rediscovered. Wyatt, in the example Grigson gives here, arranged his pentameters in *terza rima*, a viciously difficult form in English even when you cheat the rhymes, but still the naturalness of Wyatt's long iambic line brings you the sound of real speech.

I cannot with my words complain and moan
And suffer nought; nor smart without complaint,
Nor turn the word that from my mouth is gone.

Wyatt didn't always count his stresses and frequently perpetrated an unintentional tetrameter or alexandrine. A sophisticated case can be made for such lapses being intentional (as, of course, Dryden's occasional alexandrines *are* intentional), but in fact you can usually tell when a poet is careless, even when he is hundreds of years away. Chaucer set the standard: that five-beat pulse is always there, ticking along without a hitch. Nor did Shakespeare, in his formal poems, ever lose count. Donne did, though. Eager to defend him against pedantry, Donne's admirers rightly praise the vigour of his conversational rhythms. But his eighteenth-century critics were right about his roughness, which can be compensated for in his great lyrics but cracks your jaw when you try to scan his satirical couplets. Yet even the worst thicket of unspeakability is usually redeemed by the strength of his ideas, and occasionally the couplet settles into a toughly argued neatness which harks forward to Dryden, or at any rate back to Chaucer.

But he is worst who (beggarly) doth chaw
Others' wits' fruits, and in his ravenous maw
Rankly digested, doth these things out-spew
As his own things; and they are his own, 'tis true,

For if one eat my meat, though it be known
The meat was mine, th'excrement is his own.

Samuel Butler made the next big technical impact, with *Hudibras*, composed in the iambic tetrametric couplets which have ever since been known as Hudibrastics. He handled the form with specious bravura. The lines are rhythmically self-aware and there are gestures towards polysyllabic rhymes, although often these are so approximate (Bring down/kingdom) that they sound more slovenly than playful. His great virtue was to keep the argument rolling.

There is a tall long-sided dame
(But wondrous light) ycleped Fame,
That like a thin chameleon boards
Herself on air, and eats your words:
Upon her shoulders wings she wears
Like hanging sleeves, lined through with ears . . .

Admirers of Pepys will know that their hero tried long and hard to find *Hudibras* entertaining but could never stave off boredom. Modern readers should not be ashamed to concur. There is nothing wrong with sustained tetrameters – Auden has written them brilliantly in our own time and the trochaic version of the same measure is at the heart of classical Russian poetry – but there is something tedious about Butler. His small stock of ideas shows you that technique is not everything. He deserves credit, however, for being original in the way his verse moves, if in nothing else.

Cleveland was intensely satirical about the Scots.

Had Cain been Scot, God would have changed his doom,
Not forced him wander, but confined him home.
Like Jews they spread, and as infection fly,
As if the Devil had ubiquity.

Marvell merely transferred the Scots to Holland, but the high quality of his technique is at once apparent.

Holland, that scarce deserves the name of land,
As but the offscouring of the British sand,
And so much earth as was contributed
By English pilots when they heaved the lead,
Or what by th' ocean's slow alluvion fell
Of shipwrecked cockle and the mussel shell
This indigested vomit of the sea
Fell to the Dutch by just propriety.

The imagery has the luminous precision you would expect in his lyrics, but are agreeably surprised to find being lavished on a baser purpose. Marvell is already giving satire a good half of his talent, and with Dryden we see the whole gift being applied. When we get to Dryden it is like the sun coming up.

Shadwell alone, of all my sons, is he
Who stands confirmed in full stupidity.
The rest to some faint meaning make pretence,
But Shadwell never deviates into sense.

Saintsbury, who remains the highest authority on English prosody, wrote a little book on Dryden (in the English Men of Letters series) which can confidently be recommended as the best apprcciation of Dryden's originality. Dryden's technical assurance in the satirical couplet, Saintsbury argues, depended on his long theatrical training. Having written thousands of couplets to be spoken aloud, he was ready, when he came to satire comparatively late in life, to give it a uniquely dramatic voice, 'a sort of triumphant vivacity'. Grigson awards Dryden a generous selection but one is bound to feel that it is still not generous enough. The man who made English prose a fit instrument for argument did the same for English verse.

Rochester introduces a new element – satanic pornography.

Nor shall our love-fits, Chloris, be forgot,
  When each the well-looked link-boy strove t'enjoy,
And the best kiss was the deciding lot
  Whether the boy fucked you, or I the boy.

But he could handle the couplet with a conversational elegance not shamed by Dryden.

> Huddled in dirt the reasoning engine lies,
> Who was so proud, so witty, and so wise.

In Swift there is so much disgust that the self-delighting element is hard to find, but his pungent accuracy of form eventually tells you that it is there.

> All human race would fain be wits,
> And millions miss, for one that hits.

These lines are from a long poem called *On Poetry: A Rhapsody*, which Grigson prints entire. Written in faultlessly propelled Hudibrastics, it is interesting all through – as good today as when it was written. Grub Street is portrayed as a pit of squalor but there is no missing the fact that Swift liked it that way: with no dunces to aim at he would have been a marksman without targets.

Edward Young's *Night Thoughts* were hugely successful at the time but are forgotten now, although occasionally there is some academic attempt to revive interest in them by placing them in their context, etc. The selection here provided is enough to show that Young was as flat as he was perfect.

> Some go to church, proud humbly to repent
> And come back much more guilty than they went.

After yawning over his smartly turned banalities it is a relief to get to Pope, who is perfect too but immeasurably more highly charged.

There is no call to insult the reader by rehearsing what can be said in Pope's praise, but it is worth venturing that there are things to be said against him. In the *Epilogue to the Satires* he showed signs of wanting to be dramatic: he split lines up between characters, achieving the same quick shifting of attention that the French dramatists, following classical models, had traditionally employed. But he lacked Dryden's long training in theatrical speakability. Pope's couplets are exquisite in themselves, but they tend to remain themselves:

they only effortfully accumulate into speech. There are any number of academic studies to justify Pope's rhetorical monumentality but the net effect of it is of something hard to read out.

Nevertheless Pope's virtues look all the more supreme for being excerpted. The character of Atticus in the *Epistle to Dr. Arbuthnot* is a more subtle job of psychological penetration than anything that had occurred in satire before. As for the couplets, they are so highly tuned you can say nothing against them except that they sometimes take English too far towards Latin – you have to re-read in order to sort out the subject from the object. At their best, they strike the exact balance between compression and naturalness: the syntax is as complex as it could possibly be while still being intelligible at first reading.

> Beauties, like tyrants, old and friendless grown,
> Yet hate to rest, and dread to be alone,
> Worn out in public, weary ev'ry eye,
> Nor leave one sigh behind them when they die.

The tiny clockwork is wound almost to the point of jamming in the first three lines and then goes zing in the fourth, which has an internal rhyme to help celebrate its own speed. Pope exhausted the possibilities of the end-stopped, or heroic couplet, which since his time has never been fully revived as a form by anyone except Roy Campbell. The way ahead was through the romance couplet, with all its turn-overs and polysyllabic rhymes – a form as easy to write badly as Pope's is difficult to write well.

Charles Churchill, dead in 1764 at thirty-three, is one of the might-have-beens of English poetry. Those who are convinced that he had greatness in him will find their belief borne out by the selection given here. He wrote the romance couplet at full tilt, but with all the judgment necessary to produce an easily speakable verse paragraph.

> Far, far be that from thee – yes, far from thee,
> Be such revolt from grace, and far from me
> The will to think it . . .

He was the master of the conversational style. Also he had a large spirit, even to the extent of finding a good word for the Scots.

> The Scots are poor, cries surly English pride;
> True is the charge, nor by themselves denied.
> Are they not then in strictest reason clear
> Who wisely come to mend their fortunes here?

In the vivacity of Burns you can already hear something of Byron's impetus, in the bite of Landor something of his attack, and in Thomas Moore something of his urbanity. But Byron not only sums them all up, he leaves them looking as pale as his own skin. With Byron the sun comes up again. The selection from him is long and could have been longer. Technically his couplets are familiar.

> Blest be the banquets spread at Holland House,
> Where Scotchmen feed, and critics may carouse!

But Byron soon learned to save his couplets and use them as fireworks tied to the tail of longer stanzas, usually the *ottava rima*.

> For glances beget ogles, ogles sighs,
> Sighs wishes, wishes words, and words a letter,
> Which flies on wings of light-heeled Mercuries,
> Who do such things because they know no better;
> And then, God knows what mischief may arise,
> When love links two young people in one fetter.
> Vile assignations, and adulterous beds,
> Elopements, broken vows, and hearts, and heads.

From the formal angle this has everything. Technical lapses in Byron can never be attributed to ignorance, only to the sheer speed with which he wrote against deadlines. As Auden told him in 'Letter to Lord Byron', he was master of the airy manner. His poetry might be an arrangement of prose, but it is an arrangement of fully developed prose, and it is a fully developed arrangement.

In Byron, satire was whole. After him we must be content

to see it splitting up. Shelley is bitter about Castlereagh, Praed is whimsical about Whigs and Tories, but satire was only a part of Shelley's poetry and Praed's meticulously turned *vers de société* was only a part of satire. There are poems by Thackeray and Dickens to show that they would have written great verse satires if they had not written great prose ones. Browning, not present here, put the romance couplet to such fluent use in narrative poetry that the heroic satirical couplet would sound archaic ever after. By the time you get to Belloc, the self-delighting element has become self-regard: Belloc was a mighty versifier but only rarely did he manifest that unstudied intensity by which the true satirists use their form to speak naturally.

In the pages devoted to modern times there are absences to regret and presences to deplore, but on the whole Grigson has stayed true to his code, which has always been to spurn what he calls 'fudge'. Wyndham Lewis, his mentor in fudge detection, is represented by a long selection from *If So the Man You Are*. Lewis could count to five, but sometimes forgot to. Ezra Pound simply couldn't: there is a large chunk of *L'Homme moyen sensuel* to prove that a decently turned couplet was beyond him. There are only two of Sassoon's war satires. Norman Cameron, for some strange reason, is missing entirely. The selection from e. e. cummings leaves out 'POEM, OR BEAUTY HURTS MR. VINAL', the most comprehensively satirical piece he ever wrote. On the other hand it is good to see Edgell Rickword represented. A first-class critical intellect until he turned Marxist and threw it all away, Rickword was an original poet particularly adept at Hudibrastics, which he wrote with an acrid flourish.

Roy Campbell wrote end-stopped couplets with a consciously archaic Popishness but some of his best poety is couched in them. A pity that there is nothing here from *Flowering Rifle*, in which he mounted his most telling attack on the left writers of the 1930s. Nor does the selection from MacNeice quite make up for the absence of anything from *Autumn Journal*; which struck a note unheard since Goldsmith.

The omission it is impossible to forgive, however, is that of A. D. Hope. As an Australian poet, Hope guessed the penalty he would pay for never moving to England, but it is ridiculous that he should have to go on paying it at this late stage. Young critics can perhaps be forgiven for pretending that they haven't heard of him but it is most decidedly not all right for Grigson to ignore the most accomplished verse satirist since Auden. Hope's 'A Letter from Rome' would on its own have been enough to earn him a prominent place in this anthology.

> Just think of Bede the Tourist! – I, you see, am
> Not drunk, but just a little 'flown with wine' –
> Bede came to Rome and offered his Te Deum,
> Fresh from a land as barbarous as mine,
> Made one remark about the Colosseum
> And plodded back to Jarrow-on-the-Tyne.

But there can be no quarrel with the dominating presence in the last part of the book – Auden. Composed in an ebullient rhyme royal, 'Letter to Lord Byron' celebrates Byron's tone and recreates it at the same time. Auden wrote the poem in a tearing hurry while he was in Iceland with MacNeice. It has its blemishes but still seems to me the ideal way to look at the world when the world looks determined to fall apart.

> The match of Hell and Heaven was a nice
> Idea of Blake's, but won't take place, alas.
> You can choose either, but you can't choose twice;
> You can't, at least in this world, change your class;
> Neither is alpha plus though both will pass:
> And don't imagine you can write like Dante,
> Dive like your nephew, crochet like your auntie.

Here again it could be said that this is only prose. But there has always been a kind of poetry which is only prose – prose squeezed until it sings. The satirical tradition is a tradition of clarity. Sometimes the clarity is a window on nothing, at other times it is too dazzling to reveal anything, but on occasions you can see the whole world through it.

Geoffrey Grigson has collected enough of those occasions in this book to make it among the most commendable achievements in his long career of service.

(*New York Review of Books*, 1981)

All the Facts

W. H. Auden: The Life of a Poet **by Charles Osborne (Eyre Methuen, London, and Harcourt Brace Jovanovich, New York)**

C. Day-Lewis: An English Literary Life **by Sean Day-Lewis (Weidenfeld & Nicolson, London)**

THE REVIEWS of two recent biographies – Charles Osborne's *W. H. Auden* and Sean Day-Lewis's life of his father, *C. Day-Lewis* – have been nearly as interesting as the books themselves. MacSpaunday remains a bone of contention for the British literary intelligentsia, perhaps because his collective reputation is mixed up with memories of the 1930s, a period which throws a long shadow, to the extent that nobody is certain whether all the spies have yet been flushed. The amount of embarrassed soul-searching which is evidently involved makes me very aware that I am from another country. But it sometimes happens that the foreigner's view gains clarity from detachment. What matters most about MacSpaunday is that at least two of his components wrote enduring poetry. Whether Auden will be thought of as the genius and MacNeice as merely the master craftsman is a question not likely to be answered just yet. My own guess is that MacNeice will eventually be regarded as Auden's equal, if not in stature then at least in individuality. The only reason he was ever ranked lower was that he never influenced anybody, since he worked tricks that only a first-rate verbal talent could even try to copy. Anybody could try to copy Auden.

That was why all the young writers were ready to agree that Auden spoke for his generation. They thought they could talk that way too. Even at its least artful, the poetry of a man like MacNeice reminds the dabbler that he has no gift; even at its most artful, the poetry of a man like Auden makes any reader feel like a writer. The changes that make common phrases memorable seem so small, so easy. He was recognised immediately as a magician, but always those who did the recognising thought of him as *their* magician. Why, this man says our thoughts aloud! Hence the possessiveness. And they are possessive about him still. In nearly all the reviews of Charles Osborne's book the chief concern has been that Auden, their Auden, should not be traduced.

Well, he hasn't been. Osborne's book is light-toned and often distinctly unscholarly, but it has caught the man. That it did not also concern itself with catching the great poet was perhaps a tactical error. Tom Paulin, in the *New Statesman*, caned the book for leaving out Auden's high seriousness as an artist. He did not consider the possibility that Osborne was showing good manners in taking that for granted. There is also a possibility that Osborne simply did not recognise high seriousness in Auden, but this seems unlikely, since he has been so good at recognising it in Verdi. Books with the appropriate gravity will come in time – probably too gravid and certainly too many of them. This one has the gossipy actuality of a lived life. As with Isherwood's *Christopher and His Kind*, there is not much that it shirks. Auden comes out of it as a sad man in old age, and not very appealing in his prime – if what you want from genius is good behaviour and easy manners. According to this account his homosexuality hurt nobody, not even himself, but he had an overbearing manner and a full catalogue of disgusting personal habits to go with it, most of them focused on the unassuageable need to cram things into his mouth. He blamed untimely weaning – a tip to his biographer, who sensibly starts at the beginning.

Auden's childhood was apparently very happy, like Benjamin Britten's. For both of them there seems to have been enough love and encouragement to suggest that the middle class is a useful one for talent to be born into. A homosexual mentor called Michael Davidson helped to guide Auden's precocious mental development, but there was no suggestion at that stage of rebellion against his upbringing. Unusually among bright lads, Auden honoured his parents from the start. He always held that a child deserved as much neurosis as it could stand, but it is hard to see where his own share might have come from if he had not been homosexual. Even then his originality was mainly the concomitant of talent. Most of his eccentricities sprang from dedication. His version of Oxford aestheticism mainly confined itself to a strange choice of clothes. Probably he just bought the first clothes he saw in the window and put on the first he found in the morning. There was no lobster-walking: the poses he struck were all intellectual. What wowed his contemporaries was the way he said things, especially when he wrote them down. They found him overwhelmingly original and obviously they were right. His decisions were different from theirs. He was being driven by the complicated instinct of a great gift. When he got interested in Emily Dickinson and Wilfred Owen, or decided to ape Eliot's eclectic references by sowing his own work with scientific phraseology, he was not making arbitrary choices but following an impulse. His friends, not following an impulse but making arbitrary choices, were bound to be bowled over. Osborne paraphrases their worship, which few of them have ever made any secret of. Stephen Spender is disarmingly frank about his adoration in *World Within World* and Day-Lewis went on record with his immortal 'Wystan, lone flyer, birdman, my bully boy!', which is an easy line to laugh at but should remind us that hero worship can look quite logical when there is a real hero about. Day-Lewis wasn't alone in the sentiment – he merely had the misfortune to put it in the most durably excruciating form.

Wystan was a *Wunderkind*. The question turns on how long he remained a *Kind*. It is usually true that the bigger the talent, the slower it ripens into wisdom. Auden's was a prodigiously creative mind at play. Among the things it played with was politics. Nowadays there are serious people who find it hard to forgive the 1930s intellectuals for their infatuation with Communism, but if the serious people were as serious as they think they are they would do a better job of imagining the past. Osborne has been punished in some of the reviews for missing the nuances of the English class system. As his fellow Australian I suppose I could be convicting myself of an equal obtuseness by saying that I can't see he has missed much. He has brought out the cosy, resolutely chauvinistic insularity in which the young middle-class English poets could rebel against their comfortable upbringing by condemning what they conceived to be a capitalist society. He has also assumed, surely correctly, that the young people of the time had good reasons for supposing that the capitalist system would not be able to sustain itself, and no inkling as yet that democracy – or capitalism, for that matter – was not really susceptible of being analysed on materialist lines. Backing Communism looked like the only way to fight Fascism.

Nowadays it is easy to think like George Orwell. At the time you had to be George Orwell to manage it. A more damaging criticism of Auden is not that he was a dedicated revolutionary but that he was only playing at it.

By Osborne's account, Spain turned Auden away from radicalism rather than towards, while China, which he visited in the company of Isherwood, finished him with politics altogether. 'Thin gardeners watched them pass and priced their shoes.' 'All Dung' and 'Y Hsiao Wu' had a wonderful time in the Shanghai massage parlours but All Dung's net conclusion seems to have been that the world-scale political struggles already well under way had little to do with him: his shoes were too expensive. In other words he realised that he had been a bourgeois liberal all along. To the cold eye this might look like an even deeper descent into frivolity but Osborne prefers to believe that Auden was simply facing facts. The flight to America was away from politics and towards art, the thing he was good at.

Up to this point, it seems to me, Osborne's view is not only sympathetic, it has the additional merit of being right. Auden's callow demand for the death of the old gang was silly if sincere, and cynical if a pose, but the important point is that he was out of all that soon enough. He can hardly be much blamed for toying with, as a young man, what artists like O'Casey, Brecht, Aragon, MacDiarmid and Neruda went on supporting into old age. That he still seems blameworthy is because he spoke for England. MacNeice did a more thoroughly vituperative job of castigating a privileged society than Auden ever did but MacNeice spoke for himself – he lacked Auden's fatal resonance in the collective consciousness. Auden's ideal of a new order had more to do with homosexuality than with state ownership of the means of production. It *had* to be vaguely put. His mistake was to believe that his soul was his own. His emigration to America was widely regarded as treason then and in some quarters still is now.

Benjamin Britten went to America too. For a while he and Auden worked in the same house: 7 Middagh Street, Brooklyn Heights. The place was a hot-bed of genius. Osborne seductively evokes the creative hubbub, with talented people scratching away behind every door. One of them was Gypsy Rose Lee. (Considering the proclivities of most of the male residents, one can only conclude that she had come to the wrong house, but perhaps she needed a rest.) Auden was an able housekeeper, thereby proving that his otherwise slovenly habits were largely a matter of choice: he begrudged wasting his powers of organisation on everyday affairs. Britten, on the other hand, couldn't abide mess. But the chief difference between them was that Britten's embattled country drew him home, eventually to the Order of Merit, a knighthood, and the universal esteem of his grateful compatriots. He didn't come home to fight, but he did come home. Auden, who knew he couldn't fight either, thought he might as well stay where he was.

He was never quite forgiven for it. P. N. Furbank, reviewing this book in *Quarto*, argues with some force that he never forgave himself either, and lived unhappily ever after. Most of the evidence, however, suggests that Auden was pretty good at not noticing his own blunders. Indeed the most repulsive item of behaviour which Osborne has to recount concerns what sounds like monumental insensitivity in just this matter. Donning American uniform in the last months of the war as part of the Strategic Bombing Survey, Auden made a lightning tour of Germany and stopped off in England to tell his erstwhile countrymen that compared with what had happened to continental Europe they had never suffered at all. He said this while helping himself to generous portions of their rationed food. Arrogance is often a cover-up for guilt but it is still arrogance. A decent silence would have been not just better manners but less blasphemous. Osborne has credit coming to him for not trying to soften this nasty episode. It is recorded that upon being told by an angry friend to hold his tongue, Auden looked contrite. Probably he had fallen into the trap which lies in wait for anyone deficient in self-esteem – the belief that one's opinions do not matter. And if one is in possession, as many artists are, of an *ad hoc* personality, it is often hard to remember that ordinary people pride themselves less on their work than on the consistency of their conduct, judging others by the same criterion. By the time the play-actor finds himself held in contempt, it is usually too late to remind his audience that he was only talking for effect.

Auden seems to have got crankier as he grew older. Perhaps the personality was transferring itself from the work to the man. Osborne has plenty of stories to tell, including the startling information – it was certainly a new one on me – that Auden had a heterosexual affair with a comely American lady called Rhoda Jaffe. But it took Chester Kallman to bring him what measure of domestic bliss he ever found. The friendship conferred all the blessings of stability. Apart from the aesthetic aspects – Kallman might have started off playing a credible Tadzio to Auden's Aschenbach but he did not age gracefully – the only thing you could say against their relationship was that it was a permanent terminus. Homosexual marriages are between lovers, and as Marina Tsvetaeva put it in her touching little handbook for lesbians, *Mon frère féminin*, lovers are children and children don't have children. Nevertheless Auden seems to have obtained from the long alliance an enviable amount of peace and quiet. Those who believe that Auden's work went flat after the war should at least consider that the reason might not necessarily have been that he was cut off from his roots in England. Perhaps he had found contentment – traditionally a great enemy of lyric poetry.

My own view is that Auden got sick of his own winning streak. He took a moral stand against his early work, which he now conceived of as having created excitement through playing fast and loose with the truth. His later work eschews suggestiveness, some might say at the price of losing all poetic interest. There is good reason, I think, for saying that anyone who can't appreciate what Auden is up to in his later work probably can't appreciate his earlier work either, but there is no denying that Homer occasionally nodded. Osborne is commendably strict with the looser work, and rightly dismisses *Academic Graffiti*, which is an exercise in that least forgiveable of all literary genres, the unfunny joke. He also shows, arrestingly, that Auden didn't have a clue about how to translate *Die Zauberflöte* so that a singer could sing it. I would have liked to have heard more on this point, since Osborne, with his operatic connections, is well equipped to punch a large hole through Auden/Kallman's loudly flaunted expertise as librettist.

The end came at Christ Church College, Oxford, and was very messy. Osborne tactfully scamps the full story of what happened between Auden and the young man he reported for the alleged theft of his wallet, but there is already more than enough sadness in the fact that the great poet ended his life as a bore. The needle got stuck. He gave the same few monologues interminably and unasked, so that eventually the Fellows had to tell him to put a sock in it or else quit the table. The man who had once spoken more excitingly than anyone wound up unable to amuse a pack of dons. Like Mencken's semantic asphasia, the punishment seems Dantesque in its cruel appropriateness.

But what was he being punished for? Surely not homosexuality. He often counted himself unlucky to be so, but we all gained by it. Before the Wolfenden Report, if English homosexuals wanted to write public poetry about love then they had to write obliquely or else get arrested. Compelled to indirectness, Auden invented a new style of verbal architecture, so uniquely of its time that it will sound original for ever. Also the search for boys got him away from home. He saw the world, learned about it quickly, and stopped being silly soon enough. The worst you can say is that he suggested a greatness he never quite attained, but that might be just another way of saying that he set a pace not even he could match. Verdict: bent but outstanding.

Cecil Day-Lewis, on the other hand, was straight but average. Sean Day-Lewis has done a more thoughtful job of recounting his father's life than Osborne has done with Auden's. Indeed he has written a truly distinguished biography.

What tells against it is the irredeemable commonplaceness of the subject. All this book's reviewers seemed confident that Day-Lewis's reputation had vanished The reputation was put there in the first place by reviewers not very different from them. Day-Lewis deserves respect as a man of letters who carried out his duties conscientiously; most of the poets praised today will be lucky if the same is said of them. As for his poetry, at its best it showed either an unforced knack for metaphor (as when he called the darkness in cinemas 'furs they can afford') or, even better, an avoidance of effects in favour of sparely articulated argument ('That we who lived by honest dreams/Defend the bad against the worse'). But he reached maturity late and was always in danger of slipping back. His most common state was a protracted version of an adolescence that had never been very judicious in the first place. The young Day-Lewis bought the whole radical package, Communist Party-card included. Less forgivably, he gave advice in metrical form.

> Don't bluster, Bimbo, it won't do you any good;
> We can be much ruder and we're learning to shoot.

What makes this even more foolish than Auden's death of the

old gang is its absolute deafness to tone. That is also what makes it less sinister.

From the political viewpoint Day-Lewis was a chump, but not even that definition should be pressed too hard. He simply had a sheltered upbringing, in a sheltered class in a sheltered land. Young people with that background didn't have to be ignorant about state terror in order to misunderstand totalitarianism. They could be told all about it and still misunderstand. It wasn't cynicism, it was innocence. Few of us are innocent now but we can claim no credit, nor should we be quick to condemn those who were silly then. It was Day-Lewis's personal misfortune that he sounded sillier than anyone else of comparable intelligence. He got out of the Communist Party but his bellicose utterances about learning to shoot were not forgotten when the real shooting started and he found he had no stomach for it. He spent a day in the army before being rescued by Harold Nicolson at Rosamond Lehmann's instigation. The revolutionary poet sat out the war in the Ministry of Information, writing captions for its illustrated publications. Day-Lewis was no doubt right to declare himself useless as a soldier. His biographer, however, might have been a bit slower to endorse this opinion: part of the point of the call-up was that you had to serve, ready-or-not, and if you ducked out then somebody else had to face the bullets meant for you.

Rosamond Lehmann was one of the seven mistresses Day-Lewis laid claim to as a lifetime's total. Professor John Carey, who is apparently set on adding unintentional humour to his repertoire of comic effects, adduced this figure as evidence that Day-Lewis had the morals of a tom-cat. Perhaps in Professor Carey's part of Oxford the tom-cats are unusually well-behaved. Morality has a lot to do with opportunity. No man scores points for chastity if women do not like him. Women obviously liked Day-Lewis very much indeed. He could easily have bedded seventy or even seven hundred. Instead he confined himself to the ladies whose photographs adorn this book. Beautiful without exception, they are an impressive bunch, culminating in Jill Balcon – not, on the face of it, the sort of woman who would give herself to a humbug. He did what he could to keep them all happy, with deleterious effects on his digestive tract. In January 1945, while the Germans were counter-attacking in the Ardennes, Day-Lewis got sick-leave from the MOI: he was worn out from guilt about making love to Rosamond Lehmann. And, of course, from writing captions. But in this connection, as in every other, his most reprehensible act was to express himself in verse. Mistresses found that they were losing their attraction for him when they read about it in some sonnet sequence. His poetry was a direct expression of his life. That was one of the two main things wrong with it.

The other main thing was that he was short of inspiration. But most poets are short of that. The reviewers have searched hard in both these books for the man behind the work. In Day-Lewis's case the man is fairly easily detected but with Auden there always seems to be a discrepancy between the man people who knew him think they remember, and the poet that even people who never met him feel they know exactly.

What has been illuminating about the critical reception for both books is the concern with conduct. Britain has been lucky in her poets: there have been comparatively few shady characters. But a side effect is that criticism tends to remain an occupation for gentlemen, who rarely feel bound to discuss such a sordid matter as talent. If English literary history offered a few more examples of good writers who were bad hats, there would be less agonising over the routinely fallible behaviour from which nobody is exempt, and more willingness to get on with the genuine critical task of investigating the individual talent which scarcely anybody possesses.

(*Encounter*, 1980)

Flights of Angels

***The Drawings by Sandro Botticelli for Dante's Divine Comedy* with an introduction by Kenneth Clark (Thames & Hudson, London, and Harper & Row, New York)**

THE COFFEE-TABLE art book and the standard scholarly work are usually two different things, but occasionally the one volume must serve both purposes, to the benefit of the layman, even if the scholar feels let down. Speaking as a layman, I can only say that if I had not already possessed a coffee-table I would have been willing to construct one, merely for the purpose of receiving *The Drawings by Sandro Botticelli for Dante's Divine Comedy*. Visually, if not verbally, this must be one of the most resplendent books ever to have been made generally available. The price might seem high, but your local library will be getting a lot for its money. Just to make a preliminary acquaintance with the drawings takes weeks, they are so finely detailed – although Botticelli's authority for the task convinces you at first glance.

Until the advent of this volume, a first glance was the most you could hope to get. The original drawings are in Berlin and the Vatican. Lippmann's edition of 1877, reproducing the drawings full-size in collotype, has always been a specialist tool: you need a crane to turn the pages. Some of the drawings, painfully reduced, were in the Nonesuch Dante. Dover's paperback of selected reproductions could give you only some idea. Now here are all the surviving drawings in their proper order, in photographic copies as near to full-size as is convenient, with the narrow tonal range of ink and vellum faithfully adhered to. The more you look, the more you see, and the more it becomes evident that Lorenzino de' Medici – Lorenzo the Magnificent's inspired cousin –

commissioned the right man to illustrate Dante. Since Lorenzino also commissioned the 'Primavera' and the 'Birth of Venus', his track record with regard to Botticelli may confidently be said to have been pretty good.

As Lord Clark points out in a typically comprehensive (though atypically stilted) introductory essay, Botticelli was an obsessive student of Dante. Like Michelangelo – whose Dante drawings are lost, if they ever existed – Botticelli had an intellectual commitment to the *Divine Comedy*, not just an emotional response. The task of illustrating the poem called on the full resources of both mind and heart. Everything he had to offer went on show. His full mental range, which is locked together so tightly in his paintings that only the erudite iconographical studies of scholars like Wind can spring it all loose, is in these drawings spread out so as to be easily intelligible and all the more wondered at.

It is not a matter of technical equipment. Botticelli knows and cares little about dramatic relief: though enormously more resourceful, he is still recognisably in the same world as Giotto. It took Gustave Doré, who in terms of theatricality was only a step away from Walt Disney, to echo something of Dante's immediate impact. But Doré echoed that impact romantically, by lighting a selected subject and casting the surroundings into shadow. Dante is never like that, and nor is Botticelli. It might be disappointing that Botticelli does not figuratively reflect the heroic stature Dante gives Farinata (*Inferno* X) or Ulysses (*Inferno* XXVI) but such losses in drama are more than made up for by the uniformly clear intensity of his draughtmanship – a linked narrative providing the exact graphic equivalent of Dante's closely focused language, which illuminates everything it touches.

Yet even with that said, it is still remarkable how often Botticelli *does* manage to capture something of his author's dramatic power. When Virgil and Dante catch a lift from the flying monster Geryon in *Inferno* XVII, Dante achieves the most amazing effects of flight: Geryon backs off from the rim of Malebolge and turns down and away like a glider. Botticelli gets the same effect by drawing Geryon in several positions, sliding back at a shallow angle and then tilting impassively down, the long hair on his eerily human head suddenly tousled by the air-stream and the rising thermals from the Eighth Circle. I must have looked at the drawing dozens of times before noticing what the wind does to Geryon's hair. Botticelli's *thoughtfulness* strikes you over and over again – an inexhaustible subtlety, delicacy made robust by force of imagination.

The gravity-defying ascent of Dante and Beatrice in *Paradiso* I is registered by Botticelli in a design that uncannily forecasts Michelangelo's visions of Christ floating from the tomb. The whole of the High Renaissance seems implicit in these drawings. Lord Clark points out the connection between Botticelli's and Leonardo's angels and indeed it is hard to miss: there is one in the drawings for *Purgatorio* XII that sharply recalls the Uffizi 'Annunciation'. But the drawings would count as a teeming source-book of concrete images even if they connected up with nobody except Botticelli himself. Nobody could look at Matilda gathering flowers in *Purgatorio* XXVIII without thinking of the 'Primavera'.

Botticelli's failures are few, and were sometimes Dante's in the first place. The two-page fold-out Satan (*Inferno* XXXIV) is an ape-suited heavy, but Dante's version is (whisper it) not much better. In the vexed case of Beatrice's arrival (*Purgatorio* XXIX and XXX), Botticelli actually comes close to redeeming the one unarguable flop in the whole poem. It is reasonable that Dante should weigh Beatrice down with allegorical trappings, but disappointing – and I can't believe it was anything else even at the time – to make her look like, of all things, an admiral. Botticelli has done a good job of injecting life into the symbolism and would have pulled off an unequivocal triumph if only he had done more for Beatrice's personal appearance. Instead of making her look like an admiral, he makes her look like Mr Roy Hattersley – a step in the right direction, but not far enough. Later in the drawings, however, she is suitably beautiful, especially in the sphere of Jupiter (*Paradiso* XX).

The true disappointments lie in the scenes unattempted,

or else gone missing. There is no drawing for *Paradiso* XXXI, in which Dante, at the height of his lucid imagination, describes Paradise as being like a giant white rose, with angels diving through it like bees. Imagine what Botticelli would have done with *that*. The drawing for *Inferno* V was purloined long ago – not surprisingly, since Paolo and Francesca have always been everybody's favourite Dante pin-ups.

Indeed Paolo and Francesca are as far as most non-Italians ever get with Dante, so it is doubly a shame that Lord Clark writes about Virgil talking to the tragic lovers. In fact it is Dante who talks to them: Virgil talks only to Dante. A venial slip, but indicative of a general bittiness in editorial control. Word-wise, the book is a dog's breakfast. Scholars are not likely to appreciate George Robinson's commentary if there are any more howlers like the one in his exposition of *Inferno* XIX, where the Pope upside down in the hole is identified as Boniface III. Even as a misprint for Boniface VIII, this would not pass, since the inverted pontiff happens to be Nicholas III, who mistakes *Dante* for Boniface VIII.

Let any such errors be corrected, however, and the volume would still be lumbered with John Ciardi's translations from Dante, of which the best you can say is that they are not as bad as Dorothy Sayers's. What the facing pages need, instead of the verbal ballast they have got now, is the relevant passages in the original language; a prose translation of established quality, such as Sinclair's; and a commentary which conveys something of what humanist scholars like Sapegno have done to synthesise the critical tradition. But failing all that, the book as it stands is still a treasure-house. Those unacquainted with Dante will find out a lot about Botticelli, and may rest assured that the more they get to know about the poem, the more they will be gratified by how the poet's luminous originality survives undimmed in the artist's disciplined fragility of line.

(*New Statesman*, 1977)

As a Matter of Tact

***Responses: Prose Pieces 1953–1976* by Richard Wilbur (Harcourt Brace Jovanovich, New York and London)**

THERE is nothing surprising in the fact that the most intelligent, fastidious and refined of contemporary American poets should produce intelligent, fastidious and refined prose, but it does no harm to have the likelihood confirmed. This collection of Richard Wilbur's critical writings is an immediate pleasure to read. Beyond that, the book provides an absorbing tour of Wilbur's preoccupations, which admirers of his poetry had already guessed to be of high interest. Beyond that again, there is the harsh matter, steadily becoming more urgent, of whether or not the study of literature is killing literature.

In America, the place where crises burst first, it has long been apparent that the output of critical works from the universities, most of them uttered by intellectually mediocre student teachers, has reached the proportions of an ecological disaster. Yet here is one book, written by a Professor of English at Wesleyan University, which would have to be saved from the holocaust if President Carter were to take the sensible step of rationalising his energy programme by ordering all academic writings on the subject of English literature to be fed directly to the flames, thereby ensuring that useless books, inflated from only slightly less useless doctoral theses, would find at least a semblance of creative life by providing enough electric power to light a pig-sty, if only for a few seconds.

But then Wilbur is no ordinary professor. His university career has really been a kind of monastic hideaway, where he has been able to hole up and contemplate his principal early experience, which was the Second World War in Europe. Military service was Wilbur's first university. If for ever afterwards he was a writer in residence, at least he was writing about something that he had seen in the outside world. In the deceptively elegant symmetries of Wilbur's early poetry could be detected a pressure of awareness which amply warranted his retreat to the cloisters.

While his contemporaries held the mirror up to chaos, Wilbur took the opposite line: the more extreme the thing contained, the more finely-wrought the container had to be. Berryman and Lowell went in for stringy hair, open-necked shirts, non-rhyming sonnets that multiplied like bacilli, and nervous breakdowns. Wilbur, on the other hand, looked like an advertisement for Ivy League tailoring and turned out poems built like Fabergé toy trains. I think there is a case for arguing that by the time the 1960s rolled around Wilbur had cherished his early experience too long for the good of his work, which in his later volumes is simply indecisive. But earlier on he was not indecisive at all – just indirect, which is a different thing. The poems in *The Beautiful Changes*, *Ceremony* and *Things of This World* sound better and better as time goes on. Where his coevals once looked fecund, they now look slovenly; where he once seemed merely exquisite, he now seems a model of judicious strength; as was bound to happen, it was the artful contrivance which retained its spontaneity and the avowedly spontaneous which ended up looking contrived. There is no reason to be ashamed at feeling charmed by Wilbur's poetry. The sanity of his level voice is a hard-won triumph of the contemplative intelligence.

Selected from twenty years of occasional prose, the essays and addresses collected in *Responses* combine conciseness with resonance, each of them wrapping up its nominal subject while simultaneously raising all the relevant general issues – the best kind of criticism for a student to read. A lecture like 'Round About a Poem of Housman's' could be put into a beginner's hands with some confidence that it would leave him wiser than before, instead of merely cockier. Previously available only in that useful anthology *The Moment of Poetry*, the piece gains from being set among others from the same pen. It is an excellent instance of close reading wedded to hard thinking. The general statements are as tightly focused as the specific observations, which from so sensitive a reader are very specific indeed. By attending patiently to Housman's delicately judged tones of voice in 'Epitaph on an Army of Mercenaries', Wilbur is able to show that the contempt superficially evinced for the hired soldiers is meant to imply an underlying respect. The casual reader might miss this not just through being deaf to poetry, but through being deaf to meaning in general. 'A tactful person is one who understands not merely what is said, but also what is meant.' But meaning is not confined to statements: in fact the sure way to miss the point of Housman's poem is to do a practical criticism that confines itself to paraphrase. A song like 'It's Only A Paper Moon' and a poem like 'Dover Beach' can be paraphrased in exactly the same way. (This seemingly off-hand illustration is typical of Wilbur's knack for the perfect example.) It follows that meaning embraces not just statement but sound, pacing, diction. Thus the subject expands to include questions of why poetry is written the way it is. How much can the poet legitimately expect the reader to take in?

Yeats, for example, overdoes his allusions in 'King and No King'. It is one thing for Milton to expect you to spot the reference to the *Aeneid* when Satan wakes in Hell, but another for Yeats to expect you to know a bad play by Beaumont and Fletcher. For one thing, you can see what Milton means even if you have never read Virgil, whereas Yeats's point seems not to be particularly well made even when you have Beaumont and Fletcher at your fingertips – in fact pride at being in possession of such information is likely to colour your judgment. (Says Wilbur, who *did* possess such information, and whose judgment *was* coloured.)

It is worth pausing at this juncture to say that in a few paragraphs Wilbur has not only raised, but to a large extent settled, theoretical points which more famous critical savants have pursued to the extent of whole essays. In *Lectures in America* Dr Leavis argues, with crushing intransigence, that Yeats's poetry needs too much ancillary apparatus to explain it, so that when you get right down to it there are only two poems in Yeats's entire *oeuvre* which earn the status of a 'fully achieved thing'. Wilbur takes the same point exactly as far as it should be taken, which is nowhere near as far. Possessing tact himself, he can see Yeats's lack of it, but correctly supposes this to be a local fault, not a typical one. If Dr Leavis is unable to consider such a possibility, perhaps it might be of interest to Professor Donoghue, who in a recent issue of the *New York Review of Books* was to be heard complaining about Yeats's limitations at some length. It is a bit steep when an academic who devotes half his life to a dead poet starts doubting the poet's merits instead of questioning the effects of his own bookishness.

As for Wilbur's reference to Milton, well, it is very relevant to some of the positions adopted by Dr Steiner, whose important gift of transmitting his enthusiasm for the culture of the past seriously overstepped itself in Milton's case. Perhaps goaded by the misplaced self-confidence of a student generation who not only knew nothing about the history of civilisation but had erected their doltishness into an ideology, Dr Steiner declared that you couldn't tell what was going on in *Paradise Lost* unless you were intimate with the classical literature to which Milton was alluding. Wilbur's fleeting look at this very topic helps remind us that Dr Steiner got it wrong two ways at once. If you *did* have to know about those things, then Milton would not deserve his reputation. But you *don't* have to know, since the allusions merely reinforce what Milton is tactful enough to make plain.

Such matters are important to criticism and crucial to pedagogy. For all Dr Steiner's good intentions, it is easy to imagine students being scared off if they are told that they can't hope to read an English poet without first mastering classical literature. Wilbur's approach, while being no less concerned about the universality of culture, at least offers the ignoramus some hope. Anyway, Wilbur simply happens to be right: poets allude to the past (his essay 'Poetry's Debt to Poetry' shows that all revolutions in art are palace revolutions) but if they are original at all then they will make their first appeal on a level which demands of the reader no more than an ability to understand the language. Which nowadays is demanding a lot, but let that pass.

'Poetry and Happiness' is another richly suggestive piece of work. Wilbur talks of a primitive desire that is radical to poetry, 'the desire to lay claim to as much of the world as possible through uttering the names of things'. Employing the same gift for metaphysical precision which he demonstrates elsewhere in his essay on Emily Dickinson, Wilbur is able to show what forms this desire usually takes and how it affects the poet's proverbial necessity to 'find himself'. I don't think it is too facetious to suggest that this might be a particularly touchy subject for Wilbur. Complaining about the lack of unity in American culture, he seems really to be talking about his own difficulties in writing about the American present with the same unforced originality – finding yourself – which marked his earlier poems about Europe.

In the following essay, a fascinating piece (indispensable for the student of his poems) called 'On My Own Work', he rephrases the complaint as a challenge. 'Yet the incoherence of America need not enforce a stance of alienation on the poet: rather, it may be seen as placing on him a peculiar imaginative burden.' It is a nice point whether Wilbur has ever really taken that burden up. I am inclined to think that hc has not, and that the too-typical quietness of his later work ('characteristic', in the sense Randall Jarrell meant when he decided that Wallace Stevens had fallen to copying himself) represents a great loss to all of us. But we ought to learn to be appropriately grateful for what we have been given, before we start complaining about what has been taken away.

'It is one mark of the good critic', Wilbur observes, 'that he abstains from busywork.' Except for the essays on Poe, which tend to be repetitive, this whole collection has scarcely a superfluous sentence. When Wilbur's critical sense lapses, it is usually through kindness. He makes as good a case as can be made for Theodore Roethke's openness to influence, calling admirable what he should see to be crippling. But even full-time critics can be excused for an occasional disinclination to tell the cruel truth, and on the whole this is a better book of criticism than we can logically expect a poet to come up with. If there is a gulf between English and American literature in modern times, at least there are some interesting bridges over it. The critical writings produced by some of the best American poets form one of those bridges. Tate, Berryman, Jarrell, John Peale Bishop, Edmund Wilson – those among them who were primarily critics were still considerable poets, and those among them who were primarily poets have yet managed to produce some of the most humane criticism we possess. With this superlative book, Richard Wilbur takes a leading place among their number.

(*New Statesman*, 1977)

These Staggering Questions

**_Critical Understanding: The Powers and Limits of Pluralism_ by Wayne Booth
(University of Chicago Press, Chicago and London)**

PREVIOUS books by Wayne C. Booth, especially *The Rhetoric of Fiction*, have been well received in the academic world. Since it first made its appearance in the early 1960s, *The Rhetoric of Fiction* has gone on to establish itself as a standard work – a touchstone of sanity. Probably the same thing will happen to the book under review. *Critical Understanding* is such a civilised treatise that I felt guilty about being bored stiff by it.

I had better say at the outset that I didn't find *The Rhetoric of Fiction* too thrilling either. A prodigious range of learning is expressed in hearteningly straightforward prose, but the effect is to leave you wondering what special use there is in presenting the student with yet another codified list of rhetorical devices. Separated from the works of fiction in which Professor Booth has so ably detected them, these devices are lifeless except as things to be memorised for the passing of examinations. There is also a strong chance that any student who spends much time studying rhetorical devices will not read the works of fiction, or will read them with his attention unnaturally focused on technical concerns.

Worrying about what students might do is the kind of activity which such books – even when they are as well done as Professor Booth's – inevitably arouse. But any student who could get seriously interested in *Critical Understanding* would have to be potty or else old before his time. You can't help wondering why it is thought to be good that the study of literature should so tax the patience. After all, literature doesn't. Boring you rigid is just what literature sets out not to do.

It could be said that abstract speculation about literature is an activity impossible to stop, so that we should give thanks to see a few pertinent books cropping up among the impertinent ones. It could be said, to the contrary, that the whole business should be allowed to sink under its own weight. By now the latter argument looks the more attractive, if for no other reason than that life is very short. But for the moment let us assume that good books like this are justified in their existence by the corrective they offer to bad books like this. Let us be grateful for Booth's civilised manner and powers of assimilation. The question then arises about whether his argument makes any sense in its own terms.

Critical Understanding purports to help us think coherently about 'the immensely confusing world of contemporary literary criticism'. There is nothing immensely, or even mildly, confusing about the world of contemporary literary criticism. The world of contemporary literary criticism does not exist. There is only criticism – an activity which goes on. It goes on in various ways; ways which it suits Professor Booth's book to call 'modes'; 'modes' which he thinks are hard to reconcile with one another, so that a world of confusion is generated, to which we need a guide. He is a very patient guide, but in the long run it is usually not wise to thank someone for offering to clarify an obfuscation which he is in fact helping to create.

Critical 'modes' have no independent existence worth bothering about. They are not like the various branches of science – an analogy Professor Booth seems always to be making in some form or other, even while strenuously claiming to eschew it. The various branches of science are impersonal in the sense that anybody qualified can pursue them. But a critical 'mode' is never anything except an emphasis, usually a false one. It is an expression of the critic's personality. The critical personality is the irreducible entity in criticism just as the artistic personality is the irreducible entity in art. Critical 'modes' can be reconciled with one another only by taking the personality out of them. Since there is no way of doing this without depriving them of content, they remain irreconcilable. You can call it confusion if you like, but to worry about it is a waste of time.

Professor Booth has all the time in the world. There is not room in this article or indeed in the whole paper to demonstrate by quotation his strolling expansiveness of argument. To summarise his line of thought is like trying to scoop air into a heap. But as far as I understand *Critical Understanding*, it offers pluralism as the solution to the alleged problem of reconciling the various critical 'modes'. Three versions of pluralism are examined, belonging respectively to Ronald S. Crane, Kenneth Burke and M. H. Abrams. Professor Booth does his best, at terrific length, to reconcile these three different pluralisms with each other, but finally they don't seem able to settle down together except within the even bigger and better pluralism which is Professor Booth's own.

In Professor Booth's amiably loquacious style of discourse very little goes without saying, but if anything were to, it would be that pluralism is better than monism. Professor Booth defines his terms with both rigour and subtlety. Trying to convey his definitions in a sentence or two, one is bound to play fast and loose. But as far as I can tell, a monist believes in his own 'mode' and can't see the point of anybody else's. The pluralist might favour a 'mode' of his own but he is able to admit that the other fellow's 'mode' might have something in it. I keep putting inverted commas around 'mode', not just because of my uncertainty as to what a 'mode' is, but because of strong doubts about whether there is any such thing. I suspect a critical 'mode' is a critical method. If it is, then it is necessary to insist once again that there is really no such thing. There is just criticism, an activity to which various critics contribute. It is neither monism nor pluralism to say this: it is just realism. A critic's method might help him to find things out but we don't wait for his method to collapse before deciding that he is talking rubbish. Nor is it our method that detects faults in his method. We reason about his reasoning, and that's it.

Professor Booth's pluralism has a plural nature of its own, alas. When he means by pluralism that there is a multiplicity of valid critical modes or methods and that some of these might be irreconcilable, I am afraid he does not mean much. When he means by pluralism that the only real critical mode or method, criticism, is pursued in different ways and areas by various critics, he means something, even if not a lot. The latter interpretation of the word, however, would not yield up a long book, or even a long article. The first interpretation has the advantage of providing limitless opportunities to burble on. It offers all the dangerous excitement of the Uncertainty Principle.

Professor Booth is a trained thinker and I am not, so he knows at least as well as I do that the theory of Relativity in physics lends no support to the concept of relativism in metaphysics. No relativist could have come up with Relativity. Einsteinian physics are no excuse for treating reality as a piece of elastic. Nor is the Uncertainty Principle any excuse for thinking that a proposition can hover between true and false. Einstein didn't like the Uncertainty Principle very much, believing that the Old One does not play dice. Unable to arrive at a Unified Field theory which would reconcile his own theories with other theories which seemed equally powerful, he was constrained to see his own proofs within a pluralist frame. For Professor Booth, this fact is too tempting to resist. Try as he might, he can't help suggesting that

Einstein found certain lines of inquiry inconsistent with one another. He wishes his own pluralism on Einstein.

But Einstein's pluralism, in so far as it existed, had nothing to do with finding certain lines of inquiry irreconcilable with one another. He never gave up on the possibility of a Unified Field. He just gave up on his own chances of finding it. Einstein believed that there was only one mode or method of scientific inquiry – scientific inquiry.

Different things which had been uncovered by scientific inquiry might be hard to match up with each other – hard even for him – but there was no reason to think that scientific inquiry would not be able to match them up eventually, although probably part of the result would be to open fresh gaps. That was the extent of Einstein's pluralism. It was the humble admission, by a supremely realistic thinker, that not everything could be done at once by one person. It had nothing to do with superficially exciting notions about the irreconcilability of modes. Einstein thought too concretely to get interested in stuff like that.

Lesser minds are perhaps more susceptible. Pluralism might be on the verge of becoming a fad, like ecology or macrobiotic diet. Beyond that, it could easily become a cult, like Scientology. It would be a pity to see Einstein posthumously co-opted into the role of L. Ron Hubbard. The same thing could happen to Sir Isaiah Berlin, who has been getting praise in the reviews for his alleged pluralism. To a certain extent he has brought this on himself, for appearing to be impressed by Machiavelli's discovery of incompatible moralities. Machiavelli thought, among other things, that the Prince needed to be cruel in order to be kind – in other words, that ends justified means. When it comes to practice, the evidence in favour of this proposition is not noticeably better than the evidence against it, especially if Italy is your field of study. Anyway for the decent politician there is no choice: he tries to do the liberal thing in small matters as in large, just as Sir Isaiah himself would, if he was put in charge of a state.

Sir Isaiah's cast of mind is better represented by his admiration for Herzen, who distrusted the idea that good ends could be brought about by bad means. Sir Isaiah's pluralism is really just the ability to get interested in a lot of different fields. What makes him a distinguished thinker is the way he combines vitality with range and penetration. It would be sad if his sympathy for Machiavelli reinforced the notion that there is some sort of philosophical endorsement to be had for living your life to a double standard. Sir Isaiah, or any other considerable thinker who finds himself saddled with the description 'pluralist', should do his best to buck it off. On those terms, pluralism can make any featherbrain a philosopher.

Professor Booth is a solid enough thinker, but he is far too apt to proclaim himself stymied when faced with the huge task of bringing order out of chaos. It would be better for his own morale, although it would lead to much shorter books, if he realised that the chaos is a mirage and that the order he brings out of it is largely uninformative. He pronounces himself daunted by the challenge of reconciling all the differently valid ways of critically responding to a poem. The luckless poem chosen for purposes of demonstration is Auden's 'Surgical Ward'. Auden would probably have some short, sharp things to say if he were to rise from the dead and join the discussion. He might as well: he can't be getting much peace down there, when you consider how much he is being talked about up here.

Scrupulous in his pluralism, Professor Booth offers us his educated guess at how each of his three paradigm thinkers would approach this poem. We have to take it for granted that he is faithful to their respective modes, although an independent observer might point out that the modes can't be up to much if somebody else can take them over so easily. Be that as it may, it turns out that the three modes scarcely even begin to jibe, whereupon the awed Professor Booth gives forth plangent threnodies, of which the following is merely a sample: 'Regardless of whether Ronald Crane finds any one sonnet or an entire sequence to be a beautiful construct, or whether Kenneth Burke finds Auden grappling effectively with the task of curing his or the reader's ills, the "Abrams test" remains: Does an intelligent, sensitive and informed historian find the sonnets responding to years of inquiry and to his effort to write a major history of the poem-as-moment? It is in the nature of the case that we shall quite probably never know the answer to that question.'

Clearly Professor Booth envisages a discussion that can never end. The reader might have difficulty in seeing how it can even start, if it has to be conducted using terms like 'a major history of the poem-as-moment' or (from elsewhere in the book) 'the need for overstanding'. But for the moment-as-moment we can grant that Professor Booth has brought us face to face with the unknown, perhaps even the unknowable. After all, a poem is much more complicated than a cone in space. Professor Booth makes much of this cone. If an observer sees the cone from end on, he thinks it is a circle. If the observer sees the cone from the side, he thinks it is a triangle. How can the observer be sure what he is seeing?

The answer is that he has to go on looking from different points of view, but not necessarily indefinitely. If *we* found out that the thing was a cone, why shouldn't he? Eventually he will either find out what we know or will just act on less-than-complete information. But there is no great mystery. Here as elsewhere with Professor Booth's examples, it is necessary to point out that the matter he has raised is a mare's nest. When the observer sees the base of the cone and calls the object a circle, it makes just as much sense to say that he has got things right as that he has got things wrong. He has *begun* to get things right, and within a reasonable time could well arrive at a proper identification of the object. That might open additional questions – such as what the cone is made of, or who put it there – but to say that a discussion never ends doesn't mean that we don't reach conclusions. Indeed if we didn't reach conclusions along the way there could be no discussion.

A poem is certainly a much more complicated thing than a cone in space, but there is less, rather than more, reason for carrying on as if it presented a challenge to the 'inadequacy' of our modes or methods. Unless the ordinary reader is mentally defective he starts getting the poem right straight away. He might not be very sure of what it is, but he can immediately start being reasonably sure of what it isn't. After a glance at 'Surgical Ward' you can see that there are a number of things it might be about. But that number is small compared with the large number of things it is manifestly not about. It is not about the fall of Rome, for example. Auden wrote a poem about that subject, but this one is not it.

So the reader, though he might be puzzled, is not completely in the dark. He can see roughly what area of experience is being talked about, and will probably concede that the reason why he can't see more clearly is that what is being talked about is something oblique, which is doubtless why Auden has expressed it in the form of a poem. He will give Auden credit for knowing what he is trying to get at, and will be slow to cross the line into that speculative territory where it is possible to suggest that Auden doesn't know what he is up to and that the poem's deepest and truest meaning is something the author had no knowledge of. The ordinary reader's ordinary reading is already a very decisive business.

Indeed it is not all that easy to see the inferiority of what the ordinary reader does by reading intelligently to what the professional critic does by applying his mode or method. A critic would have to be pretty conceited to imagine that he does a better job than the ordinary reader of deciding what the poem is about. For one thing, the ordinary reader might be more responsive than the critic.

A public, however small, is what establishes a poem, or any other work of art, as worthwhile. This public might be so small as to consist entirely of critics, but such is rarely the case. Criticism might guide the public's attention to the work of art, but unless the public responds then the work of art is a dead duck. To the public's response there is always something that informed criticism can add, but it is never as much or as important as what the public has decided on its own account. Sensibility comes first and most, formal intellect last and least. An extreme case is that of Mallarmé, who was derided as nonsensical even by fellow writers. But there was always a public who stuck by him, out of faith that anything which sounded so lovely must mean something. The meaning of some of Mallarmé's poems will never be entirely clear. This represents, if you like, a genuinely endless challenge to criticism. But it would be a very trivial critic who believed that the real work of appreciation had not already been done, long ago and by nameless amateurs.

A good critic is always an ordinary reader in the first instance. A bad critic, not being that, is usually obliged to come up with an angle in order to stay in business. If he contented himself with saying what he found to be true, he would sound platitudinous to everybody else, like that guileless American professor of drama who discovered Jimmy Porter's monologue to be composed of both long and short sentences. So he relies on his mode or method to produce impressive results on his behalf. Structuralism, in this regard, is the greatest invention since pig Latin. It can make any idiot sound unfathomable.

'When a man talks of system,' said Byron, 'his case is hopeless.' To the extent that they are systems, critical modes or methods are aberrations. They are usually ways for mediocrities to make themselves sound interesting. Occasionally a first-rate critic is to be found promoting a mode or method but the mode or method has little value in itself except as a change of tack. The critical responses occasioned by the mode or method will be of value only to the extent that they express the critic's individuality, always supposing that he possesses such a thing. Valéry (whose *Introduction à la poétique* Professor Booth might care to reread, in order to study the virtues of a short book) believed that a writer's artistic personality was a different thing from his personality in everyday life. He was preceded in this belief by Croce, for whom the separateness of the real-life personality and the artistic one was fundamental to his aesthetic system. It was, and continues to be, a good principle, but in practice Croce didn't hesitate to blame Verlaine's artistic inadequacies on the immorality of the poet's private life. Croce sabotaged his own system because he had something he couldn't resist saying. He thought that the test of aesthetics lay in the ability to write criticism. In fact, however, his criticism does not always square up with his aesthetics. If it did, it would not be live criticism, which finds its consistency in its own vitality, and not in relation to a supposedly logical framework.

Professor Booth's three exemplary thinkers all seem to possess individual critical minds. Hence it is no mystery that their separate lines of approach are hard to match up. The mystery would be if the opposite were the case. Nevertheless Professor Booth agonises about 'these staggering questions' over many pages assigned to each thinker and many more pages assigned to the supposed conundrum that what they have to say as individuals is hard to reduce to a single order of collective sense. Crane's pluralism, it emerges, has mainly to do with approaching poetry in terms of poetics. He is a 'splitter', meaning that he makes precise discriminations. Burke's pluralism takes more heed of something called 'dramatism'. He is a 'lumper', making large claims about what the poem 'does for' the writer and the reader. Abrams takes a more historicist approach. But they are all three pluralists about modes and methods within their respective spheres, and since Professor Booth finds himself bound to be pluralist about *them*, he ends up worried about whether he has involved himself in an infinite regress, although he has apparently failed to notice the further possibility that somebody else might come along and start being pluralist about *him*.

Perhaps he is trying to thrill himself about the chance of being sucked down a black hole. For those of us with less time on our hands his dilemma looks to be no big deal. From his summaries of them, the three thinkers seem fairly human. Crane, indeed, sounds too finely discriminating to be summarised at all. As I remember his work from my student days, he commands the rare power of straightforward critical argument. The reason why Crane would not be capable of Burke's perfectly recognisable brand of hoopla has nothing to do with modes or methods. Crane has got his head screwed on. Apparently Burke has never abandoned his belief that his invented line 'Body is turd, turd body' says something penetrating about Keats.

'How can we choose among criticisms,' asks the blurb anxiously, 'if we reject the scepticism that would cancel them all?' But these are false alternatives. It is not scepticism that would cancel all 'criticisms', it is simple realism that denies independent existence to any such entities. Criticism is not a science. Scientific truths would still be true if there were no humans. Critical truths are by and about minds. In order to pursue critical inquiry, humans sometimes produce systems of thought. These systems of thought may yield a certain amount of truth, from which in turn we may assimilate as much truth as we are capable of apprehending. But to set about reconciling the systems themselves is like drawing up plans for a centralised world laundry.

Criticism is simply a talent, like any other talent. Some people can tell chalk from cheese just by looking at them. Others can't tell the difference even when they taste them. But to say that criticism is simply a talent doesn't mean that a talent is something simple. A talent, both to those who possess it and to those who appreciate it, feels as rich and various as life itself. The question of whether or not critical talent is an allotrope of creative talent is beyond me. The fact that the two talents are so often present in the one head leads me to suspect that they are the same thing in different forms. Perhaps the gift of scientific investigation is yet another form. But I don't need to wait for these suspicions to be confirmed or denied before suggesting that criticism and art have a certain relationship to one another which can't be reaffirmed too often, since it is in the interests of mediocre practitioners in both fields to mix up what ought to be kept separate.

Criticism is not indispensable to art. It is indispensable to civilisation – a more inclusive thing. When Pushkin lamented the absence of criticism in Russia, he wasn't begging for assistance in writing poems. He wanted to write them in a civilised country. Literary criticism fulfils its responsibility by contributing to civilisation, whose dependence on criticism in all its forms is amply demonstrated by what happens when critical inquiry is forbidden. Being indispensable to civilisation should be a big enough ambition for any critic. Unfortunately some critics, not always the less gifted, want to be indispensable to art. In Great Britain the extreme case of this aberration was F. R. Leavis, who behaved as if creativity had passed out of the world with D. H. Lawrence and could only be brought back by the grace and favour of his own writings. A powerful critical talent who destroyed his own sense of proportion, Leavis was our brush with totalitarianism: we caught it as a mild fever instead of the full attack of meningitis. His career was the clearest possible proof that the course the arts take is not under the control of criticism, which must either pursue its own ends or else turn silly.

Professor Booth is too humble to be a dictator. He knows his place. The worst thing you can say about him is that his place sounds so comfortable. As George M. Pullman Distinguished Service Professor of English at the University of Chicago he is obviously doing all right. Most young academics, I fear, would like to be him. It was almost better when they wanted to be F. R. Leavis. At least what they got up to in those days could not be mistaken for anything useful, mainly because anybody who could submit himself to such absolutism had to be self-selectingly obsequious. But nowadays you can build an impregnable career out of polite waffle. If Professor Booth wants to be worried about something, he should worry about that. He should turn his attention to the sociology of academicism.

Nobody objects to proper scholarship. The literary community would be sunk without it. As a denizen of Grub Street I become more and more aware that a thick fog would soon descend if scholarship and learned commentary were not kept up in the universities. Grub Street and the university make a bad marriage but a worse divorce. One can be glad that the universities continue to produce a steady output of solid work. One can even be glad that the livelier academic wits continue to moonlight in Grub Street, even though some of them – especially the ones based in Oxford – seem bent on staying precocious until the grave. But what makes the heart quail is the exponentially-increasing amount of abstract speculation in book form, most of it emanating from proponents of one mode or another. There have been important books of speculation about literature, but they have usually been written by such men as Auerbach and Curtius –

mature, greatly learned critical minds who affirmed the permanent values of civilisation by their response to the historical forces which threatened it with annihilation. Those who spent their lives in universities did so as real scholars, not as arid metaphysicians in opportunistic search of a marketable subject.

The PhD system continues to breed thousands of young academics who have no intention of ever setting foot outside the university for the rest of their lives. Not many of them could write an essay you would want to read. Knowing this – or, even worse, not knowing it – they write whole books that aren't even meant to be read. In both America and Britain it has become standard practice to publish PhD theses as books. A great many of these publications are abstract metaphysical speculation of no value whatsoever. Some comfort can be taken from the fact that nothing is directly threatened except the forests that must be felled to make so much paper. Graduates in English show no sign as yet of emulating those Italian sociology students who would sooner blow your kneecaps off than argue the point. But in the long run it can't be good that boys and girls are being encouraged to pontificate at book length on topics about which wise men and women would consider it presumptuous to venture an aphorism.

Also there is the likelihood – some would say it is already an actuality – that the sheer volume of interpretation on offer will become a demand creating its own supply. The best route to success for a dull artist might be to create a work that needs interpretation. On the other hand, the bright artist might go out of his way to avoid the attentions of the waiting owls. The result could be a seriously split literary culture, with the dummies pretending to be clever and the clever people masquerading as oafs. We have seen something like this already in the determination of Amis and Larkin – both of them deeply cultivated – to sound like philistines rather than co-operate with the kind of academic industrialism which separates the work of art from the common people. Durrenmatt forecast just such a schism when he made his resonant comment about the necessity to create works of art which would weigh nothing in the scales of respectability. Dodging respectability can be quite fun but with the onset of middle age it tends to get wearing.

Critical Understanding is about as good a book as you can get of its type, yet there is nothing in it which could not have been said in a compressed, allusive article a few thousand words long. In my copy pages 347–78 were missing but I can't say I was sorry. There were still nearly four hundred pages left, scarcely one of them without its suavely muted cry of anguish about the problem of being pluralistic without being eclectic. There is no such problem. To be pluralistic without being eclectic all you have to be is consistent. But really you don't have to worry even about that. Consistency comes with the ability, and vanishes with the lack of it, to see things as they are.

(*London Review of Books*, 1980)

Part Four

THE GIANT IN THE EAST

Nabokov's Grand Folly

Eugene Onegin: A Novel in Verse
by Aleksandr Pushkin, translated from the Russian, with a commentary, by Vladimir Nabokov (Routledge & Kegan Paul, London, and Princeton University Press, Princeton, New Jersey)

Nabokov Translated: A Comparison of Nabokov's Russian and English Prose **by Jane Grayson (Oxford University Press, London and New York)**

IN THE week of his death, it is instructive to remember that Nabokov's translation of *Eugene Onegin* was a project dear to his heart. Expert opinions of the recent second edition were not much more favourable than they were for the first, mainly because the translator had not done enough to eliminate what were earlier judged to be eccentricities of diction, while the commentary obstinately remained unmodified in all its idiosyncrasies. There is undoubtedly a sense in which the whole enterprise is a great folly. But even those Russianists who have been most inclined to question Nabokov's success in transmitting the essence of Pushkin are usually willing to concede that this cranky monument of scholarship might at least come in useful to the beginner.

As it happens, I am in a position to test this idea, being very much a beginner with Pushkin, and therefore in dire need of a good crib. Pushkin is never wilfully complicated, but his simplicities can be highly compressed. There are times when even an advanced student of the language is certain to need help, while the stumbler is likely to bog down completely. I should say at the outset that in several respects

Nabokov's Folly serves the turn. It is a work to be valued, although even the tyro is bound to find it silly as well as brilliant.

The ideal crib, of course, should merely be the servant of the original. But Nabokov was incapable of being anybody's servant, even his admired Pushkin's: in paying homage to his giant predecessor he did his best to keep his own ego in the background, but ever and anon it shouldered its way forward. Nabokov's theory of translation was based on 'humble fidelity' to the original, yet try as he might to give us nothing more pretentious than a word-for-word equivalent, he still managed to make Pushkin sound like Nabokov.

Nor is the commentary free from quirks. In fact it is largely made up of them. He has set out to be more scholarly than the scholars; it is doubtful whether anybody else inside or outside Russia knows as much about Pushkin; but you don't have to know a thousandth as much to realise that Nabokov is no more *reasonable* on this subject than on any other. I switch to the present tense because it would be unfitting to talk about the author of so cantankerous a commentary as if he were not alive – he is at you all the time, continually asserting himself against those hordes of translators and academics who have either misunderstood Pushkin or, worse, understood him too quickly. But there are limits to how far insight can go without common sense to back it up.

Following Gautier, Nabokov thought the ideal translation should be an interlinear lexicon. The theory is ably expounded by Jane Grayson in her painstaking *Nabokov Translated*, a book which has the additional merit of showing that in the case of his own writings the master is tactfully flexible about putting it into practice. But where *Eugene Onegin* is concerned there can apparently be no departure from dogma. Throughout the commentary, Nabokov is forever telling you the words he *might* have used in the translation if he had set out to do anything so misguided as convey the spirit of the original. But no, he has resisted against overwhelming odds: awkwardness is not only not to be avoided, it is positively to be sought, if that happens to be the price of exactitude.

There is something in this view, although not as much as Nabokov thinks. It is true that a translator who sets out to render the 'spirit' is likely to traduce the original author. But Nabokov's paroxysms of accuracy traduce Pushkin's spirit as thoroughly as any academic poetaster has ever done. He makes Pushkin sound like a Scrabble buff. Certainly there are words in Pushkin that don't now mean what they once did, and even words that would have seemed odd at the time. Hence the modern foreign reader's need for more help than an ordinary dictionary can provide. But none of this means that Pushkin wants to be puzzling. On the contrary, what impresses you about him is his unforced naturalness of tone. The sad thing about Nabokov's translation is that he is not really capable of echoing such a quality. Instead, he dithers pedantically in the very area of verbal sophistication which for Pushkin was never more than a playground.

It is well known that Nabokov keeps saying 'mollitude' where either 'bliss' or 'languor' would have done. Sometimes you can make a better case for 'bliss' than for 'languor' and sometimes vice versa, but what nobody normal can doubt is that there is no case to be made for 'mollitude'. Yet after all the uproar which greeted his use of 'mollitude' in the first edition, here it still is in the second, having the effect, every time it appears, of wrinkling the reader's brow. The idea behind using 'mollitude' is evidently to convey something of the Russian word's Frenchified feeling. But 'mollitude' does nothing to make the English reader think of French influence. It just makes him think about the weight of the OED.

At least he can find 'morgue' in the *Concise*, defined in roughly the same way Nabokov uses it, to mean 'arrogance'. But arrogance is scarcely the first thing an English reader thinks of when he sees the word 'morgue'. He thinks of dead bodies on zinc tables. Why not just use 'arrogance'? The answer, I'm afraid, is that Nabokov wants to indulge himself in the Euphuism of 'I marvelled at their modeish morgue'. (In the introduction we learn of Onegin and Lensky that 'both are blasé, bizarre beaux'. Always the virtuoso of his adopted tongue, Nabokov never quite grasped that half the trick of composing in English is *not* to write alliteratively.)

Why use 'trinkleter' where 'haberdasher' would have done? Why 'larmoyant' for 'lachrymose'? What does 'debile' give you that 'feeble' doesn't? Why 'cornuto' for 'cuckold'? Certainly the Russian word has horns which the Italian word reproduces. Unfortunately the Italian word is not in English. Nor is Nabokov correct in supposing that there is any word in *Inferno* III, 9, which might mean 'forever'. He quibbles so relentlessly himself that you would have to be a saint not to quibble back.

On this showing, Nabokov has no call to despise those less informed translators who have had the temerity to cast their versions in rhyme. His unrhyming version sounds at least as weird as the very worst of theirs. But as a crib it is the best available, especially in this second edition, where each line matches a line in the original – even, in many cases, to the extent of reproducing the word order. Worse than useless for the reader without Russian, for the learner Nabokov's translation would be just the ticket, if only the commentary were better balanced. But Nabokov's ambitions as a scholar are thwarted by his creativity. He starts shaping the facts before he has fully submitted himself to them. He is immensely knowing, but knowingness is not the same as knowledge.

Expending too much of his energy on being bitchy about other writers, scholars and critics, Nabokov the commentator sounds at best like A. E. Housman waspishly editing an obscure classic. At worst he sounds like A. L. Rowse trying to carry a daft point by sheer lung-power. Calling Dostoevsky 'a much over-rated, sentimental and Gothic novelist' is dull if it is meant to be funny and funny if it is meant to be serious. We are told that Balzac and Sainte-Beuve are 'popular but essentially mediocre writers'. I can't pretend to know much about Balzac, but I am reasonably familiar with Sainte-Beuve, and if he is mediocre then I am a monkey's uncle. Madame de Staël is thoroughly patronised ('a poor observer') without any mention being made of the fact that Pushkin himself thought highly of her. As for Tchaikovsky's version of *Eugene Onegin*, it is not a 'silly opera'. It is a great opera.

But most of this is casual snidery. Distortions of Pushkin's meaning are less forgivable. Commenting on the exchange of dialogue between Tatiana and her nurse, Nabokov, forgetting even to mention *Romeo and Juliet*, concentrates on discrediting the official Soviet view of the nurse as a Woman of the People. Yet that view is part of the truth. When the nurse talks about being given in marriage without regard to her own wishes, she is illuminating the condition of slavery. Tatiana might not be really listening to her, but Pushkin is listening, and so should the reader be. This acute social awareness runs right through Pushkin, building up all the time, until in the later prose he provides the model for the social consciousness of all the Russian literature to come. There is nothing naïve about taking cognizance of this elementary fact. Nabokov is naïve in trying to avoid it. Pushkin really *is* the Russian national poet, even if the Soviet regime says so. Above all, he is the national poet of all the people who have been persecuted by that regime in the name of an ideal of justice which Pushkin's very existence proves was once generous and merciful.

Nabokov seems determined to miss the point of what is going on even among the main characters. He tells us all about the books Tatiana has read but fails to notice her gifts of psychological penetration. He can't seem to accept that Tatiana ends by slamming the door in Onegin's face. He claims to detect in Tatiana's final speech 'a confession of love that must have made Eugene's experienced heart leap with joy'. Incredibly, the moral force of Tatiana's personality seems to have escaped him. Nor can he see that Onegin is arid and Lensky fruitful; that the difference between them is the same difference Pushkin saw between Salieri and Mozart; and that the outcome is the same – envy and revenge. Presuming to avoid sentimentality, Nabokov's homage diminishes its object, limiting the reader's view of the range of emotion which Pushkin embraced. Pushkin's artistic personality was the opposite of Nabokov's. Pushkin had negative capability. Not that Pushkin can be equated with Keats, even if you think of Keats's sensibility combined with Byron's airy manner. *Eugene Onegin's* stature is

Shakespearean: you have to imagine a Shakespeare play written with the formal compactness of a poem.

On technique Nabokov gives us what we had a right to expect from the man who invented John Shade. (If only Shade, instead of Charles Kinbote, had written this translation!) There is a long disquisition on prosody which is ruined by pseudo-science. (The spondee is proved mathematically not to exist.) But when Nabokov calls Pushkin's tetrameter 'an acoustical paradise', and takes time to examine the miracle of simple words producing great sonorities, he is writing criticism of the first order. He is also good on trees, houses, carriages, visitors' books, methods of travel, manners – although even here he can't resist going over the top. He finds himself saying that Pushkin was not especially sympathetic with the Russian landscape. There is a certain pathos about that, as if Nabokov were trying to insert himself into the physical reality of the old, lost Russia that will never now return. A doomed attempt and a superfluous one, since by pointing to the source of its literary tradition Nabokov has helped remind us of the Russia that really *is* undying, and in which his place is now secure.

(*New Statesman*, 1977)

Pushkin is the Sea

***Pushkin: The Complete Prose Tales* translated by Gillon R. Aitken (Michael Russell, Salisbury, Wiltshire)**

***Pushkin's Fairy Tales* translated by Janet Dalley with an introduction by John Bayley (Barrie & Jenkins, London, and Mayflower, New York)**

SOME would argue that it doesn't matter whether poetic masterpieces written in languages unknown to us are translated well or badly, since what makes them poetic is untranslatable by definition. Others would argue that unless translation is done as well as possible we can't even guess at what we are missing out on. Hardly anybody argues that a translation can be the equivalent of the original. Yet in 1977 the appearance of Charles Johnston's astonishing translation of *Eugene Onegin* powerfully suggested, even to those with no knowledge of the Russian language, that Pushkin really must be as good as he is generally cracked up to be. To those even fleetingly acquainted with the original text, Mr Johnston sounded like a sorcerer. He had duplicated the intricacy of Pushkin's stanza without notably cramping its naturalness of tone. Previously, translators had sacrificed the one in keeping the other – except, of course, for Nabokov, who had sacrificed both.

On sober inspection, it became evident that not even Mr Johnston had been able to do the impossible. Inevitably he was at a loss to reproduce the full range of mimetic effects made available to Pushkin by the lexical wealth of the Russian language and by his own genius. The sound keeps running thin. But even with all objections made, it is now possible to say that for the English-speaking reader Pushkin's magnitude as a poet is at last beyond conjecture. The inference is inescapable: only a great work could inspire so good a translation.

As Belinsky pointed out, Russian poets before Pushkin were rivers. Pushkin is the sea. He is the real beginning of Russian poetry, which is really all modern. So is Russian prose, since he is the real beginning of that too. He turned from poetry to prose towards the end of his short life. Russianists who once despaired of conveying the quality of Pushkin's poetry were and are fond of saying that the quality of his prose is even harder to transmit. But as with *Eugene Onegin* it would perhaps be better to wait for a palpably excellent translation before we decide that the prose is untranslatable.

The Complete Prose Tales was apparently first published in this country in 1962 as a paperback, which meant that it was not reviewed. When it appeared in hard covers in 1966, it was once more overlooked, on the assumption that it had been reviewed before. Now here it is again, incorporating 'some slight textual revisions'. It is a worthy volume which deserves an ungrudging welcome. Here is a handy guide to the contents of such important works as *The Tales of Belkin*, *Dubrovsky*, *The Queen of Spades* and *The Captain's Daughter*, plus many slighter things. But Mr Aitken can give you small idea of what was remarkable about the way Pushkin wrote them.

Pushkin's ideal of prose was ascetic. In his poetry he might indulge himself – although even his excesses were economical – but in his prose there is always an element of mortification. 'Precision and brevity,' he wrote. 'Without these, brilliant expression serves no purpose.' His model was Voltaire, whom the French by that time were beginning to find arid. As John Bayley tells us in his indispensable *Pushkin: A Comparative Commentary*, when Prosper Mérimée translated *The Tales of Belkin* he could not resist the impulse to juice up the style. Mr Aitken does his best to reproduce Pushkin's astringency, but he has the unhappy knack of padding a line without meaning to. There is a telling example in his rendition of *The Queen of Spades* (1833). '"The game fascinates me" said Hermann, "but I am not in the position to sacrifice (the) essentials (of life) in the hope of acquiring (the) luxuries."' This statement is attributed to Hermann twice during the course of the story. It is an epigram and should sound like one. It would possibly be better without the two 'the's which I have placed in brackets, although there is some excuse for putting them in, since Russian often leaves you the choice of whether to supply an article or not. But the other two words I have bracketed, 'of life', simply don't exist in the original and I can see no good reason for adding them.

Mr Aitken is no great shakes with dialogue. When anybody talks, the results sound stilted. He thus tends to slow down a story whose whole stylistic object is to speed up. But generally he is useful on details. It is an aberration, not a characteristic, when he says of the Countess: 'she removed the patches from her face.' The reference is to the Countess's early days in Paris, when she was a young beauty, not an old boot. Saying 'the patches' makes her sound like a heavily repaired inner tube. The original word, *mooshki*, actually means stick-on beauty spots. It is true that the contemporary English word for such cosmetic aids was, precisely, 'patches', but the same word will not serve the turn now. Even this miscalculation, however, springs from knowledge more than from ignorance: Mr Aitken is a keen and helpful student of the relevant social minutiae.

Despite its testingly elliptical style, *The Queen of Spades* was a big hit at the time. Pushkin noted in his correspondence that gamblers were punting according to the Countess's system. (The letter is quoted in Tatiana Wolff's brilliantly edited compendium *Pushkin on Literature*, which I should like to recommend in passing, since it is currently still on the shelves of the remainder shops. Even those with no time to set about learning Russian will find this book a richly stimulating work of humane scholarship.) With *The Captain's Daughter* (1836), however, Pushkin went beyond where his audience could immediately follow him. Here was the most advanced example he was ever to provide of what John Bayley has definitively called 'this uniform unexpressiveness which none the less expresses everything'. Unfortunately Mr Aitken's idea of uniform unexpressiveness is too often indistinguishable from ordinary flatness. For Pushkin, 'in a twinkling' is simply too twee a way of rendering the adverb *meegum*. And what is the point of saying 'frenzy of rage' where 'frenzy' would do? It is not even accurate. The woman is in despair at suddenly having noticed her husband hanging from a gibbet. Rage would come later.

These might seem minor points but in fact they strike to the root of the matter. Gogol said that compared with *The Captain's Daughter* all other Russian stories and novels seemed like sickly-sweet pulp. Tolstoy and Dostoevsky are both in a straight line of development from Pushkin's later prose. What Pushkin offered his contemporaries and successors was the possibility – conjured up seemingly from nowhere – of a medium which would interpose nothing between the reader and reality. Mr Aitken is just one more translator who has breathed on the glass. But at least he hasn't walked straight into it.

One of the many seductive things about learning Russian is that the fairy stories are often by great writers, so that you meet the giant talents in your first year. The story of Goldilocks and the Three Bears, for example, is told by Tolstoy. Pushkin set the fashion. The official Soviet critical line on Pushkin is that as a poet of the people he was schooled in the folk heritage of the motherland by his wise nurse, Arina Rodionovna. Certainly she must have been influential in helping him to develop his feeling for the Russian language even when the official tongue for one of his rank was French. But in fact it never mattered to him what his sources were, as long as they were vital. He was a world poet before he was a national one. His fairy tales are of acute artistic importance since they are early examples of his determination to tell stories in verse. They are first steps on the way to writing a whole novel in rhymed form. Any translator who chooses to render them in prose will be leaving a lot out.

Janet Dalley has rendered them in prose. Try as I might, I can't see that the resulting book has any more to offer than the standard rhymed translations churned out by the Soviet publishing houses. Russian illustrations might be sub-Disney but they are, superficially at least, more beguiling than the Arthur Boyd lithographs which bleakly adorn this volume. Mr Boyd would have to be a lot more penetrating than he is before the reader could stifle an atavistic yearning for a beautiful princess who actually looked like a beautiful princess, rather than a bunyip's mother.

The book's introductory note is written by none other than John Bayley. It rehearses the same points which are to be found more fully developed in the relevant section of *Pushkin: A Comparative Commentary*, where the reader will also discover that when Bayley translates a few lines of a Pushkin fairy tale for purposes of illustration, he comes up with far better results than those to which he is lending his imprimatur here. Bayley, too, is translating Pushkin's verse into prose, but at least the prose is accurate. In *The Golden Cockerel*, for example, when Pushkin writes 'The whole capital shuddered', Bayley renders it as 'The whole capital shuddered'. Janet Dalley gives us 'The whole crowd shuddered in horror.' She tells you what to feel.

Pushkin never did. He was a universal artist. In the Soviet Union the whole tendency of Pushkin studies is to make their hero a progressive. He *was* progressive – all the subsequent debates on reform and revolution begin within the boundaries of his work – but he was conservative as well. He was everything. Even at their most scrupulous, Soviet studies of Pushkin inevitably belittle him. Hence the importance of his foreign reputation. There is a sense in which Professor Bayley in his book and Edmund Wilson in his essays give the English reader an estimation of Pushkin which is truer than any Soviet reader is in a position to appreciate.

Unfortunately there is also a sense in which, no matter how good the translations get, the full majesty of Pushkin must remain unknown to anyone who can't read Russian. I can only conclude by pointing out that not even Russians can read Russian without learning it first; that once you have made a start it turns out not to be as difficult as it looks; and that some of the rewards come surprisingly early. Russian literature might show every degree of refinement but it is simple at the core, because it all springs from Pushkin's example. Genius is elementary. Pushkin is like Homer,

Dante and Shakespeare: when he mentions something, you see it. It follows that to learn even a few lines of him in the original is to see that much of the world afresh.

(*New Statesman*, 1979)

Voznesensky's Case

Nostalgia for the Present by Andrei Voznesensky, edited by Vera Dunham and Max Hayward (Doubleday, New York)

The Making and Unmaking of a Soviet Writer by Anatoly Gladilin, translated by David Lapeza (Ardis, Ann Arbor, Michigan)

TWELVE years ago *Antiworlds and the Fifth Ace*, a bilingual volume to which several distinguished poets contributed translations under the editorship of Max Hayward and Patricia Blake, left nobody in doubt of Andrei Voznesensky's invigorating talent. This new volume, in whose editing the admirable Mr Hayward again had a hand, provides further evidence of Voznesenksy's high gifts. He is blessed with such a way of putting things that he can vault the language barrier as if it were a low fence. In a poem called 'Winter at the Track' he talks of a frozen bird hanging in the air like an ornament, and a dead horse on its back with its soul sticking up out of its mouth like a corkscrew from a penknife. All he means is that the temperature is forty-five below zero centigrade, but somehow the simplest statement comes out like a burst of coloured lights. Going overboard about Voznesensky seems, at first reading, the only decent thing to do.

But after intoxication comes the hangover. Viewed soberly, Voznesensky's poetry has the same limitations as most other Soviet literature which has ever been officially published, except that in his case the limitations are even more glaring. Lesser talents might profit from not being allowed to speak out directly: they can palm off evasiveness as ambiguity. But Voznesensky is transparently a case of the poet who, in Mayakovsky's famous phrase, stands on the throat of his own song.

With good reason, Voznesensky is a hero to all those in the Soviet Union who want their poets to tell them the truth. But at the risk of his career, freedom, and perhaps even his life, he has never been able to do much more than drop hints. Reading his work through from the beginning you can see that what ought to be his main subject matter is hardly there. When the subject is the history of his own country, everything he has to say is tangential. And eventually, because he is unable to state the plain truth about his own time and place, he is unable to state the plain truth about any other time and place. The result is a kind of false complexity, a string of profundities that do not add up to much.

Voznesensky emerged in the early 1960s, supposedly a new heyday for Russian poetry. Anatoly Gladilin – then a participant, now in exile – tells something of the story in his little book *The Making and Unmaking of a Soviet Writer*. Yevtushenko, Voznesensky, Rozhdestvensky, Okudzhava, and Bella Akhmadulina were the five young poets whose names were always mentioned together. Poetry meetings were mass rallies of the best and the brightest. The poets were treated like rock stars. At the wheel of a car full of lusty bards, the beautiful Akhmadulina glamorously collected tickets for speeding. Undoubtedly the whole upsurge of lyrical afflatus had great symbolic importance for performers and spectators alike. Bliss was it in that dawn to be alive, etc. All concerned had some justification for feeling that they were at long last talking about the reality of Soviet life, and not the illusion.

But in fact not much got said. In 'Babi Yar' Yevtushenko condemned a Nazi crime, not a Soviet one. The poem lent itself to interpretation as an attack on the anti-Semitic prejudices of some of the Soviet authorities. No doubt it took courage on Yevtushenko's part even to go that far. But at no point could he allow himself to suggest that the history of the Soviet Union has been largely composed of similar atrocities. If he had written a poem about, say, Kolyma, it would have been a real literary landmark, since that would have been a case, like *One Day in the Life of Ivan Denisovich*, of Soviet literature facing up to Soviet reality. But all 'Babi Yar' does is face up to Nazi reality. In other words, it shells the ruins. One doesn't necessarily condemn Yevtushenko by saying that he has a sure instinct for what he can get away with: if we were in his position, we would probably like to have that instinct ourselves. But it needs to be remembered that he has always had more than his own innate silliness to help make him banal. Censorship breeds platitudes as surely as salt water brings rust.

Voznesensky started off with a creative imagination that left Yevtushenko's in the shade, but if you take a hard look at *Antiworlds and the Fifth Ace* you will not find much light being cast on Soviet life except by reflection. 'Master Craftsmen', dated 1959, presents a seemingly bold manifesto:

> For an artist true-born
> revolt is second nature:
> he is both tribune
> and troublemaker.

The word which Max Hayward translates as 'troublemaker', *bunt*, actually has connotations of rebellion and mutiny, but perhaps it was right to tone the idea down. Even in his earliest, brashest poems, Voznesensky's defiance of Soviet authority is very generalized. 'Shame on fat-bellied bureaucrats!' he storms. But most of these criticisms fall well within the limits of the ritual beefing which Soviet citizens have always been allowed to indulge in during periods when the regime feels itself safe. It is often possible to get away with bitching about shortages, rapacious builders, bad service, or shoes that leak. It is rarely possible to comment in any open way about organized repression, even when it occurred in the past. Voznesensky's early poems are no exception to this rule. He says nothing explicit about the excesses of the Soviet government, even when the excesses were Stalin's. He says nothing because the opportunity to tackle such subjects was not on offer – a subject in itself, which could not be tackled either.

So the truly subversive moments in *Antiworlds* are all indirect. Instead of condemning Stalin he comes out with a no-holds-barred, knock-down-and-drag-out assault on Peter the Great. Peter the Great is portrayed as a monster engaged in butchering his erstwhile favourite, Anna Mons. In real life Anna Mons died a natural death. But here she is being bloodily executed while the crowd abuses her as an 'Anglo-Swedish-German-Greek spy'. Stanley Kunitz translates this last term as 'dirty foreigner', but perhaps it would have been better to have employed some such stock phrase as 'running dog of Imperialism', since Voznesensky, with judicious choice of official language, is partly alluding to the Great Terror of the late 1930s. So at any rate, the critic V. Nazarenko assumed when he accused Voznesensky of 'trying to express certain ideas of universal application'. It is hard to see why V. Nazarenko should have got his highly orthodox knickers in such a twist. If Voznesensky had to libel Peter the Great in order to get in a fleeting reference to the most important single fact of Soviet history, then there was little danger of certain ideas of universal application being expressed in a way noticeable to anybody not equipped with V. Nazarenko's ideological mine-detector.

In 1963 Khrushchev cracked down on the young artists. On 8 March of that year he abused Voznesensky in public. The scene is recorded by Gladilin with suitable emphasis on Khrushchev's porcine features, which apparently exuded lard at the critical moment. But in Voznesensky's case, as in everybody else's, the boom was being lowered on nothing more dangerous than an outburst of youthful self-consciousness. 'The Call of the Lake', a typical Voznesensky poem of 1965, would probably not have been any more searching if he had written it in 1962. Dedicated 'to the memory of the victims of fascism', it is about Jews murdered by the SS – i.e., it is 'Babi Yar' all over again. Which is not to say that the subject is trivial: only that Voznesensky, like Yevtushenko, inevitably treats it that way, through being unable to speak the truth about events closer to home.

I am afraid that *Nostalgia for the Present* has all the disappointing aspects of *Antiworlds* plus a few new ones. But first we should remind ourselves that Voznesensky remains a talent of the first class. His books are important, whatever use he might be making of his gifts. Vera Dunham and Max Hayward have risen to the occasion. The notes are comprehensive and the list of translators is mainly just as distinguished as in *Antiworlds*, although the odd ageing beatnik seems to have joined the party. Voznesensky's verbal facility still seems unimpaired.

Beginners with Russian should beware of falling for what sounds like musicality: they could be making the same mistake as all those Frenchmen who thought that Poe wrote subtle verse. But even the fledgling can tell that Voznesensky's tricks with alliteration are something better than mere echolalia. He has an effortless mimetic knack. The humbler translators have done their best to transmit some of this, but even when they despair of the attempt there is still a lot of straightforward imagery which would be fascinating in any language. Those without any Russian will find plenty to enjoy. All they will need is a receptive heart for the poet's unbounded charm. In 'From a Diary' we find him lying on a bed with a young lady citizen of New York.

> Who in his right mind would have thought
> That here in New York we'd lie upon
> This pillow one day, opened out
> Like a Russian–English lexicon?

No wonder the girls go crazy about him. There is more of the same in 'Christmas Beaches', where yet another young lady is to be found prostrated on a bed beside the poet, with the shadow of the shutters lying on her 'like a striped sailor's shirt'. Not even the combined efforts of Robert Bly and

Lawrence Ferlinghetti can destroy the economy of an idea like that, although elsewhere in the same poem they manage to make Voznesensky sound like somebody who used to hang out with Jack Kerouac.

> Hundreds of times they've buried us with their so wise
> plaster castigations!
> Wise men, our happiness bugs you.

Which is not quite it. But other translators do better. Richard Wilbur has the formal skill to find technical equivalents for Voznesensky's symmetrical compression. In his version of 'Phone Booth' he maintains the high standards set by himself and Auden in *Antiworlds*. In an ideal world, Wilbur would be first choice to translate all of Voznesensky's overtly formal poetry. When William Jay Smith attempts to mimic the precisely balanced stanzas of '*Ispovyed*', for example, the results can only be described as blah.

Looseness of construction does not matter so much on those numerous occasions when Voznesensky himself is writing in the open, declamatory tradition pioneered by Mayakovsky. But even in those instances it is necessary to say that William Jay Smith introduces an unwarranted element of flatness. When Voznesensky says that gulls' footprints look like mermaid's triangles, Mr Smith starts talking about 'the print of their sex', which sounds like Anais Nin working to a tight deadline. Mr Smith's industry is to be admired but one can be forgiven for wishing that he did not translate quite so many of Voznesensky's poems. One sometimes recalls the deadly example of Professor Singh, who by unflagging effort has almost succeeded in convincing us that Eugenio Montale writes the Italian equivalent of giftless academic English.

Yet the preponderance in *Nostalgia for the Present* of Mr Smith's worthily unexciting contributions is a subsidiary matter. The whole book is rich with fine conceits. By now Voznesensky has been hailed as a cultural hero all over the world. He hails the world right back. He loves Paris in the springtime, he loves San Francisco in the fall.

But again he has not very much specific to say about the Soviet Union. Sloth, bribery, and regimentation all get it in the neck. He mocks the thousands of geniuses who make up the Writers' Union. There is a deserved hymn, with no sensitive names mentioned, to the Russian intelligentsia as the collective guardian of human values. But that's about it. All other criticisms are indirect at best. More often they are just vague.

Arthur Miller, in his introductory note, gets it exactly wrong when he talks about poems that 'cut close to the bone on sensitive public issues'. The sensitive public issues remain safe when knives are as blunt as these. In 'On the Death of Shukshin' Voznesensky mourns the famous writer/actor as 'the conscience of the nation'. But Shukshin died of natural causes and his quarrel with authority was about the pollution of Lake Baikal. There is a poem called 'Requiem' but the title is the only thing it has in common with Akhmatova's majestic poem of the same name. Akhmatova's poem has never been published in the Soviet Union. There is no reason why Voznesensky's could not be put up in bronze beside the Tomb of the Unknown Warrior. It is just a lament for dead servicemen. Again, it is necessary to say that there is nothing trivial about this subject but that Voznesensky makes it so, by being unable to lament all those civilians who died for no good reason.

'Ice Block' is a poem about 'man's guilt before nature'. It appears that man should feel particularly guilty about – Dachau. Of Vorkuta or Karaganda, no mention. The inevitable effect is to deprive Dachau of some of its context and therefore of much of its meaning. In 'Darkmotherscream' Marina Tsvetaeva gets in very obliquely, and it is hard to avoid the conclusion that it is possible to mention her only because she killed herself, and was not, on the face of it anyway, killed by somebody else. (Tsvetaeva committed suicide in Yelabuga in 1941. Several of Voznesensky's contemporaries, most notably Akhmadulina, have written poems about her, but always without going into much detail about what brought her to such a pass.)

The nearest thing to a straight statement is 'Book Boom',

which honours Akhmatova. It is pointed out that Akhmatova, once persecuted, is now published.

> Those who once attacked her –
> as if to atone for their curse –
> stand, a reverent honor guard,
> for a single volume of her verse.

But speaking as one who owns a copy of the 'black, agate-colored tome' he refers to, I can only feel sorry that he is unable to mention the salient fact about it, which is that it is expurgated, like every other edition of Akhmatova's poems that has come out in the Soviet Union. 'Those who once attacked her' *still attack her now*. That is the point and Voznesensky knows it is the point. But he is not allowed to say so in public. Still, at least there is a vague hint that some form of repression might just possibly have occurred once upon a time.

All these hints and evasions are unsatisfactory but you can't ask the man to put his head on the block. The culprit is the Soviet Union, not Voznesensky. Alas, there are other sad aspects of the book in which the culprit is Voznesensky and not the Soviet Union. The star status which Voznesensky has enjoyed on his trips to the West might not have swelled his head, but it has certainly inflated his rhetoric. In numerous poems about his junkets abroad he almost achieves the difficult feat of sounding as fatuous as Yevtushenko. In an awful poem called 'Lines to Robert Lowell' he apostrophises History ('You, history, are the moan/of crucified prophets'), congratulates the Poet for his propensity to suffer ('The poet thrusts his body/like a tolling bell/against the dome of insults'), and holds a meaningful dialogue with his means of transport ('And you, my plane, where are you flying/in this darkness'). The original has 'my poor plane' but the translators, Louis Simpson and Vera Dunham, knew where to call a halt.

There is worse to come. Aping Lowell's portentousness, Voznesensky is at least in no danger of slumming. Unfortunately he is equally thrilled by the profundities of Allen Ginsberg, as in 'American Buttons'.

I love Greenwich Village
with its sarcastic buttons.
Who's the shaggy one who showed up
cock & balls in dark glasses?
It's Allen, Allen, Allen!
Leap over Death's carnival,
Allen, in your underwear!

The same poem instructs us that it is 'Better to stick your fingers in your mouth and whistle/than to be silent *booboisie*'. The translation is by Ferlinghetti, but really this stuff is not up to even his level. It might as well be Yoko Ono talking. It is not because of jet-lag, hash, or willing American maidens that Voznesensky can so readily pick a side in such an inane debate. Nor, I think, is it a result of the parochialism from which even the most astute artists in a closed society are bound to suffer. He ends up making empty remarks about the US because he started making empty remarks about the USSR. The more he travels, the less he has to say. There is no mystery about the reason. Had he tried to say anything definite, the Soviet authorities would have arranged a different form of travel for him, within the borders of his own country.

There is something terrible about hearing a poet of Voznesensky's ability say vaporous things about world merchants of death, etc. Nobody ever expected Yevtushenko to become a mature artist. But of Voznesensky it was the least we could expect. Yet on this showing he has not done so. The fact is sad but not surprising. For a poet, to be denied one word means that all the others are not enough. Voznesensky has been denied the most fundamental truths about the country in which he grew up. Unable to be frank about those, he is unable to be frank about anything else either. Without the possibility of frankness there can be no true ambiguity, obliqueness, subtlety, or depth. There can only be obfuscation.

People should give up talking as if in the case of the Soviet Union the second law of thermodynamics has been suspended. The notion that poetry benefits from repression is essentially vulgar: it is a version of the equally vulgar idea that politics are not real unless they are extreme. The mass audience for poetry in the Soviet Union exists only because of the fleeting possibility that in poems some elementary truth might be mentioned, or at least alluded to, or anyway not denied outright. Poetry which exhausts most of its energy hinting at some forbidden topic is inevitably trivial. It is balderdash to suggest that the Soviet authorities repress poetry because they take it seriously. All they take seriously is what poetry might bring with it – open discussion of the historical facts.

Officially approved Soviet literature has cretinised itself. It couldn't have happened any other way. Voznesensky is a talent in the great modern tradition of Blok, Gumilev, Pasternak, Mandelstam and Akhmatova. But he does not look like becoming an *artist* in that tradition. The evidence suggests that the necessary qualification for attaining poetic maturity after the Revolution is to have been born and raised before it happened – by now an unlikely possibility. The conditions for nurturing a lyrical gift no longer exist. Unofficial poetry, though it produces a good deal to be admired, is not really a substitute. In the 1973 Harper & Row bilingual anthology *Poetry from the Russian Underground* (when I was in New York in March the Strand bookshop still had a few copies marked down from $10 to $3.95) Voznesensky and all his friends are represented. Along with Akhmatova's 'Requiem', an anonymous song about Kolyma stands out for its directness. Half the other poems in the book are busy condemning American policy in South East Asia, defending the Decembrists, or pointing out that the crucifixion of Jesus Christ was a bad thing. Even those poems which attempt to deal directly with the Great Terror seem predicated on the assumption that no coherent political analysis is possible. It all happens in a dream.

For the moment Voznesensky has had most of his privileges suspended by the Soviet authorities. While he has made brief trips abroad, he has been denied permission to give readings at home – for a Soviet poet, no light punishment. The immediate cause of all this disfavour was Voznesensky's temerity in publishing a cluster of unofficial poems in the *samizdat* magazine *Metropol*. It could be that I am missing some hidden meanings, but as far as I can see these unofficial poems are not very different from his official ones. The most subversive poem of the bunch seems to be the one addressed to Derzhavin, the favoured court poet in Catherine the Great's time. Voznesensky puns on his name (which is like one of the words for 'power'), compares the old boy to a double-headed eagle (the imperial symbol), and congratulates him on at least being able to talk to himself.

The implication is that a poet of the present day can't be frank even when alone. What we have to imagine is a country where to write such a poem is correctly regarded as an act of daring not just by the authorities, but by the poet himself. Grote ended his *History of Greece* at the point where – he took the idea from Homer – even those who thought they were free were really slaves.

Unofficial poetry is a brave try. But most of it is written by official poets leading double lives, with the implication that their official lives are fake. Worse circumstances for the production of poetry would be hard to imagine. Poetry is not just facts, but it can't start without them. It is no use saying that Voznesensky might simply be an apolitical poet. If he can't *choose* to be apolitical, we can never tell. In a long and scrappy poem called 'Story Under Full Sail', printed near the end of *Nostalgia for the Present*, Voznesensky gives the game away.

> It's shameful to spot a lie and not to name it,
> shameful to name it and then to shut your eyes,
> shameful to call a funeral a wedding
> and play the fool at funerals besides.

The speaker is the nineteenth-century buccaneering court chamberlain Rezanov, but it might as well be the poet himself. Stanley Kunitz has been unwarrantedly coy in translating *nye iskorenyat* as 'to shut your eyes'. It means 'not to root it out'. With typical obliqueness, but this time with real point, Voznesensky is saying that the Soviet Union must face the truth about its past. Until that happens, every aspect of Soviet life will go on being distorted, the arts not least. When the alternatives are death, exile, or silence, we should be glad that Voznesensky has settled for stardom. But he could have had stature, if only things had been different.

(*New York Review of Books*, 1979)

Transparent Petropolis

Osip Mandelstam, poems chosen and translated by James Greene (Elek, London, and Shambhala Publications, Boulder, Colorado)

Osip Mandelstam: 50 Poems translated by Bernard Meares (Persea Books, New York)

By now half a dozen different selections from Osip Mandelstam's poetry have been translated into English with varying lack of success. The better attempts seem to have been made in the knowledge that failure was inevitable. The worse have a deadly cockiness. The two most recent volumes, one by James Greene and the other by Bernard Meares, are humble enough – in Mr Greene's case only just humble enough – in their approach. It might also be said that they are diffident enough in their results. A pity, really, that neither David McDuff nor the Clarence Brown/W. S. Merwin team translated a more complete corpus back in 1973. As things stand, their pioneering selections still look more authoritative than anything which has happened since, but new books can, and will, go on appearing, so long as each new translator is able to convince himself that he can offer an illuminating recension.

The case of Nadezhda Mandelstam shows how important it can be for translation to be done with proper reticence. Her two great prose works *Hope Against Hope* and *Hope Abandoned* are both translated by Max Hayward, whose tactful fidelity could scarcely be improved upon. If we should ever lapse into taking his self-effacing gift for granted, a glance at Mr Robert A. McLean's translation of Mrs Mandelstam's *Mozart and Salieri*, which emerged from Ann Arbor university in 1973, would quickly jerk us awake. The first sentence is sufficient warning. 'Mandelstam was a hopeless debater, but he did not bite at just any bait.' You don't have to be a good writer to see that the original word must be translated as 'incorrigible' rather than 'hopeless', or that a clangorous echo like 'debater' and 'bait' must be avoided. Just not being a bad writer would do. It would be better to leave the text untouched than bruise it with such a ham fist.

There is an even stronger argument for leaving Osip Mandelstam's poetry undisturbed. Even people who read translated prose without a qualm are worried, when they read translated poetry, about whether they are getting anything worth having. An irrefutable case, from the aesthetic viewpoint, can be mounted against the very idea of translating poetry. Yet when it comes to the point nobody lives by aesthetics alone. Criticism includes aesthetics, but is something larger, just as culture includes criticism but is something larger still. In the end we want to know as much as we can about what is going on in the major poetry even of languages we can't read. The real questions concern the means of finding out. By now it is generally agreed that a plain translation, provided it does not make a fetish of plainness, is better than something poetic but not poetic enough.

James Greene is an honest and dedicated servant of Mandelstam, but he is also a bit of a poet on his own account. His book is equipped with a posturing foreword in which he explains, among other things, that he has found it necessary to leave parts of certain poems untranslated, since he could not find the poetic equivalent. The implication seems to be that for the other parts he *has* found a poetic equivalent. All this would sound very silly if there were not also a foreword from Donald Davie to remind us of what real silliness sounds like.

Professor Davie hails the uniquely European, rounded

formal completeness which he sees as Mr Greene's unprecedented contribution to the task of translating Mandelstam. According to Davie, the American idiom (exemplified by Brown/Merwin) is 'discontinuous'. As wielded by Mr Greene, the British idiom does 'what by its very nature the American idiom could not' – i.e. it corresponds to the European, self-contained form of Mandelstam's poems.

There is something to this notion. In much of his work Mandelstam really is a formalist, a fact of which Davie, in his time a redoubtable formalist himself, is very properly aware. The formal element is certainly what is missing in the translations by Brown/Merwin and McDuff. But a single glance shows it to be even more missing in the translations by Mr Greene. He is even more discontinuous than they are. Probably Davie, flying in the face of his own arguments, likes what Mr Greene has written because it sounds Poundian. 'Previous British versions have been wooden,' proclaims Davie: 'this one *rings* – it is bronze, properly Roman bronze.' Pound used to talk the same way about Mussolini's speeches, and with the same justification. Mr Greene has his poetic virtues, but the clonk of timber, rather than the ring of bronze, is likely to be aroused by the testing knuckle.

Mr Greene may have left bits of certain poems out, but at least – like Brown/Merwin and unlike McDuff – he has given his chosen poems the appropriate numbers, so that they can readily be traced in Volume 1 of the three-volume *Sobranii sochinenii*, the monumental Collected Works edited by Struve and Filippov. Checking with the originals soon shows our translator to be deficient in that very sense of form which both he and his mentor, Professor Davie, are convinced is vital to the task. 'Faithful as never before,' declares Davie. But look at No. 6 (from *Kamen*), a small poem written in 1909. Neither Brown/Merwin nor McDuff includes this poem, so it is useful to have it translated, but from Mr Greene's version you would think the original was fragmentary, asymmetrical – in a word, discontinuous.

April-blue enamel:
Inconspicuous

And pale,
A birch-tree hammocks in the evening sky.

This gives you some idea of the stanza's component images but none at all of its form. If Mr Greene has to be preoccupied with Ezra Pound, it would be better if he could echo the strict-form Pound rather than the free-form; but really the model he should look to is one of Pound's own models, Gautier, whose *Emaux et Camées* are a near equivalent of the way the young Mandelstam packed highly condensed imagery into a strict, symmetrical, exactly rhyming form. Another instructive example is Baudelaire, whose interest in Petrarch adumbrates Mandelstam's own.

One of the ways in which Baudelaire transmits innocence in the midst of squalor is by confining his scabrous view of life within strict Petrarchan forms. If you subtract Baudelaire's wilfully perverse element, Mandelstam's own interest in Petrarch yields the same result: the more diversely inclusive his view of the chaotic world, the more likely he is to express it through the familiar simplicity of classical form. The same applies to his lasting involvement with Dante.

Mandelstam's famous definition of Acmeism – as nostalgia for a world culture – is embodied in the formal element of his work from beginning to end. The Acmeist manifestos commonly expressed their rejection of the symbolist movement by calling for a clear, simple intelligibility of image. In that sense, Acmeism was rather like what we know as Imagism, and commentators are right when they point out that Mandelstam – whose imagery can be the reverse of clear – was not an Acmeist. But Mandelstam never courts obscurity. You always get the sense, when he is saying something in a complicated way, that there is no other way to say it. You always feel the presence, in his poems, of a central, controlling simplicity of spirit – and their unpretentious outward form is usually the medium through which you first feel it.

In the Russian tradition, Mandelstam harks back to Derzhavin and Tyutchev, both of whom dedicated their long lives to verbal refinement and a ceremonial style. In the

European tradition – the world culture for which he was nostalgic – Mendelstam harks back to almost everyone. He was a great student of poetry. Above all he was a great *technical* student. Just as Virgil absorbed Homer's technical substance and Dante absorbed Virgil's, Mandelstam absorbed everybody's. With the present disintegrating all around him, Mandelstam reaffirmed the integrity of the past. Any translation which fails to reproduce the architectural poise and balance of a Mandelstam poem might still give you a hint of his child-like nature, but is bound to miss out on the timeless confidence which makes that child-like nature so robust.

Because Mandelstam is as solid as a rock. If he ever sounds babyish, it is only because the translators are unable to find an equivalent for the centripetal force holding each of his poems together. In the modern art of Western Europe, the Blue Rider painters are the people most like him. Klee, in fact, is an extremely instructive parallel case. Klee's vision was that of a prodigiously gifted infant, expressed with all the technical command of a mature artist. Mandelstam is like that, except that the pressures working both within and without are multiplied by many times. There is no sentimentality in Klee: you can tell just by looking at him that his ceremonies of innocence have nothing to do with cuteness. Nor is there any sentimentality in Mandelstam. When he says, in one of the poems of his second exile, that if he is born again he hopes it will be in the form of children's games, the idea seems perfectly right, and poetic in the sense that no other way of saying it would do. But to preserve Mandelstam's purity of soul without making him sound winsome, the translator simply must reproduce something of his formal power.

Perhaps it can't be done. But some translators do it better than others, and you can't have greater and lesser degrees of nothing. In his version of 'Silentium' McDuff has at least retained a four-line stanza, even if he hasn't found any rhymes for it. Mr Greene doesn't even give us that much, although the way he couples the two words 'lunatic' and 'lilac' provides a momentary hint of Mandelstam's verbal delicacy. But even if you capture the verbal delicacy (and Brown/Merwin still do a better job than anyone else), the verbal delicacy doesn't mean much without the verbal strength. The wealth of exquisite interplay within Mandelstam's lines is always contained by stanza forms which either rhyme as solidly as Baudelaire's or else – in the larger poems which will probably remain, to the Western reader, the most inaccessible part of Mandelstam's achievement – possess the gravid syntactical coherence of a strophe by the mature Yeats.

Occasionally, as in 'The Lutheran', Mr Greene attempts a four-line form, even equipping some of the stanzas with rhymes, or anyway half-rhymes. But on the whole he is too much of a reductionist to feel comfortable about writing anything that might sound like padding. He is no end of a leaver-out. When he puts something in, it is usually for purposes of clarification, although some of his clarifications muddy the issue. It is all right to put some snow into No. 84, since I suppose we need reminding that in Russia it often snows in winter, but I can't see what the 'canvas' is doing 'shrouding' Hellas in No. 78.

The latter is one of Mandelstam's most famous early poems – his wife speaks of it in one of the many interesting critical disquisitions contained in her memoirs – and I really think that the Brown/Merwin version (McDuff does not attempt it) serves the turn as well as any. Merwin, who can be considered as the versifying partner in the Brown/Merwin combination, is almost as much of a putter-in as Mr Greene is a leaver-out, but at least Merwin, with Brown helping, knows that when Mandelstam refers to the flight of cranes he means the cranes in Dante, *Inferno* V. In his first stanza Greene refers to them as 'birds'. They are cranes in the second stanza, but why not in the first, where Mandelstam is so obviously combining one of Homer's most resonant images with one of Dante's? The shrouding canvas is small recompense for such a loss. After all, Mandelstam is not just a 'literary' poet in the sense of someone piling allusions together. He is proclaiming the continuity of human imagination.

Mr Greene's language keeps getting the fidgets, for the good reason that he is all too often trying to find another way of saying what another translator has said already. To take another well-known poem, in No. 89 (from *Tristia*) the first line is translated by McDuff as 'we shall die in transparent Petropolis', which is literally what Mandelstam wrote. Mr Greene's version opens thus: 'we shall leave our bones in transparent Petropolis', which is at once fancier and more commonplace than the original. One of the troubles about the reductionist impulse in poetry is that it becomes so concerned with local intensity it forgets how to make an ordinary statement. This quirk becomes a double handicap when translating Mandelstam, since among his denser passages of imagery he includes lines which are obviously meant to be as plain as day. Greene translates the first line of 'Tristia' (No. 104) as 'I have learnt by heart the lesson of goodbyes', which is almost as much his own idea as Mandelstam's. There is a special Russian word for 'by heart' and Mandelstam does not use it in this line. Nor does he use the word for 'lesson'. He uses the word for 'science'. Brown and Merwin stick closer to the original, thus: 'I have studied the science of goodbyes'.

Perhaps Mr Greene just didn't want to sound like Brown and Merwin, but the inevitable side-effect is that he sounds less like Mandelstam than he should. He deserves credit, however, for at least trying to stay within hailing distance. Mr Bernard Meares really lets rip. Same poem, same line: 'I've acquired the craft of separating', which sounds like the boast of a drunken milkmaid. Mr Meares's volume is sumptuously produced in the American manner, but in their local detail his translations are so self-assertive as to amount to 'versions', and the cold truth is that any 'version' of Mandelstam is bound to be inadequate simply because no poet in the West has been through a comparable experience. But one great advantage Mr Meares's translations do have – they are, where appropriate, formally exact, and thus transmit something of the tension, fundamental to Mandelstam's poetry, between expectedness of form and unexpectedness of content.

Meares's book has a first-rate introduction by Joseph Brodsky, who thereby refutes his own argument that criticism of Mandelstam will always fall short. He says penetrating things about the importance of the city of Petersburg to Mandelstam's view of the world; he is, as you might expect, informative about the Russian poetic tradition of which Mandelstam is an heir and culmination; and he is deeply and comprehensively right about the significance of Mandelstam's personal fate. If Mandelstam had had merely political objections to the Soviet regime, Brodsky argues, he might have survived. But what he embodied was lyrical intensity, and since lyricism is the ethics of language, his very existence constituted an intolerable threat.

A lot could be said about such an analysis, but the first thing to say is that it is up to the subject. Leaving aside Professor Davie's strange utterances, there is little in Mr Greene's translations and notes, devoted and painstaking though they are, to show that he is fully aware of Mandelstam's true magnitude as a historical figure. He unblushingly quotes Robert Chandler's opinion that Mandelstam, during his second exile in Voronezh, was 'like Pound in the Detention Camp at Pisa, knowing that he might die at any moment . . .'. Not even Davie, who has a bee in his bonnet about Pound, would be capable of so disproportionate a comparison. For all Mr Greene's display of learning and energy (he seems to have asked half the poets and professors in the world to read his manuscript), there is something immature about his whole approach to the subject. Nobody could object when, for purposes of elucidation, he gives us a passage from Pope's Homer instead of just a reference to Homer, and then identifies the passage as emanating from Alexander Pope, in case we should think that someone else called Pope had translated Homer too. There is something charming about that. But there is nothing charming about sheer political obtuseness. It can certainly be proposed that Mandelstam was not a man of his time, but to grasp the full meaning of that proposition you have to be capable of imagining what his time was like.

This is not to say that Western opinions of Mandelstam

don't count. In fact they are the only kind that do: not even Brodsky, if he were still in the Soviet Union, would be able to speak of Mandelstam as he now does. Leaving aside Brown's Cambridge monograph and his introduction (written in English) to the *Sobranii sochinenii*, his introduction to the 1973 *Selected Poems* (now available as one of the Penguin Modern European poets) gives us a better idea of Mandelstam's importance than any essay which has emanated or is likely to emanate from the Soviet Union. I have the one and only Soviet edition of Mandelstam beside me as I write. It, too, came out in 1973. It is a handsome job, like all the books in the *Biblioteka poeta* series. But there are poems missing, and the introduction is pitiably mendacious. You would think, from the official account, that Mandelstam had silenced himself.

It seems unlikely that the Soviet regime will ever find a plausible way of coming to terms with Mandelstam. This volume was the best they could do, and after trying it once they have never tried it again. Someone must have realised that you can't make Mandelstam ideologically clean just by leaving out his more questionable poems. He is not like Akhmatova, who has been given just such treatment, with results that the Writers' Union and all the other hack institutions involved obviously regard as successful, since there are pop editions coming out all the time. They all have similar lying introductions, but you can easily see the rationale behind the selection and rejection of poems. Akhmatova's work springs directly from her life and times. If you leave out the poems which explicitly protest against the brutalities of the regime, you are left with poems which in the regime's eyes can be given a *nihil obstat*, since they relate to the shared patriotic experience of the common people. You would think, from the Soviet editions of Akhmatova, that the central experience of her later life had been the siege of Leningrad, and not the fact that Stalin locked up her son and threatened him with death. You get a hopelessly distorted picture, but you get the sort of picture that the regime can sanction. With Mandelstam, no matter how much you take away, the results are still subversive. His lyricism is as indefinable as music and even more impossible for a totalitarian state to put up with.

But it isn't my purpose here to draw distinctions between Mandelstam and Akhmatova. The first thing to say about them is that they are together, not apart. As with Mandelstam, so with Akhmatova, all the important scholarly work has been done in the West. When you look at Struve and Filippov's two-volume Akhmatova *Sochinenia*, standing in its off-white binding beside their black and gold three-volume Mandelstam, and then count in the two volumes of memoirs in which Nadezhda Mandelstam does so much to illuminate all the ways in which the lives of these two great poets are linked, you wonder if any age, let alone ours, can match such a concentration of creative intelligence.

Getting at it across the language barrier is, however, not easy. But I can promise anyone who would like to learn Russian that the rewards are worth the effort. I myself set out to learn something of the language simply because I could no longer bear being left out of whatever it was that Edmund Wilson and John Bayley appreciated in Pushkin. By the time you can read Pushkin, you can certainly make a beginning on Akhmatova, especially if you can equip yourself with *Poems of Akhmatova* (Atlantic-Little, Brown, 1973), an exemplary parallel text with translations by Stanley Kunitz and an introduction by Max Hayward.

Turning from Akhmatova to Mandelstam, however, you find out with a shock that Russian is an even more copiously subtle language than you at first thought. It is like learning enough Italian to read, say, Moravia's short stories, and then tackling the poetry of Montale – you can see the shape of the sentence but the words in it are all unfamiliar. Or suppose you were a Japanese professor of English who was up to reading A. E. Housman, and then you took your first look at Dylan Thomas. If you can imagine being bamboozled by Montale's highly specific vocabulary, and then bamboozled all over again by the way Dylan Thomas ropes everything in instead of trying to make straight sense, you can imagine something of the bewilderment which a first encounter with Mandelstam in the original language is likely to induce, even when (especially when) you flatter yourself that you have got to at least an intermediate stage with Russian.

But in this case perseverance will never disappoint. Quite the contrary. Most of us grow out of Dylan Thomas, finding his little-boy act too embarrassing to stomach or else deciding that he never meant as much as he wanted to. But Mandelstam is a true innocent, with an innocence that could see everything and remain ingenuous. He will never stop reminding you of Montale, because Montale similarly emphasises the redemptive quality of inconsequential things – that amulet in his poem about Dora Markus is the kind of token which turns up in Mandelstam time after time, and the children in 'Caffè a Rapallo' might be playing one of the very games which Mandelstam saw as the only repository for his doomed soul. In a rhetorical age, the age of Fascism, Montale defended the classical succession by retreating to a hidden world of things too trivial for any tyrant to care about. Mandelstam is a lot like that, except that the tyrant is more powerful and the retreat goes further.

But the retreat always feels like an advance. Mandelstam is so successful in establishing his irrelevance to the State that he convinces you of the State's irrelevance to him. Another poet he calls to mind is Rilke, but without the whine. Rilke's lament for the collapse of Western civilisation is chiefly inspired by the possibility that the noblewomen he has spent his life sucking up to will no longer invite him to their castles for the weekend. Mandelstam was a long way beyond that. He had a world view.

The miracle is that the world ever came to hear about it. We can allow ourselves to be thrilled by the fact that so much of his work survived, but should never forget that its survival was an accident. As Nadezhda Mandelstam frequently points out in her memoirs, only chance could save you. In this respect the grandeur of the Struve/Filippov editions of Mandelstam and Akhmatova is misleading. You can hold the original volumes of both books in the palm of your hand. *Kamen* is a pamphlet. Akhmatova's *Anno Domini MCMXXI* (datelined 'Petropolis') is no bigger than a pocket diary.

Their littleness got them through. Perhaps there is a lesson for us in that. If the historical experience which has already overwhelmed half the world is on its way towards us, a low profile might be the thing to adopt.

But even supposing that the free human mind has come to the end of its time, Mandelstam is one of those supreme artists who convince you that there is such a thing as poetic immortality, and that it is at one with the simplest forces of creation, so that nothing can destroy it. He says in one of his poems that the horse's gallop goes on being audible after the horse lies dead. The metaphor certainly applies to him, although no horse ever had to die as horribly as he did. But he somehow convinces us that the same metaphor applies to the whole of humanity. History came to its conclusion before Mandelstam's eyes: if this wasn't universal destruction, then what was it? And yet when he listened to what was left of existence, it still had a singing voice.

(*New Review*, 1978)

Voices from the Pit

To Build a Castle – My Life as a Dissenter
by Vladimir Bukovsky, translated by Michael Scammell
(Deutsch, London, and Viking, New York)

Alarm and Hope **by Andrei D. Sakharov,**
edited by Efrem Yankelevich and Alfred Friendly, Jr.
(Collins, London, and Knopf, New York)

BEFORE the Revolution, there was Russian literature. Since the Revolution, except for an early and brief period when the good writers were as optimistic as the bad, there has been, for the most part, the literature of Russian dissidence. Its qualities and categories are hard to define, but lately the sheer output has become difficult to keep up with even for the expert, while the layman must simply resign himself to leaving most of it unread – a harsh fact, when you consider that there is hardly any such thing as a dissident book which is not written at the risk of its author's neck.

Vladimir Bukovsky is the bravest of the brave, but if his book told us nothing new there would be a good case for leaving it to one side. Luckily the fancy title is no guide to the book's true worth, which is considerable. *To Build a Castle* takes an assured place alongside such volumes as Evgenia Ginzburg's *Journey Into the Whirlwind* or Anatoly Marchenko's *My Testimony*. It is one more, and this time a very recent, chapter in the terrifying story – by now several generations long – of what Soviet political repression actually feels like to the people it happens to.

In addition to the inside knowledge he provides, Bukovsky has a capacity for moral reflection that almost lifts his work to the level occupied, in their different ways, by Nadezhda Mandelstam and Solzhenitsyn. If, finally, we decide that he doesn't quite reach that altitude, it might have something to do with the limitations of his virtues. There is something of the star soloist about Bukovsky. He can speak for himself and he can speak for a principle, but in speaking for ordinary people he sometimes seems to lack the capacity for self-forgetfulness.

Perhaps he is just young. Bukovsky was born in 1942, which makes him about three years younger than the present reviewer, to whom the worst thing that has ever happened has been a sinus operation. Bukovsky was first arrested for taking part in protests when he was still in high school and has spent most of his adult life in prisons and psychiatric hospitals, the latter being specifically designed to give their victims an even worse time than the former. He has dared the Soviet authorities to do their worst and they have done it. In some ways he is so grown up that the ordinary Western reader loses touch with him. In other ways he has had no life at all. It is not surprising that there is something overbearing about his ego. Nothing else but concentrated, unrelenting selfhood could have sustained him.

The literary result, however, is an intensified version of the same tone projected by Solzhenitsyn even at his most sympathetically generous – you feel that an extreme experience has lifted the man talking to you on to a higher plane and left you on a lower one. Only Nadezhda Mandelstam can take us all the way inside the nightmare, since as well as sharing her husband's status of victim she shares ours of onlooker. Her *Hope Against Hope* is the great book of modern Russia and indeed, I think, of our time. But it would be foolish to expect that the Soviet Union could go on producing, even by reaction, such finely tuned contemplative minds as hers. Her roots are in the old intelligentsia. The more recent antibodies are typified by Bukovsky – unbreakably self-confident, suicidally courageous, and frighteningly strange. You could with some hubris just about convince yourself that in the same circumstances you might have behaved as well as the Mandelstams. But only a monster of conceit could identify with someone like Bukovsky. He is practically a different species of human being – a spiritual mutant.

The most easily recognisable parts of Bukovsky's book are the long, detailed accounts of what happened to him in Vladimir Prison, the Leningrad Special Mental Hospital, and other punitive institutions. All of this took place after the Stalinist era was supposed to be over. In Vladimir Prison Bukovsky spent eighteen months of a two-year stretch on 'strict regime'. He has something of Solzhenitsyn's knack for the detail that jolts your imagination. It might not sound very impressive, he argues, when prisoners complain about having their old newspapers confiscated. But if they have nothing else to sleep on except a bed of steel rods, taking their padding away can turn ordinary bad nights into out-and-out torture. Tiny privileges, revokable at the jailer's will, make the difference between ordinary regime and strict regime. Effectively, strict regime is as close to death as you can be brought without dying.

The mental hospitals offer all the dubious attractions of the prisons plus a variety of extra features which make it hard even for toughs like Bukovsky to fight back. In prison you get thrown into solitary confinement but your mind is your own to control if you can find the trick of doing so. In the mental hospitals there are sulfazine, haloperidol, and a murderous treatment which involves being wrapped up in a wet sheet that suffocates you as it dries. Prisoners who are driven crazy by these techniques automatically confirm the theory of the eminent Professor Timofeyev – i.e., that dissidence is caused by brain disease.

According to Bukovsky – and there is every reason to think that his analysis is right – the Soviet system after Stalin is just Stalinism refined. The common people can't be aroused from their lethargy because they know too well what would happen to them. 'They keep quiet because they know, not because they don't know.' Anyone with any brains sees through the propaganda sooner or later. Everyone understands the joke about how to enjoy the material benefits of socialism: plug the refrigerator into the radio. But to dissent is to flay a stone.

Nevertheless Bukovsky dissents, in the peculiar way of his generation. The most interesting, because least familiar, parts of his book are about what it was like to grow up during what the rest of the world regarded as the Thaw. It is clear from his account that the system didn't change: it merely opened up just far enough for an alert youth to see it for what it was. Bukovsky and his friends started a secret organisation. It survived by dint of doing nothing except stay secret. An individualist from the cradle, temperamentally averse to mere survival, Bukovsky branched out on his own and got himself into trouble, where he belonged. When he organised readings of unpublished poets in Mayakovsky Square, he was expelled from Moscow University where he was studying biology. (Like Solzhenitsyn, he was educated as a scientist, not as a literary specialist.)

Thus he embarked on a career of moral opposition, which he is convinced is the only answer. If he is right, then it is an answer only heroes can give. That marvellous organ *Literaturnaya Gazeta* at one point accused Bukovsky of organising an armed insurrection. Actually Bukovsky was armed with nothing except his will. The will and the ego being variations of each other, there is nothing reticent about this book, but even when you suspect its author of bombast you have to concede that he is a tower of strength.

One's real doubts spring from the fact that his analysis and his recommendations do not quite square up. He is obviously right about the Soviet state being a sclerotic anachronism run by time-serving hacks with brains the size and flexibility of golf balls. He wants them all to come clean about the past. But if they are the men he says they are, how can they appreciate the significance of a moral stand?

None of this is to say that a moral stand makes no sense as an act of witness, *sub specie aeternitatis*. It can also make immediate practical sense as a means of bringing Western influence into play. But as a course of action for the general run of Soviet citizens, even if they were all heroes, it looks doomed from the outset. The state, as Bukovsky himself characterises it, simply can't absorb that much opposition. It can't change in that way: all it can do is close up again and propel the dissenters into the pit. Even the tactic of appealing to the Soviet constitution can be effective only so long as the state forbears. Strictly interpreted, the Soviet constitution is like one of those joke documents invented by Alexander Zinoviev – a measure put into effect in order to find out who agrees with it, so that they can be dealt with.

Equipped with sensuous good looks and the remarkably accurate English he taught himself in prison, Bukovsky made a vivid impression when he stepped off the plane into the West. Much of that vividness is in this book, which has been translated by Michael Scammell with a nice sense of rhythm: his writing here augurs well for his soon-to-be-forthcoming life of Solzhenitsyn. (Mr Scammell might care, however, to look up the verb 'to brutalise' in some dictionary less permissive than Webster's. In the context of Bukovsky's book its real meaning is too valuable to lose.) Since his arrival in England Bukovsky has been taken up by the sort of conservative ideologists whose idea of an advanced economist is Adam Smith. He is not as silly when he sounds like them as they are when they sound like him, but he is fond of inveighing against socialism without bothering to define it. Actually a modern Western society without socialism is as hard to imagine as a modern Western society without capitalism – the two things have grown inextricably mixed up. What Bukovsky is really against is the one-party state. Everything he has to say about that is pertinent and convincing, backed up as it is by detailed personal knowledge of how it feels to have the whole monolith landing on top of you.

The latest collection of Sakharov documents has no pretensions to literature but on the scale of effectiveness it is likely to be at least as important as Bukovsky's book, simply because Sakharov is who he is. *Alarm and Hope* should be seen in continuity with *Sakharov Speaks*, which came out in 1974. A comparison of the two volumes shows a hardening of his attitude during the past five years. By now he has had ample opportunity to assess the full measure of the state's vindictive pettiness. His income is down to almost nothing, he is barred from work befitting his gifts, he is overwhelmed with demands for advice and comfort, anyone close to him is subject to cruel harassment, and the telephone rings in the middle of the night so that some pin-headed KGB factotum can give him the benefit of a sick imagination. No wonder, then, that Sakharov's views have come to resemble Bukovsky's, with the emphasis on moral regeneration. What Bukovsky was born to, Sakharov has been forced to.

Yet there is still a residue of his earlier determination to reform the USSR by practical advice. Even if the young Sakharov had not valued himself as a creative nuclear physicist, the state's esteem for him would have been enough to make him self-confident. He was the Soviet Union's scientific darling. He was elected to the Academy of Sciences at the age of thirty-two, the youngest man ever to be so honoured. He gave his country the H-bomb and in return his country gave him all the privileges it could bestow – money, car, chauffeur, country house, imported consumer goods, and a twenty-four hour bodyguard who even went skiing with him.

Sakharov had every reason to think that if he gave the state advice it would listen. And for a while it did listen. It was Sakharov's prestige in the physical sciences that halted Lysenko's comeback under Khrushchev. Before the Twenty-third Party Congress in 1966, Sakharov, with twenty-four others, called on the Party not to rehabilitate Stalin. Whatever reasons the Politburo had for not putting Stalin back on his plinth (Roy Medvedev thinks it was the foreign communist parties who worked the trick) the important point here is that it didn't happen, and that Sakharov was justified, by events at any rate, in feeling that his voice counted.

Sakharov told the Soviet authorities that unless the state liberalised itself the country would fall behind and become a second-rate power. This line of thought would probably have been enough by itself to get him into trouble eventually, even if he had not begun spicing it with indications that he had begun to distrust socialism altogether. The culminating moment was his 1968 manifesto *Thoughts on Progress, Peaceful Co-existence and Intellectual Freedom*, which is reprinted in *Sakharov Speaks*. It was published only in the West. In the Soviet Union it was swallowed up, although the ineffable *Literaturnaya Gazeta* gave it a review five years later – a spatter of abuse emanating from the editor in chief's own fair hand.

The year of the Prague Spring was a bad time for appeals to reason. Sakharov was promptly on the road to becoming the un-person that he is now, when Soviet propagandists, with typical brilliance, are putting it about that he is really a Jew called Sugarman. The best thing in *Alarm and Hope* is the title essay, in which he talks about 'the full tragedy of creative life in the socialist countries'. He is one of the embodiments of that tragedy – a genius at the mercy of vengeful dimwits. That a man of Sakharov's calibre should have to spend his most creative years taking an elementary moral stand is a measure of what the Soviet Union has done to itself.

Sakharov, like Bukovsky, is on strong ground when he emphasises the importance of standing up to be counted. Nobody could denigrate such a viewpoint even if it could be proved that it were ineffective. As it happens, there is good reason to think that moral resistance within the Soviet Union has a measurable outcome in the form of Western pressure, especially now that President Carter, in his innocent way, has restored a semblance of ethical initiative to the West. In the long term the right thing is always worth doing, but in this case there is evidence that it is worth doing in the short term too.

Yet finally it is the lingering echo of Sakharov's original message that catches one's attention. Even today he has not lost sight of the practicalities. He insists, persuasively, that the Soviet Union, no matter how offended by Western criticism, simply can't afford to break off trade. There are just too many things it doesn't know how to make. Sakharov would not still be taking this line if he did not go on believing, at some level, that the Soviet leadership might be tempted toward liberalisation by the prospect of practical advantage. In a recent statement, he insisted that Western sympathy for dissidents should not interfere with arms agreements, or issue in boycotts accompanied by ultimatums, or prevent quiet deals for the exchange of political prisoners.

This is the strain in Sakharov's thought which Solzhenitsyn has always objected to. Solzhenitsyn wants the regime discredited, not reformed. But there is at least a chance that Sakharov is being tactically sound when he goes on suggesting, in the teeth of his own latterday intransigence, that the material disparities between the Soviet Union and the West could be decisive in resolving the moral ones. If *Pravda* has to go on importing Western computerised printing machines in order to tell the population how far the West is lagging behind, the time might come when not even the Soviet leaders can live with the anomaly, and if they can't bow to circumstances will at least stop lying about them. The Soviet government was able to isolate the space programme so that the genuine cooperative effort it entailed could not become too infectious. But a full-scale computer technology just might be harder to contain.

Bukovsky started off believing what Sakharov has come to believe – that the Soviet Union is a tragic farce. Most of us agree with that. The trouble is that after we have finished agreeing with each other the Soviet Union is still there. If anything could bring it crashing down, it would probably be laughter. In the annals of dissident Russian literature, Zinoviev's *The Yawning Heights* might well prove to be not only the funniest book but the most historically influential, simply because of the hilarious neatness with which it encapsulates ideological absurdity. Yet really there is no point in wondering about how dissidence can cause a change. Dissidence *is* the change. Just by the range it has come to encompass, dissident Russian literature has begun pointing towards a time when it might be succeeded by what it was earlier obliged to replace – Russian literature. We will probably never notice the day of transition, just as we will probably never notice the day when the Soviet Union rejoins the world.

(*New York Review of Books*, 1979)

The Road to Berlin

Prussian Nights: A Narrative Poem by Alexander Solzhenitsyn, translated by Robert Conquest (Collins & Harvill, London, and Farrar, Straus & Giroux, New York)

COMPOSED and committed to memory during Solzhenitsyn's time as a zek, *Prussian Nights* is a narrative poem about the Red Army's vengeful advance into Germany in 1945. The Russian text was first published by the YMCA Press, Paris, in 1974. In the present volume we get the Russian text again, with a skilful verse translation by Robert Conquest on the facing pages. A brief – too brief – preface and a useful technical appendix, both by the translator, complete a little book which will probably not make much of a splash, if the reviews it has so far received are anything to go by.

Incidental works by or about Solzhenitsyn seem to be

coming out all the time; if people still want books from him at all, they would rather have big ones than small ones; and anyway, perhaps the whole thing is becoming a bit trite, when even Margaret Thatcher gets something of his drift and can make a pretty good shot at pronouncing his name. People think they know Solzhenitsyn's message all too well. Yet this poem, while scarcely being the key to his total achievement, can certainly be said to stand near the beginning of his development as a writer, and would deserve close attention for that reason if for no other. To pay close attention, though, you need to have absorbed what he has been saying, in his subsequent writings, about his country's post-revolutionary history. There are aspects of this poem which are clear only in the light of its author's prose. When reviewers miss those aspects, you start to wonder if they are as familiar with Solzhenitsyn's writings as they make out.

For example, doubts have been expressed about where the author stands in relation to the character – a young officer – narrating the poem. Yet there can be no real doubt. The narrator might *suspect* that there is something outrageous about the way the Russian troops are encouraged to behave, but the author *knows* there is. Solzhenitsyn has always regarded Stalin's vindictive policy against Germany as a stroke of pure cynicism. In his view, the Nazis proved themselves not just evil but stupid when they threw away the moral initiative in the course of their advance: the Soviet government deserved to lose the loyalty of its people. When it was Stalin's turn to advance, his pose of ethical superiority was a grotesque sham. It was one monster calling for revenge on another. Ehrenburg, the writer who was given the task of crying havoc, holds a permanent place among Solzhenitsyn's literary *bêtes noires*.

Sure enough, Ehrenburg turns up in this poem, conveying the author's whole ethical position at a blow. He is called contemptuously by his first name, Ilya, and described as the 'senior ham of the lot'. Nadezhda Mandelstam, in her great book *Hope Against Hope*, thought of him in the same light. Ehrenburg, to all the writers who fell foul of the regime, was perennially the supreme example of what stood to be gained and lost by keeping well in with the authorities. His presence in the poem is a clear token of what Solzhenitsyn thought about the official line on the Great Patriotic War.

But even without such obvious emblems, it should be apparent that this account of the Red Army on the vengeance trail is the opposite of noncommittal. Every line declares its author's conviction that a crime is being perpetrated. Here lies the main difference between Solzhenitsyn's poem and another narrative poem on the same topic, Tvardovsky's *Vassili Tyorkin*. Both poems are written in the same metre – trochaic tetrameters, the measure made familiar to us by *Hiawatha* – and in some ways strike the same note. But they have had, and will continue to have, completely different histories.

For the Russians, Tvardovsky's poem was the most famous to come out of the war. It is still a best-seller: my own copy, printed in 1976, is equipped with explanatory notes in English, on the sound assumption that it is a book any beginner at Russian would be glad to read. *Vassili Tyorkin* is not a work to be despised. But the view it transmits is the view of the common soldier: if you look at the last section, 'The Road to Berlin', you find that it covers the same shattered ground as *Prussian Nights*, but with none of the same misgivings about the sanctity of the task. Apart from a general feeling of war-is-hell, there is not an unsettling idea in evidence. There is no suggestion that the Russian people are in as much danger from their own rulers as from the enemy.

Although Tvardovsky purveyed the official view, he was no smooth operator like Ehrenburg. Indeed it was Tvardovsky who went on to edit *Novy Mir* and thus publish *One Day in the Life of Ivan Denisovich*, the only book by Solzhenitsyn ever to appear in the Soviet Union. Solzhenitsyn, within the limits set by his irascibility, admired Tvardovsky and wrote a resounding eulogy at his death, which was undoubtedly hastened by a broken heart, the editorship of *Novy Mir* having been taken away from him when the thaw refroze. The two men were eventually united in a common trouble. But the two poems of their youth remain fundamentally separate. There were no conceivable circumstances in which *Prussian Nights* could have been popular, or even unpopular. It just could not have existed as a publication. Even now, it tells too much of the truth. At the time, merely to have been caught in possession of the manuscript would have been enough to ensure Solzhenitsyn's arrest – except, of course, that he had been arrested already.

But from the official standpoint, the truly subversive elements in the poem would not necessarily have been the hideous accounts of rape and murder – it is just possible that those might have been thought of as rather well put. The passages which would have doomed the author are concerned with the quality of goods which the rampaging troops find lying around waiting to be plundered. The narrator marvels at barns built like mansions. German things are so *well made.* Their military cars run so sweetly. Most amazing of all, there are reams of paper and boxes of Faber pencils. Our hero has never seen paper so smooth, or pencils that can draw so finely. He has come to an unknown planet.

One of the guards taking Mandelstam into exile wouldn't believe that you could be punished for writing a poem. Mandelstam set him straight: of course you could. Just the passage about the pencils would have been enough to get Solzhenitsyn shot ten times over. Stalin was mortally afraid of his soldiers coming into contact with the West. He was already purging his army before the victory was complete. Russian prisoners-of-war (some of them march through the poem, in a solitary, funereal passage of pentameter) were brought home to be liquidated. This whole mass agony, which made nonsense of the regime's claims to be patriotic, is what Solzhenitsyn is referring to when he talks about paper and pencils. That much is made clear by his prose writings. It is not edifying to see critics sucking their thumbs and wondering what he might be on about. Robert Conquest has made the understandable mistake of writing a tactfully concise preface, but it begins to look as if he should have spelled things out.

But Mr Conquest's principal task was to translate the verse, which he has done with force and guile, preserving the wide range of tone which Solzhenitsyn commands. Even in his prose, Solzhenitsyn combines any amount of modern idiom with the whole heritage of literary Russian. Packed into tetrameters, such a vocabulary can yield a daunting variety of effects. Describing the winter, Solzhenitsyn sounds like Nekrasov in *Frost the Red-Nosed*: he consciously echoes the traditional Russian imagery of the cold. At the other extreme, a bulk sugar store burns with lilac flames – an entirely modern observation. The pictorial quality of the whole poem is an eye-opener. There is always a tendency, on the part of his detractors, to make of Solzhenitsyn something less than he is, but here is further evidence that he is something more than even his admirers thought. At the very least, this poem should help to give us an adequate idea of the creative power which the young Solzhenitsyn brought to the task of re-establishing objective truth in a country whose government had devoted so much murderous energy to proving that there can be no such thing.

(*New Statesman*, 1977)

Big Book from Screwsville

***The Yawning Heights* by Alexander Zinoviev**
(Bodley Head, London, and
Random House, New York)

SOMEWHERE in the middle of this enormous book there is a tiny story about a Soviet trainee pilot with slow reflexes. The flying instructors are not allowed to fail anybody. So they just give him his orders a long way in advance. He passes the course and goes to the front, where on his first mission he does not drop his bombs until he gets back to base. Equality has been achieved. *The Yawning Heights* is about a society which has succeeded in what it set out to do. Its author, Alexander Zinoviev, is not entirely posing when he claims to be engaged in the dispassionate analysis of a historical movement which has fulfilled its aims.

The Yawning Heights has been five years reaching us. It hardly needs saying that we are lucky to be reading it at all. The author's dateline suggests that he finished writing it in 1974. But the first Russian edition of *Ziyayushchiye Vysoty* did not come out until 1976. Published by L'Age d'Homme in Lausanne, it is a neat paperback volume closely printed on thin pages. There is a grainy full-length photograph of Zinoviev on the back. Dapperly clad, he stands in front of a squalid building which a signboard proclaims to be the Philosophy Faculty of Moscow University, where he was a Professor of Logic until the regime began treating him as an enemy. His previous books had been academic philosophical works which had won him an international reputation and abundant prestige within his own country. Like Sakharov, Zinoviev was rebelling from a position of privilege.

The Russian edition was reviewed in the *New York Review of Books* for 14 April 1977, by Aleksandr Nekrich, himself a distinguished scholar, who had sacrificed his career to the truth. Nekrich's review – which retains the status of a primary critical article – was a clear indication that a book of the first importance was on its way towards us. The French edition of the book, *Les Hauteurs béantes*, was published later that same year, once again by L'Age d'Homme. Though elegantly printed, in sheer bulk it was about three times the size of the Russian original. Since the translator, Wladimir Berelowitch, wrote with unfaltering terseness, it was already becoming evident just how much meaning must be compressed into Zinoviev's idioms and coinages. In fact the translation made embarrassing demands even on one's French. But by now there could be small doubt that the book was of capital significance. This time the photograph was a typical piece of histrionically lit Russian portrait photography, with Zinoviev looking like a cosmonaut who did not very much want to take off.

Onward to 1979. Finally the English edition appears. It is even bigger than the French one. The grainy Philosophy Faculty photograph is once again on the back, although by now it is out of date: Zinoviev came to the West last year. The layout is not at all elegant. The sub-headings which in the Russian and French editions help break up the text into sections of invitingly browsable length are here meanly set up exactly the same as the body-type, so that the whole thing flows on and on like the Don. But the translator, Gordon Clough, has done pretty well. If that sounds grudging, it should be remembered that the first translations of works such as this are crucial to their future history. Partly due to an inadequate translation, Zamyatin's *We* made little impact when it first came out in English, and thus we were deprived of a prophetic insight into the nature of the totalitarian state. Zamyatin guessed a lot in advance. It could be said that Zinoviev is merely being wise after the event. But the event is of such magnitude, and his wisdom is of such a unique kind, that *The Yawning Heights* can only be thought of as a work vital to the continuity of civilisation. It would have been a disaster if the translation had misfired. Luckily it sins only through sounding like a translation. Otherwise the book has survived its journey. It has been heading our way like a planet on a collision course. Now it fills the sky and we can see all the details.

In *The Yawning Heights* the Soviet Union is portrayed as a garbage-dump called Ibansk, which is a way of saying Fucktown, or Screwsville, as well as of implying that the average Russian – Ivan – lives in a place just like it. The word Swiftian can easily be applied to the physical details of Ibansk. There is a lot of human ordure lying about. Going to the lavatory bulks large amongst Ibanskian activities. It is basically a very shitty scene. But Zinoviev's whole point is that he can't really exaggerate no matter how hard he tries. Really Ibansk is just the Soviet Union with the lavatory doors taken off. The book is less a satire than a sociological treatise on the level of Weber or Pareto. Everything that happens in Ibansk has already happened in the Soviet Union. But nobody has previously managed to make an entirely coherent picture of it.

An Ibanskian in the street shouts 'Arrogant blockhead!' and is immediately arrrested for insulting the Leader, even though he was only abusing a workmate. Everyone in Ibansk understands how things are. They just can't face the facts any other way except a few at a time. Much of the book is made up of dialogues and speeches in which characters with names like Howler, Bawler, Truth-teller and Schizophrenic severally advance their theories about the degree to which the Ibanskian official ideology has been realised in Ibanskian life. This comic symposium of voices echoes the actual history of the way we have always come to be informed about the Soviet Union. Since 1917 there has been incessant argument about whether the Soviet Union is communism gone right, communism gone wrong, or communism not yet arrived. But in Ibansk such a discussion is shown, often by the very terms in which it is conducted, to be camped in the air. Ibanskian socicty has its own imperatives which ideology exists only to serve.

The first imperative is that mediocrity shall prosper. Those who stand outside or above are dangerous because they are in control of themselves. Moral worth is automatically subject to persecution. The Boss (Stalin) rose to the top because he was a complete nonentity. Hog (Khrushchev) repudiated the Boss only in order to preserve power. In Ibansk the only reason there is no unemployment is that everyone is engaged in the imitation of work. Real work requires a limited number of people, but in the imitation of work there is no limit to the number of people who can be employed. Everything is deliberately kept inefficient. Inefficiency leads you 'to reduce to a minimum your number of contacts with people on whom you depend for anything; i.e., it leads in the final analysis to a self-imposed restriction of demand' (page 284).

Few protest because nearly all are involved. Truth-teller (Solzhenitsyn) and the other dissidents are wrong to suppose that the government is oppressing the people. The government is expressing the people's will. Even the intelligentsia polices itself. With mediocrity the universal norm, material inequality is more important than ever. By struggling for their fair share of unfair advantages, the intelligentsia put a trump card into the hands of the leadership and automatically eliminate potential trouble-makers from among their own number.

In Ibansk the leaders are decorated for being leaders and then decorated again for being decorated. Whatever is achieved is achieved in spite of them. 'But things still get done. They can't all be like that.' 'They are all like that.' (page 371.) In the arts, the mere fact of becoming known is a guarantee of bad faith. The sculptor Dauber (based on Zinoviev's friend Ernst Neizvestny) spends most of the book trying to be defiant. He ends up carving busts of the Leader out of snotoplast and turdotron, convincing himself that he is carving them in a defiant way. 'The whole horror of our existence lies in the grandiose scale and inescapability of triviality' (page 481). Ibansk is one big yawn.

The above hardly begins to summarise the elaborately detailed picture Zinoviev paints of life in Ibansk. But the reader can already see that this is a fantasy whose inspiration lies in the real world. One's estimation of the book will mainly depend on whether one feels the correspondence between Ibansk and the Soviet Union to be exact. And surely, by and large, it is. 'An amoral society wastes a huge amount of energy' (page 800). Like Ibansk, the Soviet Union purposely squanders its own human resources. The destruction of talent is not incidental to the system of administration. It is fundamental. Stalin's career, to take the most extreme possible example, can't be explained in terms of variations in ideology. Variations in ideology have to be explained in terms of Stalin's career, which was solely devoted to eliminating every trace of human individuality which could not be brought under the regime's direct control. Tolstoy's portrait of Napoleon in *War and Peace* is a possible literary ancestor of the idea that the man of destiny can be a cipher. Solzhenitsyn took the same line about Stalin in *The First Circle*. But really such a view needs no credentials. In the case of Stalin it is simply right. After the early disasters in World War Two it became evident that Stalin's brains were made out of the same clay as his feet. But just because the fact became evident did not mean that it could be acted on or even admitted.

Again, Zinoviev is surely right about what Sakharov has called 'the full tragedy of creative life' in the Soviet Union. To speak only of the arts, and of the arts to speak only of literature, it can be taken for granted that any writer over the last fifty years who has not been persecuted by the State is simply not worth reading. Learning to read Russian brings rich benefits, but the prospective student should be warned that he will not be able to retain any comfortable illusions he might have about this century being as fruitful as the last. It is like walking out of a garden into a desert. The catastrophe was already in the making before Stalin came to power. Those gullible Western authors who go on junkets to Moscow and Leningrad at the invitation of the Soviet Writers' Union, and who come home to declare themselves impressed with how *many* poets are published in *Literaturnaya Gazeta* and how *many* copies of his new book a Soviet poet is accustomed to see printed, are kept safe by the language barrier, as well as by their natural obtuseness, from realising that the Writers' Union is an organisation which exists in order to seek out talent and make certain that it is expunged.

Zinoviev deals harshly with Yevtushenko, who appears in *The Yawning Heights* as Snottyhanky, 'the favourite of young people, the secret police and the Americans' (*passim*). Yevtushenko is such a preening booby that it is easy to be tempted into feeling superior to him. A sceptical inner voice should warn us that in the same circumstances we might be even more glad than he obviously is to accept a privileged position as the crowd-pleasing bard with a licence to be just so irreverent and no more. But the point to make is that the real poets are condemned to silence. The same applies to every other area of Soviet artistic life. Even the performing artists are allowed to achieve eminence only on the understanding that they will be given no new material worth performing. It was easy to be happy for the Panovs when they reached the West but impossible to admire the ballets they brought with them. Soviet creative life is 'a tragedy of unrealised possibilities' (page 547).

According to Zinoviev, the Soviet Union is not a society which has fallen short of its ideals. It embodies them. As a linguistic philosopher with something of Karl Kraus's gift for dissecting rhetoric, Zinoviev is able to show that communist theory has always been nothing but a project. The social laws governing Soviet communism are to be deduced only from what actually goes on in the Soviet Union. This proposition, central to Zinoviev's thought, is expounded at length in a second book, *Svetloe Budushchee*, which has not yet been published in English. The Russian and French editions were both published by L'Age d'Homme last year. In French the book is called *L'Avenir radieux* and in English it will probably be called *The Radiant Future*. It tells the story of an academic whizz-kid doing what he has to do in order to get on. A friend of his writes a treatise about the real nature of Soviet life. These two main characters can be thought of as incarnating the two sides of the argument that must have raged in Zinoviev's head when he found he could no longer put up with his own success. 'Communist society', argues the friend, 'can be thought of only insofar as it is an empirical phenomenon, and not as an abstract system.'

But not even a man as clever as Zinoviev can quite escape the debilitating effects of the life he so brilliantly describes. Like Solzhenitsyn, he has to a certain extent been infected by the very absolutism which he condemns. He is hard on the dissidents. He gives them credit for bravery in such a terrible battle, but says that in the end they help to buttress the state. This is a neat argument but it is open to the same objections which Zinoviev, possibly following Karl Popper, makes to Marxism: there is no conceivable way of disproving it. Anything that opposes the Soviet state buttresses the Soviet state as long as the Soviet state is still there. Here Zinoviev fails to take the historical view, which must always allow for the unexpected consequences of actions. Moral opposition might serve the totalitarian state in the short term but could well undermine it in the long. Nor is Sakharov's standpoint to be summarily belittled. Sakharov, who has been through all the same degrading experiences as Zinoviev, has never lost sight of the possibility that the Soviet leaders, while deaf to moral arguments, might well be obliged to allow a measure of liberalism when it becomes clear that without it the Soviet Union will no longer be able to maintain itself as a first-rate power.

Zinoviev is unfair not just to the dissidents but to the intelligentsia as a whole. There can be no doubt that for Soviet artists and academics life is largely as squalid as he portrays it. But the persecuted far outweigh their persecutors, and it is a kind of materialism to suppose otherwise. Since Gumilev's murder in 1921 the Russian intelligentsia have been living in a nightmare. Without exception the outstanding talents have been killed, silenced, or exiled. The good work that has survived is scarcely a hundredth part of what would have been there if things had been different. It has been a cultural disaster without parallel in history. Yet does anybody suppose that names like Gumilev, Akhmatova, Pasternak and the Mandelstams mean less because of it? They mean more. Nadezhda Mandelstam willed her dead husband's poems to a just future. Even if it could be proved that such a future will never come, would her gesture mean nothing? It would still mean everything.

Most unfortunately of all, Zinoviev is hard on the ordinary people of the Soviet Union. By suggesting that they are unusually compliant, he comes close to resurrecting the 'mysterious Russian soul' which he is ordinarily at pains to say does not exist. If Soviet society is as he describes it, then there is no mystery about why most people collaborate with the authorities. Most people are not heroes. It is fancy talk to suggest that they are sharing power. They are sharing powerlessness.

Solzhenitsyn is right to insist that the Soviet government is an imposition, and Zinoviev is wrong to imply, even as a comic exaggeration, that nobody is innocent. Zinoviev says himself that the social laws of the Soviet Union have to be seen from the outside if you are to make sense of them. Seen from the inside, they are impenetrable. On this particular point, Zinoviev probably still feels himself to be an insider. When he was dismissed from Moscow University his friends and colleagues demanded that he be stripped of his medals. He can be excused for taking a sour view of his fellow man.

But in those areas where Zinoviev is uncharitable his arguments refute themselves. Probably it was only an element of self-contempt that ever led him to advance them. By a process which *The Yawning Heights* describes in vivid terms, merely to grow up in the Soviet Union is to be compromised. Zinoviev should take heart. The mere existence of this book shows that to dissent is worthwhile; that the intelligentsia, of which he is a worthy representative, maintains its real traditions, despite all; and that not even the Soviet Union can be entirely confident about its ability to obliterate individual thought. 'A society which officially adopts the slogan that the interests of the people transcend those of the individual is a lawless society. And that's all there is to it' (page 575). The proposition is simple but hard to take in. Nobody wants to believe that all those millions of innocent people died in agony for nothing. Not even *The Gulag Archipelago* could get the message across if you didn't want to listen. But Zinoviev has found a way of joking about it, and nothing travels further or faster than a joke.

(*New Statesman*, 1979)

A State of Boredom

Brezhnev: A Short Biography **by The Institute of Marxism-Leninism, CPSU Central Committee (Pergamon Press, Oxford)**

HERE is a book so dull that a whirling dervish could read himself to sleep with it. If you were to recite even a single page in the open air, birds would fall out of the sky and dogs drop dead. There is no author's name on the title page, merely a modest line of italic type advising us that Leonid Ilyich Brezhnev's 'short biography' has been composed 'by the Institute of Marxism-Leninism, CPSU Central Committee'. This is the one statement in the entire opus which is undeniably true. Only an Institute could write like this:

> Monumental progress in building communism has been made by the Soviet people under the leadership of the Communist Party, its Central Committee and Politburo headed by the General Secretary of the Communist Party of the Soviet Union's Central Committee, LEONID ILYICH BREZHNEV.

Monumental progress in probing the outer limits of tedium has been made by the time the hypnotised reader has slogged through more than two hundred pages of ideological prose at its most glutinous. Unable to believe that the Institute could keep down the pace, I read the whole thing from start to finish, waiting for the inevitable slip-up which would result in a living sentence. It never happened. That the book could be read from any other motive seems highly unlikely. Even the most rabid Brezhnev fan would be catatonic by the end of the first chapter.

It is safe to predict that sales will not be large. What, then, does Robert Maxwell hope to gain from the deal? Brezhnev has contributed a foreword graciously mentioning Maxwell by name. Perhaps that's enough. But leaving aside any suspicion that the chairman of Pergamon Press might have finally mislaid the last of his marbles, there are grounds for according him a vote of thanks. If nothing else had ever done so, this book would be more than enough to prove that boredom is not just incidental to Soviet life, but fundamental. Boredom is built into the Soviet system. The Soviet system runs on boredom. Boredom and the Soviet system are the same thing.

State-induced ennui on the Soviet scale is not something we can easily imagine. We think we are being bored when we chance to tune in on a television programme starring Sir Harold Wilson, or when we accidentally stumble on a short quotation from Edward Heath's latest book. Our own marxists are fond of telling us that such mendacious bathos is ultimately more corroding than whatever drabness might occasionally make itself manifest behind the Iron Curtain. But really there is no comparison. What you have to imagine is being *forced* to listen, your whole life long, to stuff like the following paragraph, chosen at random from page 61 of the life story of the General Secretary of the Communist Party of the Soviet Union's Central Committee.

> The plenum once again proved convincingly the CPSU's monolithic unity, its stand on Leninist principles, and its political maturity. It demonstrated the fidelity of the Party and its Central Committee to Marxism-Leninism and expressed the unswerving determination of Communists to adhere to and develop steadfastly the Leninist standards of Party life and the principles of Party leadership, notably that of collective leadership, and boldly and resolutely to set aside every impediment to the creative work of Party and people.

But once again it is not enough to say that the Institute's style is devoid of interest. What the Institute's style is devoid of is truth. In fact so thoroughly has the truth been siphoned out that you might even find yourself getting interested in the consequent vacuum. James Joyce used to say that he had never met a boring man, and I suppose that by the same criterion there is no such thing as a boring book: even trash raises questions – among them, the question of how it came to exist. From that viewpoint, Brezhnev's Brief Bio is unputdownable. Every euphemism, circumlocution, outright omission and flat lie is an eloquent testimonial to the Soviet government's regard for the truth. The Soviet government has such a high regard for the truth that it will go to almost any lengths to ensure that the common people never get even a smell of it. Hence the care with which the Institute makes the facts unintelligible even when they don't matter.

The Institute, in a solitary burst of candour, makes it reasonably clear that the Ukrainian town of Kamenskoye, nowadays called Dneprodzerzhinsk, was favoured on 19 December 1906 with the birth of Leonid Ilyich Brezhnev. After that the story gets a bit blurred. There is much emphasis on his early career as a steel-worker, but what really mattered was his climb through the ranks of the Komsomol and the Party. He grew up as a member of the 'first generation of builders of socialism' who 'were remodelling the country's agriculture on socialist lines and carrying out a cultural revolution'. Millions of people whose existence might have impeded such a process had already been wiped out, but there is no mention of these, beyond a blanket statement that 'trends hostile to Leninism . . . were overwhelmed in this struggle'. It could be said that those particular millions of victims have no relevance to this story. But later on there were further millions of victims whose relevance to this story is beyond question, and there is no mention of them either.

Brezhnev's heroism as a soldier during the Great Patriotic War is heavily underlined, but first there is the sensitive topic of what he was up to during the years immediately preceding. The Institute calls it 'Party work'. By 1939 he was 'propaganda secretary' of the local Regional Committee. It appears that he 'ran extensive campaigns among the Communists and all working people for the successful implementation of the tasks set by the Party.' This, remember, was the Ukraine, and the tasks set by the Party were the brain-children of Stalin. They consisted mainly of rounding people up and shipping them off to be killed. How, you might wonder, does the Institute get around the unarguable fact that Brezhnev was faithfully engaged in carrying out Stalin's lethal plans? And then as you read on and on you gradually realise. *There is no mention of Stalin at all.*

But here comes the war, during which 'Communists were everywhere in the forefront'. More to the forefront than almost anybody was Leonid Ilyich, variously 'deputy chief of the Southern Front's political department' and 'chief of the political department of the 18th Army of the 4th Ukrainian Front'. Brezhnev spared no efforts in his task of 'instilling in Soviet troops a spirit of utter devotion to the socialist homeland and hatred for its enemies'. The Institute doesn't explain why it should have been so necessary to instil this hatred, unless the devotion to the socialist homeland wasn't all it might have been.

Anyway, Brezhnev, as a leading member of the political organs, 'stimulated the morale, political consciousness, fortitude and courage of the troops in the heavy fighting'. The citation for his first Order of the Red Banner in 1942 described how he had 'often visited the troops at their battle stations'. He was 'a fearless political worker'. By 1943 Colonel Brezhnev was in charge of all the 18th Army's political instructors. The Institute seems to be in no doubt that the Party won the war with the help of the army. Nowhere is it suggested in this book, and in no book published in the Soviet Union has it ever been suggested at any time, that the Party's heroic efforts were mainly devoted to supplying deficiencies which the Party had caused in the first place.

The Party having brought the war to a successful conclusion, Brezhnev 'took part in liberating Czechoslovakia, Poland and Hungary'. With the passing of 'the cult of personality' (i.e. Stalin), Brezhnev was obliged to switch bandwagons. There is not much data from any source, and none at all from this one, on how he managed it, but connoisseurs of grotesque euphemism will be pleased to learn that as the man in charge of transforming the Kazakhstan virgin lands in 1954–5 Brezhnev inspired 'the thousands who came from all parts of the Soviet Union' with creative fervour. One of the places they came to, of course, was Karaganda.

How does the Institute deal with the awkward fact that Brezhnev was Khrushchev's man? Easy. *There is no mention of Khrushchev at all.* Instead, 'it was necessary to remove the subjectivism which was in evidence at that time'. The subjectivism having been removed, the way was eventually clear for this 'outstanding political personality of the Leninist type' to assume power. There is no telling, certainly not from this source, quite how he did it, but Brezhnev made it all the way to the top, and set about ensuring that he stayed there.

There are probably no exceptions to the rule that power corrupts, but Brezhnev can perhaps be cited as evidence that absolute power need not necessarily corrupt absolutely. His power by now is as absolute as anyone's has ever been, but he has not gone mad with it, although there can be no doubt that he is an ugly customer. Dubček and the other Czech leaders were personally favoured with a sample of what Brezhnev is like when he is putting on the squeeze, since he it was who did most of the shouting down the telephone. But generally he has gone about his business with such tact as to make it appear that a monopoly of power has dropped into his lap impelled by nothing more assertive than gravitational force.

Brezhnev, the Institute assures us, has eliminated 'the consequences of the personality cult and manifestations of subjectivism and voluntarism'. This is good to hear, even if it is bad to read. There is something to it. Compared with, say, Kim Il Sung, Brezhnev can even be said to have kept a low profile. But the appearance of this biography should be enough to start people wondering. My own view, for what it is worth, is that Brezhnev is just as keen on himself as Stalin was, but has a more acute sense of what he can get away with without having himself written out of Soviet history. He wants his immortality to last, like Lenin's.

As a philosophical brain Brezhnev is no better than Stalin. Indeed at times he sounds just like him, especially when he contends, in the same paragraph, (a) that scientific and industrial progress can be attained only through socialism, and (b) that socialism can be attained only through scientific and industrial progress. He is also as vain as Stalin: the photograph on the jacket of this book is retouched to suit the self-delusions of a man who can't pass a mirror. But he is less nuts than Stalin. During Brezhnev's reign the innocent have been permitted to live, as long as they don't heckle. Even at its mildest, totalitarianism is never less murderous than that: a society in which the rulers talk on and on without making any sense, but nobody is allowed to laugh.

(*New Statesman*, 1978)

Awkward Laughter

The Radiant Future by Alexander Zinoviev, translated by Gordon Clough (Bodley Head, London, and Random House, New York)

Sans illusions by Alexander Zinoviev, translated by Wladimir Berelowitch (L'Age d'Homme, Lausanne)

THOUGH it deserved all the praise it got, *The Yawning Heights* was nevertheless of a size bound to tell against its long-term fortune. Its successor, *The Radiant Future*, treats the same themes at about half the length. It would be nice to think that Zinoviev had now, after recovering from the initial impact of leaving the Soviet Union for the West, struck his true sense of proportion. Telling against this wish, however, is the awkward fact that we have not yet even got to the end of what he produced before being expelled from the Soviet Union, and the further fact that from his mighty output there are at least two more behemoths on the way.

L'Antichambre du paradis, a satirical treatment of the Soviet psychiatric hospitals, is of the same dimensions as *The*

Yawning Heights: presumably its appearance in English will be not long delayed. Beyond that, and looming rather than hiding, there is a two-volume blockbuster which at the time of writing has not yet appeared even in French, but whose Russian title might perhaps be translated as *The Yellow House*, although a less literal but more accurate rendition would be *The Madhouse*, since for Russians the yellow house is the slang term for the lunatic asylum. (Apparently the French translation will be called *La Maison de fous*.) In Dom Knigi, the marvellous Russian bookshop in Paris, I saw a copy of this last-mentioned whopper lying spine-up on the counter and can remember letting out a discreet groan. The man's books generate themselves like yogurt. One continues to be grateful, but with trepidation.

For *The Radiant Future* one's gratitude is unalloyed. It is nearer than *The Yawning Heights* to being an ordinary narrative and is thus easier for the reader to follow. There is a central character to get interested in and care about, even though he is not very likeable. The central character is the narrator, head of the Department of Theoretical Problems of the Methodology of Scientific Communism. (The department's offices are in the Yellow House, which suggests that Zinoviev's forthcoming works might link up in more than just a thematic way to the ones we know already.) The narrator's career as a philosopher has some resemblance to Zinoviev's own, and indeed it is possible that an element of self-hatred has been incorporated. Zinoviev has good reason to be proud of his achievements as a dissident, but he seems very slow in forgiving himself for his career as a Soviet academic. According to one of the cardinal principles of *The Yawning Heights*, it is impossible to flourish, or even grow up, in the Soviet Union while still retaining a moral sense. Therefore almost anybody you have ever heard of is automatically reprehensible.

This principle would be intolerably strict if Zinoviev did not in the first instance apply it to himself, and more rigorously than to anyone else. *The Radiant Future*, I think, is clear evidence that he does so. The book has an expiatory quality that gives it a dimension missing from *The Yawning*

Heights, in which the squalor is without pathos. The narrator of *The Radiant Future* is enough of a recognisably human character for us to identify with him and realise that his compromises might have been ours if we had shared his circumstances.

The circumstances are those of the Soviet Union nearly unaltered. For the most part of its enormous bulk *The Yawning Heights* draws on the Russian satirical tradition that goes back at least as far as Saltykov-Shchedrin's *The History of a Town*, and beyond that to the whole Western tradition of utopian satire, which is essentially a means of drawing attention to a state of affairs by exaggerating it. In Saltykov's town, all the different governors were united in the assumption that the function of the ordinary inhabitants was to be whipped. Thus was Tsarist rule satirised by exaggeration, even if the exaggeration was not great. But another, equally important, part of *The Yawning Heights* simply analyses things as they are. This part of the book grows out of the more recent post-revolutionary satirical tradition founded by Zamyatin's *We*. In this satirical tradition the true state of affairs is found to be already so exaggerated that its enormity can be conveyed only by analysis. Rather than to create a fantasy, the main effort is to understand a fantasy that is already there.

The closely argued passages of sociological analysis in *The Yawning Heights* belong to this second tradition and are, in my view, by far the most original parts in the book. As an exercise in neo-Swiftian scatological imagination *The Yawning Heights* leaves Swift's title safe, but as an analytical treatise it has great vitality. *The Radiant Future* is the same sort of thing but more economically done, since there is no supererogatory burden of fantasy. Instead of being called Ibansk (Fucktown) as in *The Yawning Heights*, or Glupov (Dumbtown) as in *The History of a Town*, the earthly paradise in *The Radiant Future* is called Moscow. The title itself is not a parodic extrapolation but an actual Party slogan. No time is wasted on thinking up accoutrements for an imaginary madhouse. The real madhouse is taken to be more than sufficient.

At first glance the narrator is ideally equipped to thrive in the Soviet academic system. He has no interest in his subject beyond the means it offers to gain advancement, usually by suppressing any signs of originality in others. We recognise the state of affairs characterised by Sakharov when he outlined the tragedy of creative life in the Iron Curtain countries. But the narrator makes one mistake. He listens to his colleague Anton instead of taking immediate steps to crush him. Anton, a revenant from Stalin's camps, has analysed the Soviet system and written a book about it. Reading the manuscript, the narrator becomes infected with Anton's penetrating realism, and the onward march of his career falters as a consequence.

> For several days I was completely under the influence of Anton's book. Although I had only had time to leaf through it briefly, I had seen a great deal in it. Anton and I had discussed these topics dozens of times. I was already familiar with everything in the book. But here everything had been brought together and set out systematically. The effect was devastating. It was the general method which produced the greatest impression. Anton did not criticise Marxism and the Soviet way of life in the way which is generally accepted everyhere. He accepted everything as fact. He even accepted our most extreme demagogic pronouncements as truth. He looked an even more orthodox Marxist than I. For example, we all moan about the collapse of agriculture, about rising prices, about waste in economy and so on. But Anton accepted as truth the statements of our leaders (he even quoted from our newspapers) to the effect that Soviet society today is more monolithic than it has ever been socially, politically and ideologically; more powerful than ever economically, and so on. And he set out the bases of Marxism in a way which can only be described as brilliant. Clearly, briefly, convincingly. And that creates a feeling of unease. It was as if you were being flayed alive, leaving your body like one vast

wound. You can't be touched anywhere without being in agony.

It is not difficult to guess that Zinoviev must have discovered the components of this simple but useful plot within his own experience. He himself was once, like Sakharov, a darling of the Soviet academic system. But he was also, again like Sakharov, a thinker original and brave enough to see past his own advantage and pursue an argument even if it led to heresy. Inside his own head he was both the narrator and Anton. The two personalities fought a battle, which Anton won, to the world's lasting benefit but with decisive effects on Zinoviev's academic career. He was stripped of his medals and ritually denounced by his colleagues, in the kind of scene which he had already said must inevitably take place if anybody in the Soviet Union gets sufficiently carried away by the truth to start telling it for its own sake. To have predicted your own fate, however, is not necessarily of much comfort on the day your time runs out.

Sometimes it is hard for us to remember that these amazing people who have had the honour to be denounced by the Soviet system still feel just as much outraged as vindicated, even when they are well aware of their own worth and of the squalid motives of their accusers. Zinoviev, a man of the highest distinction whose intellectual integrity does honour to his country, was deprived of his Soviet citizenship by personal decree of Brezhnev, whose chief quality of mind is the ability to produce speeches so boring that the *Pravda* compositors fall senseless into their key-boards when transcribing them for an indifferent posterity. If such is a comic event, it is for Zinoviev to say so. And of course the wonderful thing about him is that he says so.

Most of Anton's ideas can be deduced from *The Yawning Heights*, but in *The Radiant Future* they are laid out in a more readily appreciable chain of consequence. Once again Zinoviev insists that the Soviet Union is not a distortion of communism but an expression of it, and that Stalinism was the ideal expression, towards which Soviet society will always tend to return. (Leszek Kolakowski develops the same idea, making several references to Zinoviev, in a long and fascinating interview published in the January 1981 issue of *Encounter.*) Anton advances his thesis not as a paradox-monger but as a simple truth-teller: that the truth keeps on coming out sounding like a paradox is simply a measure of how far things have gone. The state's ideological apparatus has taken over even the terms by which it is criticised.

> Soviet history really (and not merely apparently) is a history of congresses, meetings, plans, obligations, overfulfilments, conquests of new fields, new departures, demonstrations, decorations, applause, folk-dances, farewell ceremonies, arrival ceremonies, and so on; in brief, everything which can be read in official Soviet newspapers, journals, novels, or which can be seen on Soviet television, and so on. There are certain things which happen in the Soviet Union which do not appear in the media of mass information, education, persuasion, and entertainment. But all this represents in this context an immaterial non-historic background to real Soviet history. Everything which, to an outside observer who has not passed through the school of the Soviet way of life, may seem a falsehood, demagogy, formalism, a bureaucratic comedy, propaganda, and so on, in fact represents the flesh and blood of this way of life, in fact this life itself. And everything which may seem to be bitter truth, the actual state of things, commonsense considerations, and so on, is in fact nothing but the insignificant outer skin of the real process.

Defenders of the Soviet Union say that it has a free health service. Critics say that you have to stand in line for it. Anton points out that neither side of the argument has anything to do with the truth. There is no free health service in the Soviet Union, since it is paid for in garnished wages, and thus by depressed living standards. The same applies to cheap housing. The fact of the matter is that it is not cheap. Whether it is easy to come by or not is irrelevant, and to argue one way or the other is to argue within assumptions that the regime can easily accommodate. Anton keeps on coming up with these awkward discoveries one after the other. There is no stopping him. He is a sort of holy fool. (The character of Anton, incidentally, is an instance of why it is never sufficient to deduce the chain of inspiration from the history of a genre. Many satirical works feature a truth-teller and often he is the author of a secret document. But Anton's holy awkwardness is more likely to have its origins in Bulgakov's Jesus, as portrayed in the second chapter of *The Master and Margarita*. The way Zinoviev's narrator and Anton are bound up with each other can't help but remind you of Bulgakov's Jesus and Pilate.)

Anton's talent is to see the fundamental importance of trivia. He is continually seizing on the apparently incidental and calling it essential. According to Anton nothing is essential *except* the incidental. The radiant future will never arrive and there is nothing here now except the yawning heights. The putative solidity of the Soviet achievement is nothing but hot air. Meanwhile all the abuses and atrocities, all the stupidity and chicanery, are not excrescences on the structure but the structure itself. Denunciations, for example, are not a regrettable by-product of the system but the system's bedrock. Soviet society can continue to exist only if everyone is ready to denounce anyone else. Indeed it came into existence in order for that to happen.

> There are human problems [Anton tells the narrator] which arise because of the presence within society of an actively operating system of morality and other problems which arise because of the absence of any such system. Only the former can be the basis of a great spiritual literature. Denunciation, betrayals, deception and falsehood, for example, do not engender problems worthy of great art in a society where morality does not function as a significant social mechanism. Great art is the creation of a moral civilisation, and one of its means of existence. That is why we do not have, and cannot have, any great spiritual art. We can force the entire country to dance folk dances, take up figure skating or

sing in choirs. But we will not allow great writers like Dostoievsky or Tolstoy to exist. Do I need to say any more? The facts are legion. They beg for scientific study. Yet all we do is try our best to get rid of them.

And so on. Armed with his devastating central perception, Anton is like a man with a hammer fighting one of those terra-cotta armies that the Chinese emperors used to guard themselves with in death. All he has to do is go on swinging. The state might destroy him physically but its official ideology can do nothing to defend itself. It has no intellectual substance whatever. The whole elaborate mental edifice of Marxism-Leninism amounts to nothing more than a heap of beans. Anton's idea is so simple, and yet so wide-reaching in its implications, that even he is slow to grasp it. The narrator is slower still. And perhaps Zinoviev's main reason for expressing it dialectically, through two opposing characters, was that he feared the world would never get the point if he said it straight.

One looks forward, with the tremor of apprehension I have noted earlier, to Zinoviev's forthcoming satirical mammoths. I have read a good deal of *L'Antichambre du paradis* in French but won't pretend to have got far with *The Yellow House* in Russian – Zinoviev's idiomatic language would be daunting for a beginner even if the book looked less like a brick, or in this case two bricks. But even on such scanty acquaintance it is perhaps allowable to suggest that Zinoviev has given the pill more sugar than it needs. As Anton's quoted manuscript demonstrates, the argument loses little from being stated plainly. *L'Antichambre du paradis*, with its account of the psychiatric hospitals, is really about the psychological engineering needed to produce the ideal Soviet citizen. Zamyatin's *We*, prophetically concerning itself with that very subject, is a quarter the length and four times as effective. Zinoviev is a formidable comic inventor but he would be even funnier if he understood the importance of economical writing, and even more influential if he understood his own originality, which is less for comic invention than for clearly argued analysis.

For just how good he is at that, those of his admirers who can read some French should look at *Sans illusions*, a collection of his general essays written since he came to the West. All the themes of *The Yawning Heights* and *The Radiant Future* are contained in it, shorn of fictional properties and rigorously argued to conclusions which are both logically consequent and consistently surprising. (The Moscow brand of mediocrity, for example, is defined not as an absence of talent but as a talent in itself – the talent for suffocating real talent.) It is an engrossing book which one hopes will be brought into English without delay. Among the many pleasures it offers is that of a certain measure of reassurance. In *The Yawning Heights*, Zinoviev, through one of his emblematically named characters, seemed to be arguing that the dissident movement could do nothing except reinforce the monolithic nature of the state. In *The Radiant Future* he seems to be less rigid on this point, but it is not easy to be sure. In *Sans illusions* he is explicit, calling dissidence the most important phenomenon in the social history of the Soviet Union, since it poses problems, for the first time, to communist society in its essence.

> Dissidence exercises above all an influence on the mentalities of certain milieux, and beyond that, through them, on the public at large. It would be absurd to expect immediate, visible results in exact conformation to the ideas of the dissidents. In fact it is practially impossible to follow the mechanism of this influence and to foresee its consequences. But anyway that isn't necessary. The historical experience of humanity furnishes us with sufficient reason to hope.

If Zinoviev ever believed, as he once seemed to, that dissidence accomplished nothing, he refuted himself with his own accomplishments. It wouldn't have mattered much if he had been wrong on that point: it would have been merely another instance of how hard he is on himself. Nevertheless it is a pleasure to find that he can set that particular part of his vast subject in the same illuminating perspective as he has done with all the rest. He has the gravity of a man who has lived with shame but whose pride in the independence of his own mind remains unshaken. The late Nadezhda Mandelstam, who saw the vindictive state do its considerable best to obliterate the very notion of objective truth, always held that it would return of its own accord. Zinoviev is proof that not even totalitarianism can entirely expunge the human propensity to laugh at the wrong moment.

(*New York Review of Books*, 1981)

Index